Days of Sorrow, Times of Joy

Gottahavebooks,
16 Middle Street, Great Gransden,
Cambridgeshire SG19 3AD, UK
sales@gottahavebooks.co.uk

ISBN 978-0-9933781-4-0
This edition published 2016 by Gottahavebooks

Cover and page layout design by Bounford.com

Days of Sorrow, Times of Joy

The story of a Victorian family and its love affair with China

苦日難熬　歡時易過

Days of sorrow pass with difficulty, times of joy, very easily

(Chinese proverb)

Frances Clemmow

For my grandchildren,
Emma, Alex & Skomer

"It was an experience not to be forgotten, a hard life, with much in it to sadden and depress you if you gave it the chance, but in another sense it was a grand life and one we wouldn't have missed for anything. We, there in the hospital, nurses, doctors, evangelists and other workers were drawn closer together in team work than ever before and inspired and challenged to renewed loyalty to each other and above all to our Team Leader in the great adventure."

Dr. Keith Gillison, Surgeon and Medical Superintendent,
Union Hospital Hankou, 1939
"Hankow in the Storm", in *The Chronicle of the LMS*, February, 1939, p. 31.

Contents

Foreword

The memory of the British Empire is fading now, settling like sediment in the glass. The last people still alive who actually administered the empire, who went across the world to govern, to build, to judge and to preach, is fast diminishing now. Very few today can tell us what it actually felt like to be there; how they spoke; what they really thought; what inspired them; what it meant, in Kipling's phrase, to hold 'dominion over palm and pine'.

All the more reason then to be grateful to Fran Clemmow for this fascinating book, and for her painstaking care – almost an act of piety to the ancestors, as the Chinese would say – in transcribing and putting together from a huge archive of letters, pictures and documents this extraordinary story of an extraordinary family who worked in China as doctors and missionaries over much of the century before the Chinese revolution of 1949.

The family were based in the middle Yangtze at Hankow (now Wuhan). The book gives us an intimate picture of the daily life of a missionary family beginning in the 1880s; work and leisure, the struggles in the field, the personal loss, the long sea journeys which sustained the imperial system, the blissful moments on 'furlough' back home in Calne or Scotland, which were in fact only ever breaks in the real business of life, which was service to China. It was a life where illness and disease were commonplace, and where the death of family members, and especially of children, was simply accepted as part of the job. Fran's father, for example, still jumps at the chance to go back in 1939, even during the Japanese occupation!

Supported by their religious faith, this unswerving attitude to service bred a discipline, and a kind of stoicism, which comes out vividly towards the end when fifty years after she left China, Fran's dying mother is asked why she was willing to leave her young children behind, knowing full well that she might never see them again. Her answer is simply, "I had to".

But the family story is also interwoven with the grand picture of modern Chinese history. There are dramatic first-hand insights into the sufferings of the Chinese people between the late 19th century and the Second World War. The family letters conjure up the tension of the Boxer Rising and the electric atmosphere in Hankow as the revolutionaries of 1911 begin the final awful chapter of the fall of the empire after more than 2000 years; all the more poignant with Tom's moving hopes at that moment for a new China. There are graphic glimpses of the civil conflicts and rural risings in the twenties, and then the Japanese occupation in the thirties, the 'perfect storm' which gave rise to the communist revolution. The family lived through all of this, experiencing it close up: the killings in the streets, the looting and burning of their own Hankow, when China was forced to 'drink deep of the cup of suffering' as US journalist Theodore H White wrote.

They were sent out by the London Missionary Society, which had started in China in Canton in 1807. Their goals were three: education, medicine, and, as Fran puts it bluntly, 'conversion of the heathen'. The religiosity of the late Victorians often seems very alien to us today, to be sure; but what comes out strongly from these pages, it seems to me – as in other published imperial memories, from the Raj too for example – is their humanity. For all the often racist attitudes of our great grandparents, for all their religious certainties, they were full of a love of China, a sympathy for the Chinese people, and a determination to make a better world. As Fran says in her epilogue, their educational legacy today is hard to see, especially after nearly 70 years of Communist Party rule; in religion too, though there are Christian churches in Wuhan, these are not easy times for Chinese Christians. But in medicine it is another story: their legacy is today's impressive Union hospital at Wuhan, a link now acknowledged and celebrated by the local Chinese.

So Fran's return to Wuhan and her visit to the hospital makes a fitting end to a moving story. As a memoir of a courageous British family through the age of empire it is a compelling, and often touching recessional: or, as the Chinese would say, a report to the ancestors worthy of recital each year when we give them thanks on the day of the Qingming Festival.

Michael Wood, historian and broadcaster, June 2016

The Gillison family in 1882:
Mary Agnes, Thomas, Jane (mother), John, Andrew, Jane, Marion.

Introduction

Sometimes it seems that coincidence, chance or some totally insignificant event can bring about an unexpected new area of interest in one's life. This happened to me ten years ago when, through a casual invitation from a friend, I was lent a book by the travel writer Simon Winchester called 'The River at the Centre of the World' , an account of a journey which the author took from Shanghai to the source of the Yangtze River in Central China. It was of particular interest because I was born in Wuhan (formerly called Hankow and that is the name that is most frequently used in this book), a city on the Yangtze River about five hundred miles from Shanghai. In the chapter on Wuhan, Simon Winchester wrote, among other things, about the Revolution of 10 October 1911 which actually started in Wuchang – the city on the other side of the river from Hankow – but which spread to Hankow itself and then to other parts of China. Four months later it led to the abdication of the six-year-old Emperor Xuan-Tong on 12 February 1912. While I was reading, it suddenly occurred to me that my grandparents would have been in Hankow at that time, working for the London Missionary Society and that there might be some reference to the event in the cardboard box of old family letters in our loft which no one had looked at for decades. In the box, I found two surprising letters – the first was indeed an account, written by my grandfather, describing the fighting going on outside his window in that 1911 Revolution; the second was a description of a battle that took place half the world away in South Africa, at Elandslaagte – one of the first battles of the Boer War.

The discovery of these letters was highly significant for it suddenly opened wide a window on my family's missionary past which until then had been obscured, like frosted glass. Perhaps because of my own experience as the daughter of missionaries, my views on the missionary ethic have always been ambivalent, especially in regard to family relationships. Circumstances are very different now from what they were between the years 1850–1950; the world has shrunk particularly in terms of transport and communication. Modern missionary families would no longer have to face long term separations as they did in my childhood and in that of my missionary forebears. For them it was the overwhelmingly strong conviction that what they were doing was in God's name which compelled them to carry through these separations sometimes conflicting with their equally strong natural instincts. For someone who has never been driven in that way it is difficult to understand but I have always felt that a missionary couple, who chose to educate their children for long periods thousands of miles away, could not expect their relationship with their children to be necessarily close when the family was reunited.

In my case the Second World War exacerbated the situation. We, as a family, had come back to the UK in 1938 – just in time for my sister and me to start as boarders at Walthamstow Hall in Sevenoaks (a school for the daughters of missionaries) in September 1938. In November 1939 my parents sailed from Tilbury in the S.S.Narkunda. Looking back now it seems astonishing that, with all the uncertainty of a world war just beginning, with Japan already overrunning China and having no idea of what the situation could be in five year's time, my parents taking with them their four-year-old son could contemplate a dangerous journey by sea to return to China. My mother's diary of the voyage mentions the need for a total black-out of the ship and announcements by the captain about his having to steer a zig-zag course to avoid detection by German U-boats. I have no idea of the thinking of the Missionary Societies on this point but they must have felt that the work should go on. In any case a full complement of missionaries was out in the field already and they would be expecting the return of their colleagues. What the future was going to hold for any of them was impossible to predict. I was seven years old when my parents left and fourteen when they returned and, because of the war communication or correspondence for the last three of those years was virtually impossible. From 1939 until the end of 1941 my father was able to work at the hospital fairly normally but on December 8th 1941, after Pearl Harbor, the medical staff were forbidden by the Japanese authorities to leave the hospital without a permit. Treating their Chinese patients in the city became very difficult. In August 1942 all foreign nationals were moved first to Shanghai and from there they were eventually dispersed to camps in and around the city. The Gillisons together with six hundred other internees were sent to Camp C at Yangchow, about one hundred miles from Shanghai. During the three years my parents and brother were interned we were able to exchange a few twenty-five word Red Cross messages which sometimes took many months to arrive; there is little of significance that can be written in a letter of that kind. Had the war not extended their normal tour of duty beyond five years they must have been prepared for a lengthy separation – but I, as a seven-year-old, was not. Our family was not unique in this regard. Among my peers there were some who were similarly separated from their parents and the problem of reinstating a relationship after many years was not an uncommon one. There was a story about a girl at my school whose parents were missionaries somewhere in Africa and whom she had not seen for nearly ten years. In the Reception Room at Walthamstow Hall there was a grand piano and particularly musical children were allowed to practise on it. The protocol was that were visitors shown into the room the girl should quietly collect her music and depart. On this particular occasion when visitors arrived the child acted correctly and politely left the room, only to be called back ten minutes later because the visitors were her own parents and she had not recognized them – nor they her.

As a second generation daughter of missionaries, the discovery of these old family letters gave me an insight into the lives and attitudes of an earlier generation which would not have been possible except through the intimacy of the letters. I have some memories of my grandparents although I was only four when grandmother Bessie died and five years old at grandfather Thomas's death seven months later. Childhood memories are notoriously unreliable, so appreciating and understanding that generation through the letters has been a great and rare privilege.

On the advice of a friend I took the letters to the School for Oriental and African Studies at the University of London, who did noble work assessing and cataloguing them. The librarians expressed an interest in adding them to the

School's collection so, in consultation with my brother and sister, it was decided that we would eventually donate them to the Library after I had transcribed them for the convenience and interest of the family, and this was duly done in November 2015. SOAS already holds the archives of the former London Missionary Society (now Council for World Missions) and our papers will help give an interesting personal slant to the existing official collection. Transcribing the letters turned out to be a huge but compelling task which in the event took my friend and me about seven winters to complete. The project was eventually finished towards the end

The author, Frances (*neé* Gillison), (*left*), and sister, Meili, (*centre*) on 'the school run' accompanied by their young brother Walford (*circa* 1937). Born in China, the children spent their early years there before being sent to boarding school in England. Pulling the rickshaw is Da Tse Fu, who was also the household cook.

of 2009 and consisted of over 750 items divided between three volumes entitled 'The Gillison Letters'. A limited number of copies were printed and circulated round the family and other interested parties including the SOAS. However with all the material we had we believed there was a story worth telling – this book is the result.

Not unnaturally, as the bulk of the letters were written to and by my grandparents, my grandfather Thomas Gillison is the main character in this story. However because the Gillisons were a very close knit family, the lives of each sibling were very important to the other five and this is reflected in the correspondence. Like many Scots of the time, five of the six of them moved to different continents for various reasons but their concern for each other remained undiminished. How such a diverse collection of letters came to rest in the same cardboard box will always remain a mystery.

On a personal note – I am deeply indebted to the late Barbara Bastable for the years of dedicated hard work she gave in helping me to transcribe the letters. Without her enormous contribution the project would have fallen at the first hurdle. Together we experienced a full range of emotion as, the more we read, the more we found ourselves deeply involved with the characters. There were those we grew to love and those we could not warm to; there were many whose faith, undiminished by extreme tragedy and hardship, we could only admire. It was an unforgettable experience. My thanks are also due to many friends and family who gave me both encouragement and practical help. However, I am especially grateful to Trevor Bounford who gave so generously of his time and professional expertise to iron out the creases and tranform my original manuscript into a readable book.

Frances Clemmow 2016

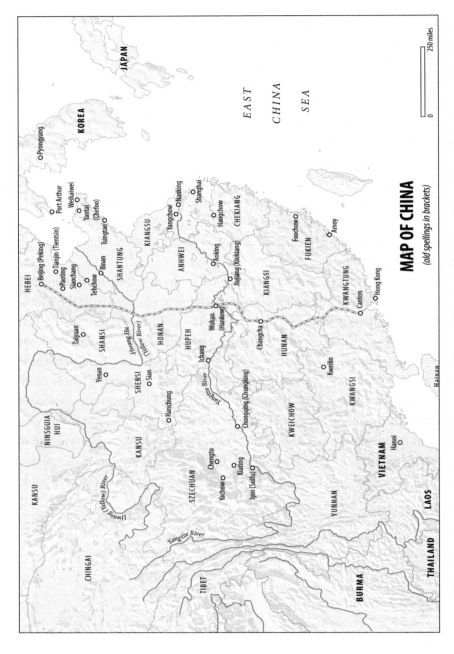

Map of China showing the location of Hankow on the Yangze River and the main railway linking Hong Kong and Peking.

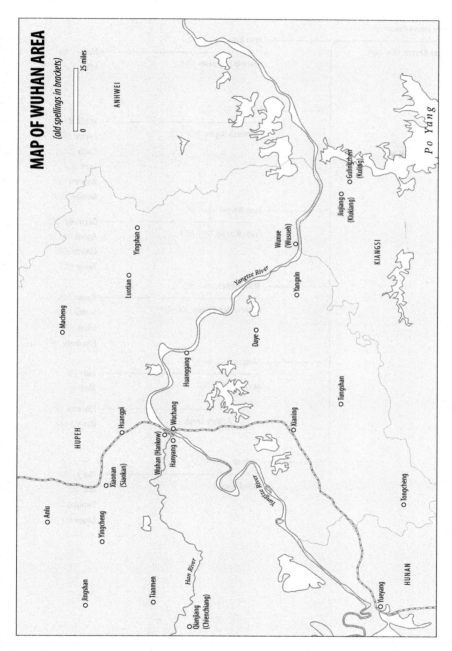

Map of the area around Hankow showing some of the places mentioned in the text.

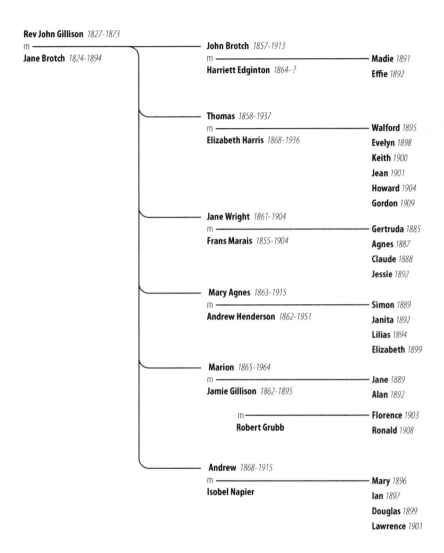

Rev John Gillison *1827-1873*
m ⎯⎯⎯⎯⎯
Jane Brotch *1824-1894*

John Brotch *1857-1913*
m ⎯⎯⎯⎯⎯⎯⎯⎯⎯⎯⎯⎯⎯⎯⎯⎯
Harriett Edginton *1864- ?*

Madie *1891*
Effie *1892*

Thomas *1858-1937*
m ⎯⎯⎯⎯⎯⎯⎯⎯⎯⎯⎯⎯⎯⎯⎯⎯
Elizabeth Harris *1868-1936*

Walford *1895*
Evelyn *1898*
Keith *1900*
Jean *1901*
Howard *1904*
Gordon *1909*

Jane Wright *1861-1904*
m ⎯⎯⎯⎯⎯⎯⎯⎯⎯⎯⎯⎯⎯⎯⎯⎯
Frans Marais *1855-1904*

Gertruda *1885*
Agnes *1887*
Claude *1888*
Jessie *1892*

Mary Agnes *1863-1915*
m ⎯⎯⎯⎯⎯⎯⎯⎯⎯⎯⎯⎯⎯⎯⎯⎯
Andrew Henderson *1862-1951*

Simon *1889*
Janita *1892*
Lilias *1894*
Elizabeth *1899*

Marion *1865-1964*
m ⎯⎯⎯⎯⎯⎯⎯⎯⎯⎯⎯⎯⎯⎯⎯⎯
Jamie Gillison *1862-1895*

Jane *1889*
Alan *1892*

m ⎯⎯⎯⎯⎯⎯⎯⎯⎯⎯⎯⎯⎯⎯⎯⎯
Robert Grubb

Florence *1903*
Ronald *1908*

Andrew *1868-1915*
m ⎯⎯⎯⎯⎯⎯⎯⎯⎯⎯⎯⎯⎯⎯⎯⎯
Isobel Napier

Mary *1896*
Ian *1897*
Douglas *1899*
Lawrence *1901*

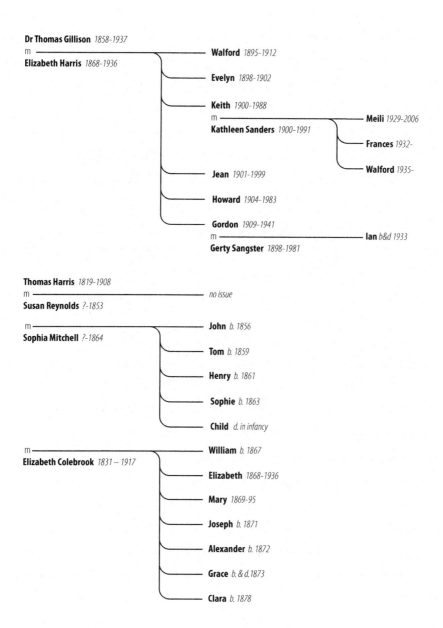

Dr Thomas Gillison *1858-1937*
m ———————————— **Walford** *1895-1912*
Elizabeth Harris *1868-1936*
———————————— **Evelyn** *1898-1902*

Keith *1900-1988*
m ———————————— **Meili** *1929-2006*
Kathleen Sanders *1900-1991*
———————————— **Frances** *1932-*
———————————— **Walford** *1935-*

Jean *1901-1999*

Howard *1904-1983*

Gordon *1909-1941*
m ———————————————————— **Ian** *b&d 1933*
Gerty Sangster *1898-1981*

Thomas Harris *1819-1908*
m ———————————————————— *no issue*
Susan Reynolds *?-1853*

m ———————————— **John** *b. 1856*
Sophia Mitchell *?-1864*
———————————— **Tom** *b. 1859*

Henry *b. 1861*

Sophie *b. 1863*

Child *d. in infancy*

m ———————————— **William** *b. 1867*
Elizabeth Colebrook *1831 – 1917*
———————————— **Elizabeth** *1868-1936*

Mary *1869-95*

Joseph *b. 1871*

Alexander *b. 1872*

Grace *b. & d. 1873*

Clara *b. 1878*

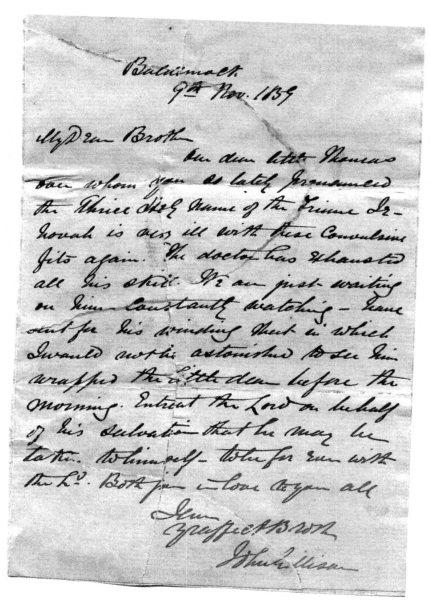

Rev John Gillison's letter to his brother.

ONE

Introduction to the family

Three letters set the scene for the beginning of this story. The Rev. John Gillison, father of baby Thomas, sent them to his brother, a fellow minister, telling him of the very serious convulsions from which his five-week-old son was suffering.

Baldernock 9th Nov 1859

Our dear little Thomas over whom you so lately pronounced the Thrice deity name of the Triune Jehovah is very ill with these convulsive fits again. The doctor has exhausted all his skill. We are just waiting on him constantly watching – have sent for his winding sheet in which I would not be astonished to see him wrapped the little dear before morning. Entreat the Lord on behalf of his salvation that he may be taken to himself – to be for ever with the Lord. Both join in love to you all

I am

Your affect Brother

John Gillison

Saturday 12th Nov 1859

My Dear Tom

    Our dear baby is still spared to us. His days have indeed been few and full of suffering. His trouble is more like what is called 'nine day fits' than any thing else. Last night he had between 5 and 8 great suffering – when he had complete relief for 4 hours – till 12, then his sufferings again began and have continued almost without intermission till now, 9.15 A.M. this morning. At the present moment they are not so frequent. On another occasion since I wrote you Jane & I were waiting beside him expecting every 5 minutes to be his last. His forehead, eyes and round about his mouth was blue and deathlike, very. I was just thinking this morning that if he was spared to us after all this, we might call him 'Little Wonder' for his agony and suffering have been continuous and extreme. The doctor expected days ago to find his little patient gone when he arrived. ....He is again resting but very weak. He takes very little support of any kind. He drank the breast this morning to our great astonishment after he was dressed. Jane is bearing up under the fatigue of both body & mind wonderfully. I have never had my clothes off since Monday – Jane only twice – though these times more for the refreshment than time she rested.

    Other people have offered to sit, but we would not feel comfortable if one or the other was not with him.

For seven days John and Jane Gillison anxiously waited by his cot until Thomas turned the corner and John was able to write to his brother again with the good news of Thomas's recovery and there was no need to use the winding sheet.

Baldernock 16th Nov. 1859

My Dear Tom

> *You will both be glad to hear that your dear little namesake is greatly*
> *better. He is almost well again. He has not had an ill turn for 20 hours*
> *never rested so quietly while sleeping nor was so good while awake since*
> *he was born as he has been during that time. We have now good hopes*
> *not only of a complete recovery but that there are none of his faculties at*
> *all impaired. The doctor now says it is impossible to say whether they will*
> *or not. My conviction along with Jane's is that he did not understand his*
> *trouble. We have been doing things ourselves through the advice of a non-*
> *professional friend from Glasgow that seem to have done him more good*
> *than anything else he has yet received – viz – hot fomentations to his*
> *bowels. I hope you will now unite with us in giving thanks that we have*
> *received him again as from the dead.*

Thomas was my grandfather and had he not survived neither I nor this book would exist. He was one of six siblings – three boys and three girls brought up by their widowed mother after the death of their father at the age of 43. John Gillison had been inducted to the Roxburgh Free Church in Edinburgh in 1872 but died of smallpox in December 1873 and Jane was left with a family of children ranging from five to fifteen to bring up on her own. Arrangements would have been made for the support of widows and orphans by Free Church funds but even so Jane had to be very careful of her money. The family lived at 143 Warrender Park Road which was a very pleasant part of Edinburgh and the terraced houses built on three floors were divided into spacious flats. With six growing children Jane needed the space but as the children grew up and left home she made a living by letting rooms to young boarders to keep herself and Andrew, the youngest child, and to pay for a living-in maid.

Jane came from a farming family in Dumfriesshire. She was one of the six surviving children of Mary and John Brotch, a Portioner (owner of a small piece of land within a larger estate), at Castlemains, Lochmaben. In the corner of an old Brotch family tree someone has scribbled – 'Jane the clever sister, Marion the skilly (*practical*) sister, Jessie the pretty sister'. Whether that was true or not we cannot tell but it makes a neat comment on the trio. Jane's niece, Mary Black (the pretty sister Jessie's daughter), was devoted to Jane and the Gillisons, and although she lived with her widowed mother, Jessie, in 1 Church Place, Lochmaben, close to the family farm, she was always ready to come to Edinburgh and help in a crisis.

A devout woman, Jane's world was bound up with the Barclay Church and its community. She was a great admirer of Dr Wilson, the minister and at Dr Wilson's request she frequently asked Tom to send reports from China for the church magazine. Until the departure of John to Australia and Tom to China, Jane had had moral support from the two older boys in the upbringing of Andrew, her youngest child. From John, who was earning, she received financial contributions. She was a formidable lady, fiercely proud of her family and their achievements, always expecting high standards and yet she was capable of both giving and receiving warmth and affection.

As there are no significant letters between 1859 and 1882 we are not told how the family lived in the intervening years at Baldernock and from 1872 in Edinburgh but by 1882 John, the eldest, was working

Jane Gillison –
widow of Rev John Gillison.

in an insurance office and was living at home. Thomas, a medical student at Edinburgh, had qualified that summer. He had offered himself as a medical missionary to the London Missionary Society and had been appointed to the London Mission Hospital in Hankow (now Wuhan) earlier in the year and preparations were well advanced for his departure in October. There appears to have been no requirement to serve any kind of post graduate hospital registration at the time.

In these days of instant communication and rapid movement all over the globe it is salutary to remember that a hundred and thirty years ago the voyage to the Far East occupied at least six weeks; that letters took a month or more to arrive and even the telegram could be a few days in transit. Furlough, or home leave, was granted about every five years but was sometimes hastened or delayed depending on the health needs or particular circumstances of the missionaries. Thomas Gillison's first leave came after nine years in China which was an unusually long period to serve without respite. Disease and death were no strangers to the missionaries of the time but everything that Fate delivered, no matter how tragic, was accepted with fortitude and did not shake their staunch beliefs. In Hankow Tom was to be the only doctor at the mission hospital and would be coping entirely on his own – it must have been a daunting prospect.

So much of a person's character comes through reading the letters but apart from two short ones to his uncle about his appointment to Hankow by the London Missionary Society in 1892, there are no letters at all from Tom written to anyone during the next nine years. It is clear, however, from the letters he received (and kept) that he inspired great affection from family and friends and enormous respect as a doctor. A keen sense of humour clearly enlivened his more serious side as is shown in the banter in the letters from his friends – particularly Philip Cousland, a fellow student from medical college.

As to the picture I shan't send it you this time as you were pleased to call my last elegantly written letter an epistolatory scrawl !!!!!!!!! An epistolatory scrawl indeed!! However I take refuge in dignified silence merely

23

remarking that yours looks as if a hen had got into the inkpot and then waltzed across your paper! so there! (N.B. these marks (!!) express indignation with the eloquence of silence!)

Philip's teasing remarks from time to time offer a glimpse of Tom's personality and interests.

> *I have been longing so for a line from you! Hope deferred maketh the heart sick. Fortunately my heart has a strong stomach & is not easily sickened. It knows your letter writing propensities well. Yes! Many a time and oft of yore had the post bag been one letter too light. But I forget & forgive. If you haven't been wasted & eaten & even if you have, you might try and drop me a note. Next week if you don't, I shan't send you a roast turkey on Christmas! Happy fellow, if you haven't been eaten you have been roasted and stewed. I daresay till you are as thin as the lamppost you used to be in collision with when you walked along the meadow walk reading diligently – you always were such a bookworm.*

For some reason John had also decided to spread his wings and go abroad to work. There are no clues as to the reason for this but sometimes the impression he gives in his letters is that money and status were of significant importance to him and he may have considered that there were better prospects in Australia. His mother, Jane, was constantly worried by his lack of a God-fearing attitude to life. It was particularly hard on their mother that he was going to Australia so soon after Tom's departure for China.

The last of the boys and youngest of the family was Andrew. Only five when his father died and fourteen when the story begins, he was still at school and needing some parental discipline and encouragement to keep his nose to the grindstone. Jane frequently poured out her possibly unnecessary worries to Tom in her letters about Andrew's lack of concentration or application to his studies. The one subject he excelled at was recitation. He was in constant demand at social gatherings and concert parties. There could have been no surprise that he decided to go into the Church for a career.

All three of Tom's sisters were destined to become governesses or teachers. By the time of the first letters of 1882, Tom's eldest sister, Jane, was already teaching at a little school at 30, George Square; Mary Agnes, at 18, was close to the end of her time at a school in Hanover, Germany and was shortly to take up a position as a governess to the family of the Rev. Guthrie in Liberton, south of the city then but now a mere suburb of Edinburgh. Virtually the only career that was open to daughters of the manse was to become a governess which, of itself, would require the teaching of foreign languages and to this end a stay in a foreign country was excellent training. How Jane was able to afford to send her daughters Jane and Mary Agnes to Germany – even for a short stay is a puzzle. By contrast it is interesting to see that Thomas's future wife, Bessie Harris, who on the other hand came from a fairly wealthy family, also received the final part of her education in Germany. In her case, however, she would not have become a governess but would have been expected to live at home after her education was complete and engage in 'good works' in the local community until a suitable marriage partner could be found for her. Bessie's father, Thomas Harris, was well able to afford for Bessie to train as a doctor as will be seen in later letters. In December 1886 Bessie, my grandmother, wrote to her sister Mary to tell her of her decision to train as a doctor and further to apply to become a lady medical missionary. She said:

> *I feel that there is nothing to tell me I am needed at home; Sophie as far as we know will be staying there, and there is little for me to do indoors except seeking my own amusement, or perhaps, to express better what I mean, if I am always at home I cannot help spending a great deal of time*

for myself as it were, and this I do not wish to do. Besides this we know that Papa is in a position to make it easy for us to do anything of the kind and also that he would not object to it. He has said to me once or twice that although we shan't have to do anything to gain our living, he hoped his girls would find something to do. Since I have been home I have felt very much drawn to 'Medical Zenana work'. It is like this, I don't think I should ever care for teaching or speaking, whereas in speaking to anyone in any difficulty or trouble (even from the little experience I have had) I feel how my whole heart goes out; and I therefore think perhaps if by being able to relieve their bodily needs I could get at the spiritual needs of any, I might perhaps be made a blessing to some poor thirsting souls. You know too how often there is an appeal made for lady medical missionaries and each time I hear it I long to go.

Mary Agnes Gillison, with the more modest background, had no option but to become a governess. She wrote a rather charming letter to Tom from the school in Germany wishing him good luck in his final examinations shortly before her return to Edinburgh:

4ᵗʰ January 1882

Just a little note to wish you all success in the two coming exams that Marion told me you were going to have. Are they class exams? No matter how much I would like to hear from you and all about how you spent your holidays, which seem to have been very nice, you are not to write till you have time. Remember and tell me how you get on next Saturday as I suppose your exam will be in the morning before my letters are posted, as I will be very anxious to know, but I have no doubt if you study well you will get on well and I won't forget you in my prayers. Last Saturday we had a very long walk to Thiergarten & I spent all our forenoon there and came home to dinner. We played all sorts of games with our German governess and enjoyed it pretty well but we were fearfully tired on the Sabbath. We went to Military Service

in the Schloss Church on Sabbath morning where all the soldiers go to church
and fill the body of the church and lots of them go in the galleries too. It
began at nine o'clock. The German officers are very conceited and just imagine
in a Scotch church anyone taking out a small brush & comb & brushing
their hair and moustache. Tell John he would see what moustaches were if he
came here. I think why they are so nice is because by the constant brushing &
twirling, whenever they come into a house they go right up to the mirror &
put all to rights before you.

Of the Gillison girls the eldest, Jane, seemed to attract the most attention of
the young men, particularly Tom's friends from medical school who regularly
called at the house – often in pairs. Perhaps they found the Gillison household
under the matriarch Jane rather intimidating and needed the support of a friend.
Mary Agnes, who was two years younger than Jane, may not have had the more
immediately pretty looks of her older sister but her photographs show serene
and handsome features. She was certainly endowed with a keen sense of humour,
plenty of commonsense and made an amusing and easy companion. The youngest
of Jane Gilllison's daughters, Marion, was still at school in 1882. She was said to
be very delicate because she had had rheumatic fever when younger which would
explain why she did not go abroad to learn a language, but as she lived to a few
months short of her 100th birthday, she may have outgrown the handicap of her
youthful illnesses. I am convinced that she played a little on her frailty to tease
her mother although there is no doubt that she suffered from frequent colds and
chest infections. Her character, as shown in the letters, suggests that she was a bit
headstrong and wilful but those characteristics probably stood her in good stead
in later life.

The official, practical and ceremonial arrangements for Tom's departure for
China were duly observed and early in October 1882 Thomas left Edinburgh,
accompanied by his mother. Jane was to see Thomas off from the quayside which
must have been a difficult and sad occasion for her. Mary Agnes, now home from
Germany and working as a governess for the family of the Rev. Guthrie at Liberton,

writes to Tom about the group of friends who had gathered to say farewell at the Caledonian station:

11th October 1882

> *What to begin to tell you about, I do not know, but I shall try and give you all possible news although the others at home will be writing and doing most of that and you will likely have the trouble of reading some things twice but that is better than not hearing them at all. To begin with we all felt desperately lonely and downcast as we plodded our way home from the Caledonian that memorable Friday evening, for it was memorable and will be long remembered by not a few I'm sure. Perhaps you did not hear that there were about forty friends in all there. It was so kind of them to come down and cheering too, as it shows a greater interest in missions and didn't the Psalm sound grand. It was very trying indeed for all of us especially, but I think everything went off wonderfully well. It was so much nicer for you to have dear Mama with you and really it is quite astonishing to see just how bravely she keeps up under every trial.*

> *I suppose the last news we shall have of you will be from Suez until your arrival (DV) at Shanghai. It is a long time to wait but we must just have patience and after that we hope to hear regularly. I got the chance of writing a little while this afternoon as I could not practise as Mrs Guthrie had some friends and now that it is dark and I've had recourse to my candle as we have no gas here I think I had better lay this aside and go downstairs as I don't wish exactly to burn out my candle. I have scarcely any time to myself now and the short time I used to have has now to be spent in reading to little Jane Guthrie, while she lies on her back. Then M^r & Mrs Guthrie were away for two days when of course I had the charge of the house which was a great responsibility – but everything got on nicely. Of course I had to have worship which was rather a thought to me at the time, but which like everything else passed away. The first evening I thought I would not trust myself without any notes, so therefore I wrote out my prayer and read it but the next morning*

*it was extempore although of course I prepared it but was very glad after
everything was over that I had the opportunity given me, still it was rather a
little trial to me before all the Guthrie family and three servants. Pray for me
my dear Tom that I set a good example before these children and that my
acquaintance with them may be blessed. There is no doubt but that it is one
of the most delightful families I could be with, but of course it has its trials like
every other situation.*

*The first bell has just rung for tea, so I must close and wishing a very
happy and prosperous voyage and may our Heavenly Father keep you and
preserve you from all danger and bless you in all your work.*

This was the letter written by Robert Robertson, a friend of Thomas's, and it too
paints a vivid picture of the farewell given to Thomas by his family and friends.
Robertson would, himself, become a missionary in China:

Oct 2ⁿᵈ 1882

*I hope you are not thinking that my late arrival at the station on the
sad night of your departure was through a wilful carelessness. I was under
the impression that you were to leave by the 'Waverley' as you did before
& landed there about half an hour before the train time & waited till 9.20.
Came the hour at the Waverley for the departure of the Liverpool train when
not seeing yourself nor anyone of your friends arrive I began to think I had
made a mistake & was told that a train left the Prince's St Station at 9.25.
I had only 5 minutes to get from the Waverley to the Caledonian Station
&, determined to see you if at all possible I got into a hansom and told the
man to drive like Jehu of old (I did not use these exact words to the man
but told him to drive fast) & just landed into the station when the train was
starting in the startling way you last saw me. I tell you I was glad to get
once more a shake of your hand. Coming along Princes Street I was in a
desperate state. I don't think the grass had much time to grow beneath the
horse's feet on the way from the Waverley to the Caledonian on the night in*

*question but possibly it might. Had I missed you I don't know if I ever could
have got over it.*

*Although I missed mingling my sweet & unsophisticated voice with
the large company in the singing of that psalm still I had the great honour
of being the last of the persons at the station to shake hands with you. I don't
know whether you are pleased at such an honour being conferred on me
or not but God foreordains whatever comes to pass. I still think I hear your
parting words of blessing ringing in my ears.*

John Gillison left Edinburgh that November escorting a young relation of the
Jeffray's whose family were providing the contacts for John in Australia. His letter
to Tom gives an interesting account of the long voyage and was written in his
beautiful copperplate handwriting;

S.S.Ballaarat

7ᵗʰ Decʳ 1882

*At 12 o'clock today we were on Lat 7.17 N Long 76.02 E and were
230 miles from Colombo.*

*We left Gravesend on Thursday 9ᵗʰ Nov, just four weeks today, sailed
down the Channel etc, etc. In this and the Bay of Biscay we were not favoured
with very fine weather, but we got nothing to complain of. John James or, as
he is now more generally called, Jack, is with me. Miss Butterworth a friend
of Mʳ Jeffray's was also actually though not nominally, under my charge.
She is a pretty young lady of about 20 or so, undoubtedly colonial, smart in
her manner, a good chat and withal a general favourite. She is somewhat like
Maggie Stuart of Helensbro' both in appearance and general conduct though
with scarcely so good a figure.*

*Well on the Thursday night that we sailed, Jack was all right and slept
well but when he got up next morning he said he felt a little sick. Nevertheless
he came down to breakfast but was compelled to disappear after eating a*

quarter of a roll. He returned & manfully tried to eat, but had to give up and
when I went upstairs I found him in a miserable condition in his cabin sitting
disconsolate with his head in his hands. Carried him out (you must know
that we have a very nice deck cabin) laid him on a long chair, wrapped him
in rugs and in general cared for his comfort. Next day, Saturday and also
Sunday he could not rise and ate little or nothing, on Monday he was slightly
better and got up. Lay on a chair nearly all day. I fed him at intervals and
in the course of the afternoon he began to take an interest in what was going
on around him. Next day he was all right. Nothing further was the matter
with him until we had got through the Red Sea and past Socotra. There the
sea was rougher and I think that combined with the heat and perhaps food
that did not agree with him laid him up for a couple of days but now he is
all right again. Miss Butterworth was never sick worth speaking of and as for
myself I did not think of it. I did my duty at table and was never absent. The
worst weather that we have had was in the Bay of Biscay. One night we had it
so 'hot' that the waves or spray splashed right up to the top of the funnels; but
our good ship was very steady and although we had the racks on the tables
on several occasions, I saw very few things broken. That night we stopped for
one or two hours as the steam steering gear gave way; but next day it was put
right. We passed Gibraltar just as it was getting dark. Did not stop therefore
failed to get even a fair view of the rock. Arrived at Malta, went on shore,
drove to Civita Vecchia, saw St Paul's Bay in the distance,

St Paul's Cathedral in the old town, St Paul's Grotto or cave, an old
Roman house, with tile mosaics & old marble sculpture much damaged and
the Catacombs. Returned by the Governor's gardens and had a walk through
the orange groves & pulled and ate as we went along. Then saw the sights
of Valetta – the Church of St John, the palace, armoury and market and
returned on board in good time for dinner. Then to Port Said. On the way
something about the engines gave way and we were unable to move for
three hours. All put right again.

This being our maiden voyage we are more liable to accidents of this nature than a vessel that has been sailing for some time. These stoppages do not include several others that we had to make on account of the heating of the piston rod of the high pressure cylinder.

Arrived at Port Said. Landed & took a walk through the town. Then through the canal, in which we lay for two nights. Arrived at Suez about 5 in the afternoon. Went on shore next morning. Had rides on donkeys – Jack on 'M*rs* Langtry', Miss Butterworth on 'M*rs* Cornwallis-West', and I on 'Lefroy'. Such a lark! Visited the native garden and saw the interior of a mosque. Backsheesh the general cry and 'swindle' the all-prevailing motto.

Returned on board. We saw the 'Maliva' coming in (The 'Maliva' was the steamer in which M*r* and M*rs* & Miss Jeffray were. They joined us at Suez.) as we were doing so, but were more than astonished, why horrified, to be informed that she had been run into by a steamer of the Clan line & had had one of her boats smashed to atoms, a large portion of the railing torn off and a big hole torn in her side, extending below the water line. At that very moment we could see her heeling over and apparently sinking but the Captain ran her on a sand bank and all lives were safe. Boats were launched from us and other ships in a twinkling: eight were off from a man-of-war the 'Carysfort' in about two minutes; but their services were not required.

In the course of half an hour or so the Jeffrays and all their luggage were on board us safe. Nobody 'of ours' appeared to have lost anything or to be put about, except one oldish lady, who had been using approved means of keeping up her spirits!! We were unable to start that afternoon as expected, in fact did not know when we would start at all. So next morning we set off to see the wreck and on arriving were about to go on board, but to our dismay we were told that our captain had gone off some little time before and that in all probability the anchor of the 'Ballaarat' was at that moment being weighed. Hastened on board and were just in time; others had a narrow squeak and two second class passengers were actually left behind to make the best of their way to Australia by any of the P & O vessels that had room for them.

The vessel that ran into the 'Maliva' was damaged considerably but was not in a sinking condition and made her way to the docks. We could not tell and when we left nobody knew whose fault it was.

Did not stop at Aden. Merely saw the bare burnt looking rocks in the distance. Passed Cape Gardafin pretty closely one morning & Socotra in the distance in the course of the afternoon. And here we are.

Of life on board ship I need say little except that we are a 'jolly family'. I am not at all tired of it. Rise about 6.30 or 7. Salt water bath followed by a rub down in fresh. Walk on deck in pyjamas until eight. Dress, breakfast at nine. Four or five things to chose from. Read, smoke, play backgammon, chess or draughts or sing or talk till luncheon or tiffin at 1. Cold meats, fowl or turkey etc. Afternoon, second edition of forenoon until about 4 when I usually have a cup of tea with one of the numerous family parties on board. Dinner at six. Eight courses or so. We have a piano on deck which was subscribed for by the passengers & bought at Malta to be raffled for before the end of the voyage. This is used for dancing two or three times a week, concerts on Mondays as a rule, and last night we had a theatrical performance & thereafter a 'Christy Minstrel' performance the latter by the Saloon stewards.

About ten or half past most of the ladies retire and the gentlemen don their sleeping dress and loll about until 11 or so. Some sleep on deck. This Jack and I do not require to do. Some of the ladies sleep in the saloon which is somewhat like a gallery to the dining saloon and opens on to the main deck. It is cooler and more comfortable than the cabins particularly when ports are closed

The sky is beautiful at night just now. The comet is visible nightly after 11. This morning about 2, I happened to get up & saw it beautifully almost overhead. Orion is beautiful. The 'plough' has almost disappeared and we have *not yet seen the 'Southern Cross'. Meteors are plentiful. Last night a green one was seen about 10.30.*

As to heat – I wore my winter flannels until we arrived at Port Said. In the Red Sea & Arabian Gulf we had a good deal of 'muggy' heat, that made one feel always dirty and ones clothes always sticky. Just now I have on a flannel tennis suit, but no underclothing and a black alpaca coat. The perspiration is standing in beads on my forehead and chin, and I require to mop it up occasionally; but I like it all the same. It is far better than the nasty East winds of 'Auld Reekie'.

I had a letter from Mama at Suez. They were all well.

I shall post this at Colombo tomorrow. J.G.B

P.S. Excuse the writing as the throbbing of the screw and the long roll of the Indian Ocean are not conducive to extra good penmanship.

Besides I wrote a letter of 21 pages to Mary Agnes this morning.

In the years that followed Jane wrote frequent letters to Tom in Hankow – often complaining that his in return were few and far between. Her letters and those of the other members of the family paint a very clear picture of the occupations and aspirations of a modest Scottish family. John, in Australia, kept in touch with his family in Edinburgh and, despite the faults his mother saw in him, he showed concern for her and sent her money from time to time.

1882 Nov 14

This is the famous photograph of the Great September Comet of 1882 taken by Sir David Gill on November 14 at the Cape Observatory. Many stars are visible in the background. John Gillison's letter of 7th December mentions sighting the comet and the passengers would have had an excellent view as the ship crossed the Indian Ocean.

Jane Gillison

Frans Marais

TWO

Jane's engagement

At the time Tom was a student, South Africans were obliged to come to Europe to train as doctors because there were no medical schools in their homeland until 1912. Tom had friends among the South African students and one of these was Francois Marais (known to his family as Frans). Tom must have brought his friends to the family home and there Frans Marais met and fell in love with Jane, Tom's eldest sister. Frans Marais had also qualified as a doctor in the summer of 1882 and following his success he did not immediately return to South Africa but took the opportunity to tour the continent. Reading between the lines it would seem that Frans's intention was to stay within a reasonable distance of Edinburgh so that he could maintain contact with Tom and thereby court Jane by correspondence until he could gauge what his prospects were. Frans Marais wrote to Thomas:

August 11 '82

I called twice to say goodbye to you. I failed on both occasions – as you know – to find you in. As a 'dernier resort' I took to writing, in order to wish you God's speed on your way & in your work. May you be the means of relieving many a poor sufferer in China, and if it so happens that, 'only one of the nine' returns to thank you and embrace Christianity, remember that they did it even to our Lord and Master.

We had a pretty rough passage across. Nearly everybody on board the vessel was sick. Dʳ Muirhead also came across in the same boat. He and a few other Gentlemen were not ill. We came together as far as Berlin. He was to leave yesterday. – As soon as the steamer left the Docks (Leith), one of the sailors smashed 3 fingers of his left hand. As I was the only Surgeon on board, I undertook to dress it. Fortunately I had some eucalyptus oil & so I could treat it antiseptically. The next day I could not see him – for obvious reasons – On Monday I saw him again, dressed his fingers, which were doing beautifully …

… Enclosed I send you a copy of my photos and one to Miss G. Tell Miss Mary Agnes she shall have one later. In return, I hope to get one from you & Miss G, if she has one to spare. Of course I can't expect one from Miss Mary Agnes before I send her one. But if she's not so particular, I'll be glad to get hers now – if she has one to spare.

Remember me kindly to Miss G & Miss Mary Agnes & to Mrs G, your youngest sister & to John.

Hoping that you will have a prosperous voyage, and be very successful in all your undertakings.

One of Jane's suitors had been Dr Underwood, a friend of Tom's, who had been smitten in earlier days. Unsuccessful but still hopeful, he had embarked on his own career as a missionary and was now appointed to work in Kiu Kiang, further up the river from Shanghai. Kiu Kiang was one of the great cities through which Tom passed on his way to Hankow and it seems he took advantage of the fact and spent a few days with his friend, helping him, briefly, with his medical work – Hankow just had to wait. At the end of December Jane wrote to Tom in some embarrassment because she had received a gift from Dr Underwood:

Edinburgh, 29th Dec 1882

I wish you a very happy New Year. It is a month since I wrote you and John, but I know that Mama and Mary Agnes are such good correspondents that you do not want for news. Many thanks for your letter from Hong Kong. It was very interesting and instructive. I hope you will always be in as good spirits. It must have been sad parting with your

missionary brethren with whom you had spent so many weeks. Last Saturday
evening I got a lovely silver necklet from Dr Underwood. It is a very handsome
and weighs over half a pound (of course you need not mention to D^r
Underwood that I told you the weight of it as if we were looking at it from a
mercenary point of view).

Tom must have been able to write or speak to Dr Underwood about it on Jane's
behalf and one supposes that she kept the necklet for Jane wrote again:

21st Feb. 1883

> *I received your letter marked 'private' today. You may depend upon me*
> *that I will burn it and not show it to anyone. Very many thanks for acting*
> *the part of a true and noble brother. It was good of you to let me know of Dr*
> *Underwood's intentions & I can never forget this kindness. The only thing that*
> *I am sorry for is that there may be a letter on its way to Edinburgh from Kiu*
> *Kiang which I would rather never see, not that it would make any difference to*
> *me, but that if such were the case, it would be anything but agreeable for Dr. U.*

The matter was never raised again.

Mary Agnes, Tom's sister, commented on the apparent social attractions of the
Gillison household to the young men of the neighbourhood:

27th Dec 1882

> *Just a word or two to wish you a very good New Year as I dare say it*
> *will be rather different this year from last as it is for us too – we miss both you*
> *and John dreadfully – but we must just try to make the best of all the comforts*
> *we have, but there do not seem to be fewer gentlemen coming here although we*
> *have only the one male representative in the house – for instance this evening we*
> *are to have a few friends & I think three gentlemen more than ladies counting*
> *ourselves. David Robertson & Margaret, the Stewarts, Philip Cousland & the*
> *Hamiltons, Pritchard & Tomory – We hope to enjoy the evening – We had a*

*grand time last night at the Lowe's. You being a great subject of conversation...
Tomory & Pritchard make their usual fortnightly call and Tomory brings us a
bouquet every time & today he gave Pritchard two lovely white camellias to bring
to Jane & me to wear tonight. He is just rather too kind ... . I wish I could fly
across to China and get a peep at you once more.*

By the beginning of December Jane's love affair with Frans Marais was blossoming.
She wrote to Tom:

9th Jan 1883

*Before I left home yesterday morning, I was cheered by hearing your
letter read. You seem quite at home already among 'the Sons of the Celestial
Empire'! How pleased you must have been to see Dr Underwood and spend a
few days with him. We feel very thankful that you and John have had such
a good passage, had it been the contrary Mama and all of us would have
passed a much duller holiday. – I often look at the 'W' [1] and think of you,
supposing our eyes will meet some fine starry evening.*

*We have had very pleasant holidays & they have passed only too
quickly. Mama is well and happy although she misses her two boys more
than I can tell. We were at a party at the Hendersons'. It was a mixture
of children and grown-up people and we did not enjoy it much – quite a
different class of people from those we would like to associate with.*

*Now I am going to tell you a secret – – – Dr Marais and I have been
corresponding for sometime & I shall leave you to imagine what it has come
to!!! Of course nothing is settled yet. He asked me to send him your address,
which I did yesterday and you will probably soon hear from himself. What
say you to all this, brother? I hope to give you more particulars in my next, so
until you hear again from me, keep all this strictly to yourself ... .*

*... Mary Agnes and I were at an entertainment in the Canongate,
but I am afraid we did not contribute much to the amusement of the people.*

We sang 'Cast thy burden on the Lord'. Mary took the alto, I soprano but somehow or other Mary did not find her note until about the middle of the piece! We flattered ourselves that the people would never notice it.

A month later events had reached a climax and Jane was anxious to tell her brother of her engagement and hoped for his approval:

6th February 1883

The last time I wrote you my mind was too much taken up with 'some other body' & I don't think I gave you many particulars about (oh!) Francis. That is what I call him as François sounds too foreign. The day you left us was a Friday, and the following Monday, according to your instructions, I sent Francis Mary's photo and my own, writing or rather scribbling a few lines along with them. On the 3rd of October he wrote to thank me for them and also said something in German about writing more but not without my permission on which he waited. This letter was lost by Marion on the way to school (as we thought, but since then it has turned up) and Mama had opened it but of course could not tell me all it contained, so I concluded that there was no need for me replying & did not do so. On the 29th of Nov I got another letter asking me if I would let him know whether I would correspond with him or not. If I refused he 'would not ask me to give any reason', but that it was too bad of me to ignore him all together. That letter Francis said was 'the result of mature consideration'. As you know we then commenced to correspond – then came 'the crisis' as he calls it during the Xmas holidays. I trust dear Tom that I have been rightly guided in this important matter. Both of us have sought guidance and I feel sure that it will be for God's glory & our own good. If you had read all his letters you would have been very pleased with them. He is coming to Edinburgh in April along with Campbell, who is engaged to a Miss Dunnachie of Glenboig near Coatbridge. It is possible that I may go out to the Cape in the autumn. McKenzie goes out then

and just a week ago Mr Lockhart told us that very likely he and Edith
would be going out to pay Anna a visit towards the end of the year. So
then if my beloved is ready for me either of those would be good escorts.
All this will likely be settled in April. Most of our friends know of our
engagement by this time & I have received lots of letters of congratulations.
Uncle David's would amuse you; it commenced thus 'Yours of the 16th
inst. To your Aunt, with the intelligence of an engagement entered into
between two parties. I hope the contract may be beneficial and profitable
(!!) to all concerned'. Now dear, I am sorry for having occupied so much of
your precious time but there is a time in one's life when such things are
excusable.

Dr Underwood was not alone in his affections for Jane. Tom's great friend Philip
Cousland and fellow student, who frequently berated Tom for not replying to his
letters, light-heartedly included himself in the long list of Jane's would-be suitors
in this letter to Tom. His letters are always highly entertaining:

Dear Tummas,

One requires to cultivate gratitude now-a-days. You may judge to
what a high state of culture it has attained in me when I tell you that
I was <u>grateful</u> – yes positively – absolutely overwhelmingly grateful for
your letter! Letter did I say? Humph! No time of course – Never plays
Lawn Tennis – Oh no! Nothing but Chinese characters & vowels from
morning to night. Dreams of them. Eats them. Drinks them. Everything
but writes & talks them. I can tell you one tip. If you write with a broad J
pen & write half text you would make 2 or 3 sentences compose quite a
respectable letter. If that wont do you can try thick paper 2 ounces the sheet
so that you can only send half a sheet at a time. Good idea that. In using
it pray make one exception & I will charge you nothing for the patent.
Apropos of Chinese characters. They are all very well in their way no doubt,
but I would in future strictly limit them to their native heath. My mental
powers are well known to you but they are really unable for the strain

*of deciphering heathen hieroglyphics. What can you mean by W.P.R. &
L.S.D.? [2] The latter is suspicious. I am truly grieved to see you referring to
it so often in your letters. It indicates a tendency to use the muck rake that
I had hoped was in a fair way of being extinguished. If you are hard up
please say so in plain English & I will do my best for you even to parting
with a shilling or two of my hard earned mammon. I always like to
cultivate a liberal spirit but I prefer to get others to give, than to give myself,
as it is good to teach others how to give.*

*No, you need not tell me of Marais' engagement – After I heard of
it I sat right down in a chair! Then I endured a fit of asthma for some time
after which I sallied forth & procured a revolver. Thereafter a shadow might
have been seen hovering around W.P.R in the evenings. At last one evening
2 figures might have been seen sitting on a seat in the meadow walk – a
sight that used to rejoice the heart of an ancient friend of mine. There was
some difficulty in making out that there were 2 figures and not one stout one.
However that point was settled by the fact that 2 heads could be made out
only they seemed to be united by some connecting medium so close together
were they! The gentle sibilations of the wind sighing thru' the trees might be
heard occasionally only, curiously enough, the meteorological report next day
said there had been no wind of any kind! But see! A dark shadow approaches
– It – But we draw a kindly veil. For further particulars see 'Weekly Scotsman'.*

Once Jane's engagement was announced and the excitement had died down, Jane
returned to the little school in George Square where she taught, eagerly awaiting
the summons from her fiancé to join him in South Africa. This would be in a
year or so, as soon as Frans could set up in medical practice and be well enough
established to afford to support a wife. Jane's mother nursed a heavy heart at the
prospect of her daughter's departure for she had already lost her two oldest sons to
foreign parts and her feelings about Jane's engagement were very mixed. She wrote
this letter to Tom at the end of January:

Edinburgh 24th Jan 1883

We were very glad to hear that you had arrived safely at Kiu Kiang and it was so nice that you could take Dr Underwood's practice. Was Mr John quite pleased that you remained? How are you doing for funds? And how will you ever be able to live and send what will pay Mr Middlemass by September?

I wish I could have helped you, but I have more than enough to do with myself and then I will have a great deal to do for dear Jane bye and bye. I suppose you will have got his (D^r M's) letter before this reaches you. The Lockhart's are very pleased to hear of the engagement, and they are coming to see us on Sat. afternoon and Mr Lockhart is going to bring a letter of Anna's description of her visit to Dr Marais' parents and read it to Jane. Your Uncle Thomas is very pleased also. He would like them to go to Fossaway in April and he thinks Jane ought to go out this Autumn with M^r McKenzie and not wait for him coming (i.e. Dr Marais) for her. I however will miss her very much but I do not wish to be selfish. God only knows what she is to be sent to the Cape for. Oh I do trust and pray that it may be to promote His cause there. I have been telling her that she might be a missionary in her own sphere. How glad I would be if this was the case. Dr Wilson is anxious for extracts from your letters for the supplement. You will need to give him as much missionary news as you can. Last Sab. our new elders were ordained under rather trying circumstances. Dr Wilson was seized with a bleeding of the nose in the interval, and Mr Stewart had to preach while Dr Wilson with difficulty got through the ordination. Those who accepted office were Messrs Bisset, Mogerson, Blyth, Hately, Scott and McAlpine. Mr Watson of Merchiston, one of the old elders, died very suddenly last week. Our communion is on Sab. and on the Tuesday following D^r & Mrs Wilson with four companions start for Palestine. He is to be presented with the 'needful' tonight. Col Young in the name of the congregation presented Dr Wilson with a cheque for £300 and he accepted it with very grateful thanks.

Marion has been at home with a cold for ten days but is a little better. Andrew is doing pretty well but I think he might study a little harder sometimes.

Lord Rosebery and the Master of the Merchant Company were visiting the school last week and Andrew was called out of his class to recite a piece to them. Some one said to him as he retired, 'You are an orator'.

Jane seems to have been sceptical about the large sum of money presented to her minister Dr Wilson from the congregation for his trip to Palestine which she ironically describes as 'needful'. Three hundred pounds in 1883 must have been a very considerable sum.

Frans Marais returned to Edinburgh in March for the first time since his written proposal of marriage to Jane. He was to stay with Mrs Gillison at 143 Warrender Park Road and get to know other members of the family. Jane writes to Tom:

22ⁿᵈ March 1883

I intended writing you a few lines last night from W.Pk. Rd & Francis was going to do the same, but, alas for good resolutions! – I went to the Waverley Station on Tuesday evening & met the Dr. He is not a bit changed, and of course seems a hundred times nicer in my eyes. My highest expectations of him he surpasses & we love each other dearly. We have much need to be thankful to our kind Heavenly father for permitting us to meet. Mama is so good and kind & does everything in her power to make him comfortable. I shall never forget the kind reception he got from my dear Mother – I must close now.

Mary Agnes writes:

As you by this time know we have Dr Marais with us. I need not say how much we all like him. He is so nice and a perfect gentleman. I have been enjoying my holidays so much but am sorry they are just at an end. He is so kind in taking us out and so interesting to talk to. I'm afraid he is going to spoil Jane, but of course he thinks that can't be. He gave her a lovely silver bracelet and the ring is also very beautiful – two diamonds and a sapphire in the centre – Both very good taste.

Tom's mother writes to Tom:

18th April 1883

Now I must tell you that I was very pleased that you approved of Jane's engagement with Marais. He has now been with us for four weeks and I can testify that I never knew a more gentlemanly man in both manner and feeling and I believe that he is a sincere Christian His friends here all speak well of him and Mr Marchand also bears the same testimony and says he 'speaks what he knows'. John has written me to ask him to insure his life in Jane's favour. When I told Francis this he said he had his life insured at the Cape for £500 and that by the law of his country if a husband died the day after his marriage every thing he had then belonged to his wife. So I do not like to press the matter further seeing she has no dowry. I expect he will pay for her passage out and I shall have to borrow for her outfit.

The D^r, that is Francis as Jane calls him, leaves us on the first of May and sails from Southampton on the 3rd in company with Campbell and Retief who gets his M.D. on Friday. Francis is going to take me to the 'capping'. Mackenzie has gone to London to be near his intended for a fortnight. He would like very much to take Dr Robertson's practice while he comes home for Dora Waugh. Jane and Francis were at Coatbridge one Sat. seeing Dr S. Campbell & his intended. She is young and sick and he is going to return to this country and her father is going to buy him a practice. The other Cape students don't think this very manly or independent in him but he told me that the recent death of his mother had altered circumstances. We had Bruce and Nellie Lockhart here one evening and both were very pleasant. Just fancy little Alice said one day to her mother, 'Oh! Mama do you know that I will just be 19 when Tom Gillison comes back again'. I hope she and many others will be spared to give you a joyful welcome.

In May Tom's sister Jane writes to him again:

Edinburgh 2nd May 1883

It is a fortnight now since I got your letter of congratulation. Many thanks for the same. I am so glad that you think so much of Frans, and that you are pleased with my engaging myself to him. He is a truly good fellow and I feel that if we are spared, we shall have a happy life together. The more I know of him, the more I like him for, under the quiet exterior, there is a true & noble heart. – I am sorry that I did not give you further particulars about what he intended to do, but probably by this time you will know more from our letters. Perhaps I had better repeat myself, or rather tell you what I thought I or somebody else had told you – To begin at the beginning Frans left us last night for London. He travelled by the L & N. Western leaving the Caledonian at 9.25 pm (the same train as you left by). He intends sailing from Southampton on Thursday by 'The Moor' for Cape Town. As you probably know it takes three weeks at most to go to Cape Town & Wellington is not more than a few hours in the train from the first mentioned place.

The people at Wellington have been longing for Frans to go out for the last few months & I suppose he will soon have a good Practice there. His parents & most of his relations live in or near Wellington. The Practice will be both Town and Country. He intends living in a Hotel or Boarding House when he goes out at first until he has made enough to procure & furnish a place of his own. Whenever he has accomplished that, I have promised that I will go out to him. Frans does not think that I shall be here much later than the end of the year. He told me that if he had gone to the Free States, he might have made £2000 a year easily, but that at Wellington he expects to be able to make £1000 per annum in a year or two. Don't say anything about this to him when you write.

Today as you may imagine, I feel very lonely or as if I had lost a part of myself. Last night we had such a meeting (farewell) at the Caledonian as you nor

47

I ever saw. There were about 40 people down to see Frans off; most of them Cape Students. Mama, Marion, Andrew, Tom Henderson, Henry, Jim as well as myself were there. If I had thought that there were to be so many to witness the trying scene, I do not think that I could possibly have made up my mind to go down to that Station – Frans was anxious for me to be there & I too, wanted to see the last of him. (You understand that in one sense I wanted to see the last of him, but not in another!) Both Frans & I stood the parting pretty well. He kissed me only four times – this Mama thought three times too often!! However, she might just have done the same had she been in my place. – When the train began to move off, the students gave three cheers & then sang 'For he's a jolly good fellow etc'. We came up from the Prayer Meeting tonight with Mrs Finnie & she has seen Frans twice. She thinks a great deal of him & said that I was a 'lucky girl'!!

Now, dear Tom, I hope you will excuse me for taking up so much of your valuable time in writing at such length about myself and that other self which you know I could not help writing about.

I am glad that you are in as good health and spirits as ever. Would you like to go to Chungking if you thought the L.M.S wanted you to do so? We all think that you would be much better in Hankow, but wherever you are most needed, I suppose you would be quite willing to go there. May the Lord guide you aright and help you with that language which to us seems to be dreadfully difficult. We do not forget to pray for you and your work. – I need not thank you yet for the things which you are sending us, as the box has not arrived. The contents will be much prized by each of us.

Marion bids me say that she has begun to study for the Locals & therefore cannot find time to write to you. She sends her love. Mama is pretty well but does not sleep much at night. Perhaps you know that she does not intend keeping a servant after the term and I do hope she won't suffer from too much work. Marion will be busy with her exam & although the family is small, there will be a good deal to do – Now I must close as it is late & Mama has given you lots of news.

Jane was to wait only just over six months before Frans Marais sent for her to join him in South Africa. It was a tremendous undertaking for a girl scarcely ever outside Edinburgh to leave her home and embrace a totally new culture, language and environment.

From Tom's mother to Tom:

17ᵗʰ May 1883

> *We have a quiet house and I miss my dear boys and girls very much. I often feel now that I would have liked had I been able to have had more of the society of my own family alone, but God did not will it so, as I saw plainly that it was my duty to keep boarders and now if the girls are to keep themselves they must go out into the world. I have truly very peculiar feelings at times and now that you are all scattering abroad, I fear never to meet all again on earth. I can only look forward to the great reunion above. I am now three score and in the order of nature, cannot expect to be spared very many years at most. That hymn 'A few more years shall roll' suits me well. Thanks for the birthday text. John wrote me that he was going to insure his life for £500 and he thought this was the best birthday gift he could give me. The girls had a good laugh at his economy!! It is very good of him however, and only what he ought to do. I am glad that the Dʳ yonder thought him 'a very good life'. He had a fine Easter holiday and went on shooting excursions.*
>
> *I must close as I have to go out about a dress for Mary for the marriage. With our love and praying that God may bless you and more.*
>
> *Dr Graham was pleased with your letter. He called here and engaged in a prayer for you.*

The following letter was the last Jane wrote to Tom before she sailed for her new home.

Edinburgh 28th June 1883

    I received yours of the 21st May in the parcel of silks on Monday. Accept of my very warmest thanks dear Tom, for your thoughtful kindness. Those lovely silks will be of great use to me, & will moreover last for a long time to come. When I got them, I went over them one by one, thinking each prettier than the other. I brought them to school on Tuesday & you ought to have heard the admiring exclamations of the girls. One said she would dance on her head if she were the possessor!! Your kind wishes were not less acceptable & I thank you for them also. – Mama will have told you that there were no stamps on the parcel & that she paid 9/4 for it. We suppose that you had entrusted the posting to a Chinaman & that – well I won't say! – Tell me Tom, did you choose the silks yourself? Or did a lady do it for you?

    We often think of you and your work, knowing that it must be pretty heavy on one so young. But dear brother, what a glorious work it is – the noblest on the face of this earth. May God bless you richly and give you 'souls for your hire'.

    My dear Frans has now started his practice in Wellington. On last Wednesday week, I got my first letter from him from the Cape but as he told me that he had written you then, I need not give you any of the details of his voyage. His friends seem to have had a time of rejoicing on the occasion of his arrival in his native land, but for all that he has not lost much time before getting registered, for he started his Practice just a week after he landed. – I suppose he will be able to tell me in the course of two months when he will be ready for me. Last night I had another long letter from him telling me how well he had got on with his practice so far, & that he had agreed to remain in Wellington.

    His sister-in-law wrote me a nice kind letter. From what I have heard from my South African friends they seem to be good people, but I shall require to be very prudent to go amongst so many 'newly acquired' relatives.

His brother-in-law has also written me three times. He is married to Frans'
eldest sister and is a teacher. The younger members of the community can
speak English, but not so the older people, & therefore it is very necessary that
I should get up the language before going out.

I am glad you liked my photo, but I intended sending you a nicer one –
the one Frans & I got taken together. You will not get it for some time, however,
as I am too near the bottom of my purse. Whenever I can find the time, I will
do you something for your scrapbook, to show that 'there is no ill feeling' as you
would say, but for the present you must excuse me.

Jane Gillison wrote bravely to Tom of her daughter's departure:

I received your letter yesterday and was so happy to think of you
writing it beside your own study fire. I am always glad to hear of you being
busy – but of course I would not like you to be overwrought. You say that
you would like more time for spiritual exercises, which are certainly conducive
to growth in grace; but dear Tom I have found the 'nearness' of a real and
personal saviour in my busiest days. For the more help we need we naturally
seek it oftener, and the more difficult our path the closer we cling to our guide.

We had a very busy time getting Jane's outfit ready, but the boxes were
taken to Leith yesterday. Charlie Cousland made all the necessary arrangements
for her and James came and painted the address on her boxes. She got one very
large tin lined one and I got the 'hold-all' made into a cabin box and a splendid
one it is. Miss Cleghorn made it up, and charged £2.6 and it is well worth it.
Then I got her a good cottage piano at Paterson's. Price £42. I gave them £15
and the balance to be paid at 1st Nov 1884. That is the time I receive the grant
from the Free Ch. Fund for sons and daughters.

Jane has got upwards of a hundred presents, a list of which she will
send you in a letter which D.V. she intends writing you on board the 'Conway
Castle'. She also got several money presents which is a great help to me in the

way of clearing off some of her accounts. She got £20 from Dr Richardson, 5 from James Reid, 4 from Mrs Colville and 2 from Kitty Scott etc, etc. So God is good and gracious to poor unworthy me. Mary Agnes goes up to London with her and Mrs Guthrie has given her her holiday a month earlier than she intended.

In the autumn of 1883 Frans Marais sent for Jane and her passage was booked for the 18th December. Jane sent this letter to Tom from her ship:

'Conway Castle' 3rd Jan 1884 Gulf of Guinea

You will be longing to have my first letter from Sth Africa, I am sure just as much as I am longing to hear from you. I left London on the 18th Dec. and on the 20th we reached Dartmouth where we remained until the 21st. This gave the passengers a good opportunity of seeing the place. It is a very interesting old place and it being the last English town in which I was, I can never forget it. On the 24th we reached Lisbon & there we had an opportunity of seeing the place. We remained in Lisbon for about 8 hours. I don't think I was ever more interested in any place in my whole life, for it was totally different from any other town I ever saw. As soon as we had landed we were fortunate enough to meet an English gentleman who said to us that as he had a few minutes at his disposal, he would be delighted to act as guide. He took us to the Market Place which is one of the sights of Lisbon & then directed us to a church called St John's – the most handsome church of its kind that I ever saw! There we saw a Portuguese wedding. The bride was anything but good looking as she had only one eye & not more than half of a nose! It would be too painful to describe any further!!!

I am enjoying the voyage exceedingly well, although I won't be sorry when it comes to an end! Of course you know why!! I expect Frans and I will remain in Cape Town for a week at first, and then we will go to our own home. We have about 20 1st Class Passengers & some of them are particularly nice. These are Scotch, English, Irish, German, French, Dutch, Portuguese, and

Brazilian. The Captain, to whom I got an introduction through Mr Lockhart, is an exceedingly nice man. He is Scotch.

We have the English Church Service read to us every Sunday by the Captain, but there is no sermon because we have no Minister on board. – In the evenings we have concerts etc. Once we had a Magic Lantern shown to us by one of the sailors. On New Year's Eve the Captain set off some fireworks, & they did look beautiful shooting out into the dark waters.

On the whole we have had an exceedingly good passage. We have had very little rough weather & consequently not much seasickness. I did not feel very well for about a week after we left England but am now all right & enjoying the voyage. – Of course you will know by this time, life on board ship is somewhat monotonous, but it is a pleasant change after a busy time.

What I consider to be the most beautiful sight at sea is the wonderful phosphorescent light, which is seen at night. We have seen a great many flying fish, porpoises & one or two sharks.

This is not a very quick vessel, so we don't expect to arrive in Cape Town before the 12th or 13th of this month. The ship is small though comfortable. I have a cabin to myself, which is a comfort in this hot weather. We crossed the line on the 2nd & did not find the heat so great as we anticipated. 83° in the shade. I cannot say that I care much for the heat or that it agrees well with me, but in time I'll find that out. The day we crossed the Line we had an opportunity of watching the usual shaving performance. Four poor unfortunates, who had never crossed before, had to undergo the process of shaving. The stewards were dressed up as different characters – Neptune, the Barber, the Doctor etc. It was very amusing indeed but unfortunately as with so many other things of the kind, there is a considerable amount of drinking connected with it.

I shall enclose you a list of my wedding presents. Now I shall write no more, but will (D.V.) finish it when I arrive at the Cape Town & when my name will no longer be Jane W. Gillison!!!!!

Jane was married on Monday 14th January and her new husband wrote this letter
to Tom:

Wellington 20 Jan 1884

> *I am finishing this letter for Jane since she has more to write than she
> has time for – She had an awful long passage – 22 days from Dartmouth.
> Arrived in Table Bay on the 12th at 11.30 am.*

> *We tried to get married the same day. But failed. We had to wait
> till Monday. During that time, she stayed at the Normal College under M[r]
> Whitton's (The Principal's) protection, who is a Scotsman. He was most kind
> to us. We were married in his house, on Monday 14th at 12. noon. The
> Captain of the Conway Castle gave her away. All went off well. After the
> marriage, we drove to Wynburg where we had lunch. Then we returned &
> left with the last train for Wellington. D[r] Retief came to Town, just to attend
> the ceremony. D[r] Nieuwoudt also came, just missed us. At the W. station,
> there were a lot of my relations to welcome my bride. From there we drove
> to Groenberg where we had a quiet party of my young friends. Here I must
> come to a close. You would rather have Jane's opinion of these things i.e, of my
> parents etc, etc, than mine.*

> *Before closing, just a few generalities. I was very busy yesterday. Was
> driving about for 7 hours. Got home at 10.15 pm. Today was not very busy.
> Jane nearly always accompanies me when I drive out. She is fond of driving
> in the country. It is great fun leaving her with the philistines while I attend to
> my patients. She gets on splendidly with her Dutch – She is looking as well
> as ever – if not far better, and no wonder considering the amount of grapes
> and peaches etc she eats per diem. I calculated that she ate 15 lbs of grapes,
> 30 peaches, 10 bananas etc etc, the other day. 'Don't believe all this Tom just
> believe half, J.W. Marais! Bad enough, anyway. F.P.M*

> *We had delightful weather all the time – only 2 or 3 hot days. Jane
> says she likes the climate, the people etc etc, very much. Says she feels quite at*

home & not a bit homesick. She is quite a favourite with my parents already. — We had only an apology for a honeymoon. My patients would not let me 'off' any longer. — We came to our own house on Friday last (18th). It is a nice house for Wellington & Jane likes it very much. I hope we'll one day have the pleasure of seeing you in it. Now I must close.

For Jane Gillison life in Edinburgh, without her three eldest children, returned to normal. Jane worried constantly about Andrew's education; the nineteen-year-old Marion by this time had left school and although living at home had a position as some kind of mother's help to an Edinburgh family called Stewart. The ever reliable Mary Agnes, still a governess at Liberton for the Guthrie family, was a tower of strength even though she was not living at home. The rest of the family continued to be busy with their own affairs and young Andrew, then aged fifteen was on holiday at the Brotch family farm in Lochmaben near Dumfries. Jane Gillison's own family consisted of eight children of whom only four reached maturity. None of them figure prominently in the letters except Jessie, the youngest member of the family. She was married to John Black and their only child, a daughter Mary was a first cousin of the six Gillison siblings. Mary, born in 1863, was their only child and she is the one member of the family who plays a very important part in this story. She never married and was a constant support to Jane Gillison throughout Jane's widowhood but, more importantly in later years, she became the hub of the extended family. It was she who received letters from the family from every corner of the globe and frequently copied those letters to disseminate the family news and there are many instances of this in the collection of Gillison letters. For years she looked after her mother who died in 1929 aged 101. Mary Black was always known to the later generations of the family as 'Aunt Molly' and I remember her as a very tall, spare, whiskery old lady – especially when she greeted you with a kiss. Her front parlour at 1, Church Place, Lochmaben was full of dark, heavy furniture, aspidistras and patterned rugs; it always felt cold, even in summer. Although she had a keen sense of humour, which made her an entertaining companion, her ideas of health, welfare and comfort remained sometimes comically fifty years behind the times. I recall an occasion when my uncle received a letter from her in the 1950s saying she was troubled with rheumatism because of a certain chill she had thirty years before. Like her mother she lived to a ripe old age and she died when in her 90s. In 1946, the summer after my parents returned from Japanese internment camp, we cycled as a family from Derbyshire to Lochmaben and stayed with Aunt Molly. She helped me to set out a family tree, which she was well qualified to do, but I deeply regret not asking her to reminisce about the family history at the same time. It was a lost opportunity.

Back in 1884, plans were made for Marion to spend three months abroad accompanied by the then twenty-one-year old Mary Black in preparation for her future work as a governess. Jane had written to Tom in May:

> *Last week Marion was keeping house at Charlotte Square, and for a day or two in the beginning of the week, she had a very bad cold. The Prof. says that she is not at all strong, and that should she think of going to the Continent she must by no means go to Germany for she could never stand it; and besides she must not travel alone as she might take on faint turns. It is just the effects of her old rheumatic complaint.*
>
> *The only thing that I see she can do is to try and get into a French Pastor's family through Mr Guthrie and get up her French so as to be able to teach it and stay at home, and try and get a forenoon's engagement as governess to little boys or girls.*

In the event Italy was the chosen spot but while the two girls were there, there was an outbreak of cholera which gave Jane considerable anxiety. However, all was well and Mary Black sent this account of the trip written in Milan in a letter to Tom. It is interesting that, although she described Milan Cathedral as very beautiful, Mary found the 'misguided' devout in the cathedral offended her fiercely Protestant soul.

Hotel Milan, Stresa, Italy 7th August 1884

Will you accept of my very best wishes for your birthday? I am really not in a letter writing mood, and pled with Marion to wait until tomorrow, but she first lectured me herself and then applied to Mrs Marrett who followed suit so effectively, that I was fain to take pen in hand. A more effective help still has just arrived in the shape of a delightful wind, which is blowing over the lake and making the lake's horses show their white manes. It is so refreshing that I feel I am a little more able to describe some of the beauties we have been seeing. Marion says she will leave me that portion of the news. I will go backwards like a crab and tell you first what I am seeing at the present moment. The lake is like a sea with angry waves and white breakers; the distant hills are shrouded in dark clouds, while the nearer ones look dark and frowning. The scene looked very different this morning when we went out for a row on the lake, which was beautifully calm and clear, and everything was smiling in the sunshine. We went round two of the Borromean Islands [3] and landed on one of them to see the beautiful gardens. The gardens looked somewhat stiff and formal from the lake but were very nice when one was in them. There were many interesting plants including the sensitive plant, the papyrus, the tea plant and also bamboos, magnolias.

Milan Cathedral was a treat. It really passes all description. The first look at it, I thought Oh! I think it is not as grand as it is called, but when I had got through it and up the 512 steps to the top, I felt I was beginning to see endless beauty and could have spent any length of time in it. The 100 pillars look so beautiful and like a forest, the windows are so exquisite, the roof so lovely both inside and out that they require to be seen for people to have any idea of their beauty. But – there is always a 'but' – it was sad, sad to see the poor misguided people crossing themselves, confessing, bowing down and worshipping images of the virgin. We also went to a little chapel whose walls were lined with bones said to be those of the early Christian martyrs.

A photograph of Mary Black in later years with her mother Jessie.

The picture gallery we liked very much. It was formerly an old palace. The pictures were by old masters, and are I was told carefully arranged according to the different school. I for one, was a little too ignorant to appreciate it. Some of them were very fine, but some we could not help laughing at, for imagine monks and priests with their hoods in Scripture scenes. The one considered to be the gem is by Raphael and is the marriage of the Virgin Mary. In it several men are breaking rods, which we did not understand. Pastor Turin explained it however. It was a legend that the Virgin had many suitors, and told them to put a rod each in the temple for a night,

58

and whosoever [sic] rod blossomed she would marry him. Of the rods being brought out Joseph's blossomed and the others broke theirs in rage. Another fine one was St Celena or something of the same like name, being tortured. Her face was exquisite, so rapt and placid.

Torre Pellice and Bobbio Pellice are both on the Pellico a tributary of the Po. They are about two hour's walk apart and are surrounded by mountains on almost every side. They are not very large or important in themselves, Bobbio being only a village and Torre interesting only because of its being the chief town of the Vaudois valleys and having their college and meeting of their Synod. The scenery is lovely and the walks endless in their beauty and variety. I was disappointed not seeing more ancient things concerning the Vaudois. [4] The only thing I heard of was a cave (in an adjoining valley) which had served as a hiding place for them. The sole article of antiquity was the remains of a wall built by Oliver Cromwell. We walked along it in honour of a fellow countryman. Now I hope you will excuse all mistakes as I have written in a great hurry, and with love and all best wishes for you and your work.

Back in Hankow Tom was stricken with a serious fever. Among the letters there was a torn sheet written in pencil on which Tom recorded the progress of his illness – as a doctor might make notes on his patient. His mother, unaware of his illness, fretted at the lack of news from China.

July 12th

Took seriously ill with relapsing fever.

July 16th

Dr Begg gave me up and said I must die before evening. Very, very weak (Sunday).

Monday July 17th

 Temperature in forenoon 105.6! – After injection of Quinine &
salicine with acid mit Hydnocell dil concentrated to 3 times strength of B.P. –
temp suddenly fell to 99.(6?) Very possibly not to do with medicine (inject^n)
Fever probably played out – Improvement slow & interrupted but sure till
10th day of fever when I was put on board the 'Ngan Kin' to go to Kiu Kiang
intending to go to the hills there.

 14th day of fever July 26th 1884 Had another relapse – 7 days of
bad fever – very weak – slightly delirious – nervous depression – About 22nd
day of fever went down to Shanghai per SS Shanghai. Capt.Martin very good
to me – Went to Chefoo with Bonsey – afterwards to Tien Sin & Pekin.

 Got back to Hankow in good health 2nd October – Praise the Lord for
all His goodness!

The fact that it took nearly three months for Tom to recover from his illness
indicates how severe it was. There were several occasions during his time in China
when he suffered from life-threatening diseases and it may be an indication that
he was fortunate to possess a strong constitution. The Rev. Arnold Foster, one of
Tom's colleagues in Hankow, writes to him:

Hankow 16th Aug. 1884

 I hope you will not have attributed my silence during the past few
weeks to any forgetfulness of you on my part. You have been much in my
thoughts & in Mrs Foster's so I cannot tell you how rejoiced & thankful we
have felt to hear of your recovery. I wrote to you nearly three weeks ago to
tell you this, but before I had sent off my note, news came of your relapse
& I thought I would withhold what I had written lest it should reach Kiu
Kiang when you were too ill to read it, – which it would have done. Now we
have heard of your arrival in Shanghai & intended departure for Chefoo, &
I hope this will find you there, better & daily gaining in strength. We miss

*you very much from Hankow for although when you are here we often do
not have much intercourse for days together, yet then the light of your cheery
countenance is continually beaming on us if only for a few minutes at a time
& I have often found that refreshing. I suppose in a letter from Hankow you
would like to hear some Hankow news, but I really do not think there is much
to send, at least if there is I hope Mr John will send it to you for no doubt he
writes every now & again both to your self and Bonsey … . I am your dear
brother, Yours affectly, Arnold Foster.*

When the news of Tom's illness reached Edinburgh it explained why the family
had not received any letters for so long. His mother writes:

Edin^r 2nd Septr 1884

> *I am feeling very anxious about you, seeing I have not heard from
> you for a month. I do sincerely trust that you are well, and that the re-
> vaccination did not sicken you or lay you up. Then again the war between
> France and China makes me also think that your letter may have been kept
> up or detained on its way. What are your feelings in regard to this war? Do
> you think it will injure your work among the Chinese? Or do you think your
> position at all perilous? I can only dear Tom cast you on our loving Heavenly
> Father's care, trusting that no evil may befall you.*

And later from Mary Agnes to her brother:

Liberton 1st October 1884

> *Almost my first thoughts were with you this morning. I wish you very
> many happy returns of your birthday. My heart is really sore for you dear
> Tom, to think of you being so ill. We can't but feel thankful now after what
> Dr U. wrote that your precious life is spared. May our Heavenly Father see fit
> to restore you to perfect health again, but of course your situation causes us no
> little anxiety. They tell me at home that if I went out to you I should be ill in*

a week or two and fit for nothing, but how I wish I could come to you, either that or that you could get a nice wife. But Mama is set upon having me with her now and I really think it would be wrong of me to leave her. You must try & write her very often as she feels very much when she does not hear from you. You will likely be back in Hankow by this time, that's to say if you are fit for work. Oh! Dear Tom, I do earnestly pray that you may be strengthened for your work. I saw in the 'Christian' a notice of the opening of the 'Sailor's Rest' in Hankow and your name as one of the speakers. You must have turned ill immediately after that, did you not? I feel so sad to think of you lying so ill with no relative near you and have often pictured you to myself, but how grand to think that there is 'one that sticketh closer than any brother,' and that you are under the same good protection in China as you would be in Scotland.

His mother writes:

Edin^{br} 26th Novr 1884

    I had your long and interesting letter last week telling me all about your illness at Kiu Kiang and I could not restrain my tears when I heard of your great suffering and extreme weakness – and alas nervous frustration. I did wish that I had been with you to wait upon you, for however kind friends may be no one can be so considerate as a mother. Still I praise God for his great goodness to you and trust you may not be troubled with the effects of your fever in your system. Have you any idea of getting a change of sphere by the time the summer comes round?

    Now I wish very much to know if you get my letters, and the Scotsman and Record etc regularly, and I am also waiting for orders about your box. I am pretty busy just now with my three boarders, and Bertie Stewart coming from school for his early dinner. Marion seems to suit Mrs Stewart in many ways as she gets to do her business, and many little things in the house besides sewing, knitting, marking etc and this morning she had to go off at 8 o'clock to take Hugh the youngest boy to school as he had taken a dislike to it! Moreover she was to sit in his class till he had his lessons and then take him home.

Andrew is working pretty well this winter but his elocutionary powers are what he displays to best advantage. He seems to desire to live to God's glory, and is affectionate to his mother which is a comfort, as I really do need a little sympathy at times.

I have retaken this house for two years from May, as I fear I shall still need to keep two boarders at least if I am to give Andrew a university education. Jack is getting on pretty well at Merchiston, but he has no great love for his master Mr B. Lockhart. Tom Henderson is working for honours, but Jamie does not display any great energy, but he is good and earnest and that seems to suit the Baptists better than learning. He has to all appearance less brain than any of the male sex here, or in his own family. He was down at Leith last night visiting the Baptist minister and his family.

The new year will have dawned ere this letter reach you and I wish that it may indeed be a happy year to you in God's service. God bless your own soul very richly and with our warmest love.

P.S. I still go on the Friday afternoons to the Infirmary – so kindly remember me and my work prayerfully.

Most of 1885 seems to have passed quietly with nothing dramatic for any of the parties to record. Jane Gillison continued to run her home with a number of boarders – not all of them ideal tenants. Mary Agnes was still a governess at the Guthries' manse in Liberton. Marion spent the time with the family of Professor Stewart and Andrew, at seventeen, had left school and was at University. Jane Marais in South Africa was well integrated into her life with Frans and was expecting the birth of her first child. Tom's mother writes to her son:

Edin 17ᵗʰ Decʳ 1885

> You will very likely have heard before this reaches you that dear Jane had a little daughter on the 4ᵗʰ inst. Frans kindly telegraphed the news but we wait with anxiety for further particulars about the first week of the New Year. May God bless her and her little babe, and may they long be spared to each other as a comfort and blessing. Andrew & I, along with Mʳˢ Cousland, are going to the Cowgate treat tonight so I must be very brief. Such changes there are there now but thank God the good work still goes on and prospers … .

> … This is the anniversary of your dear father's death and many and varied are the thoughts which arise in my mind. Time flies & I still have a little strength to 'toil on' but it is being 'weakened on the way' as I get older.

And from Mary Agnes to Tom on the last day of the year:

Edinburgh 31.12.85

> For your most acceptable Xmas gift, I send my great thanks. It is good of you dear old Tom, to think of us, when you have not too much to come and go on. In spite of my good salary, 'passing rich on £40 a year', I don't seem to have the knack of being able to save. I have so many marriage presents and also other gifts to give. Sara Richardson is to be married in the end of February and I am asked to her wedding. Maggie Dunnachie is to be married in about six or eight weeks and they will both require good presents. Dʳ Campbell visited Mama a few weeks ago and she thought him nicer than ever. His brother has died very suddenly in South Africa so Maggie and he can't come through to see us, as we expected, but I am going on Saturday to Glenboig to stay until Monday.

> Mama is very much gratified to hear so often from you. You are certainly much improved of late, which is a source of great pleasure to us all, especially when you tell us something of yourself and your work. It was rather

a blessing in disguise to get the wing of your hospital burned down. I am glad you have got it all so nicely done up now and I trust during the coming year that rich blessing may attend your labours in it

Yesterday evening we had a Thanksgiving Service in the Barclay Church, but it was really rather a ludicrous sort of meeting & most of the congregation were in a subdued giggle the whole time. Mr William Brown stood up to thank God for his happy contented disposition, another Mr Brown to thank God for Dr Moon, a Mr Bell for the bright, lively lady collectors, even although they did come for money. Nevertheless it was a very nice meeting. Tonight Andrew and I are going to the Watch Meeting at Carrubbers' Close. Andrew is to recite, as he was so much liked last Saturday when we were there for the first time. Mrs Barclay (formerly Miss Lucy Smith, who was engaged to Mr Horder) was out at Gilmerton singing at an Evangelistic Soiree for us and she heard Andrew recite there and was much taken with him. He really has a great talent for recitation and is very willing to oblige people.

Our Sabbath School at the Craigs has been given up as we could not get a suitable superintendent & for other reasons, but most of the children come to our morning Sabbath School where I now teach. Three poor girls, who were in my class at the Craigs have gathered up their pennies for several months and as a Xmas present gave me a very beautiful dark brown Oxford Bible box covered. You can't think how I prize it and what pleasure I had in teaching these girls and I know, not without profit for which I feel very thankful for it is an encouragement to speak more plainly to others.

Now, dear Tom, I must close, in a great hurry as it is post time.

P.S. I forgot to congratulate you on being Uncle Tom and the uncle of such a very beautiful child, with dark blue eyes and a great deal of character in her face, at four days old. Of course she is like every other first child. M.A.G

65

The present day interior of the Barclay Church. It is, of course, centrally heated, carpeted, with chairs in place of pews and looks very elegant but must have been very different in Victorian times as Jane Gillison mentioned in a letter in 1888 that "Andrew and I have changed our sitting in the church so we and the Douglases sit in the pew before the Hendersons. The third pew from the front. It is much warmer than our old seat."

THREE

'Grace, gumption & grit'

Because we have so many of the letters exchanged between members of the Gillison family in the first nine year period of Tom's time in China whilst almost none of Tom's own letters in return survive, there is no clear picture of how he adapted to his totally new environment on arrival in Hankow. The next generation of new missionaries automatically spent their first six months in China at a language school before being allowed to begin their chosen ministry. Tom seems to have been unceremoniously parachuted into the work of the Mission hospital where he was the sole doctor. Fortunately, blest as he was with a natural facility for languages, this did not prove to be a real handicap and with lessons with his Chinese teacher fitted into his daily routine, he seems to have been able to carry out his work at the hospital. However, the lack of Tom's letters means that we have little idea of Tom's life in Hankow nor any clear picture of his friends and colleagues in Hankow. The one missionary whose presence and influence dominated the missionary circle was Dr Griffith John.

Diminutive of stature but an inspirational preacher he was one of the most significant figures in the British Missionary life of Central China in the second half of the nineteenth century. He was a galvanizing force in the community of the mission and a much loved senior colleague and adviser. One of the most important contributions he made between 1883 and 1886 was to translate the New Testament into a form of Chinese that would be understood and accepted by the ordinary man. A translation already existed in Wen Li, a highly classical form of Chinese used for all important and classical documents, but something was needed that steered a middle path between classical Wen Li and colloquial Chinese.

Born in Swansea in 1831 his early education was limited and at the age of twelve he started work at the store of a large smelting complex twenty miles from Swansea. He attended the local Ebenezer Church where he became famous as the 'boy preacher'. After training for the ministry at Brecon College he offered his services to the London Missionary Society and in 1855, with his new wife Margaret, daughter of David Griffiths of Madagascar, a renowned L.M.S. missionary, he sailed for Shanghai. Life for foreign missionaries in the middle of the nineteenth century must have been daunting, especially in the aftermath of the British war with China from 1840 to 1842 (the Opium Wars) culminating

Taken from Rev Wardlaw Thompson's book 'Griffith John – The Story of Fifty Years in China.'

in the Treaty of Nanking which ceded Hongkong and five treaty ports for the purposes of trade. Griffith John, working at that time in Shanghai, had set his sights on taking Christianity to the three great cities in the heart of China – Wuchang, Hankow and Hanyang. Seven years after arriving in Shanghai in 1861 he set up the London Mission in Hankow.

Griffith John believed very strongly in taking the gospel to the people, standing at street corners and handing out leaflets. He made many pioneering journeys deep into the countryside and these were often fraught with danger and frequently physically hard and uncomfortable. In 1868 Griffith John, accompanied by his friend Alexander Wylie, made his first journey up the Yangtze to Chung King. The two men left Hankow early in April and arrived in Chung King on June 7th Dr John wrote to a friend:

*The perils of the journey through one hundred miles of rapids, so
strong that they tax to the utmost the strength of gangs of as many as 100
trackers towing the boats up from the bank ... . We have passed through
many scenes of danger on the way. The gorges and rapids are as dangerous
as they are grand – fine to look at, but not always comfortable to encounter
and pass through.*

The journey up the Yangtze nowadays is one of the standard tours for visitors to
China. The colossal Three Gorges Dam was designed to transform the provision
of electricity for millions of Chinese and has also proved to be a huge tourist
attraction. Opinion is divided about the wisdom of this because of the damage
to the environment caused by the flooding. The upheaval of more than a million
people forced to move from their homes and livelihoods on the river banks to
great cities like Shanghai imposed on them an entirely alien way of life.

In 2006 my brother, sister-in-law and I, as the descendents of the first President
of the Union Hospital Dr Thomas Gillison, were honoured to be invited to the
140th anniversary celebrations of its founding. We took the opportunity to see
some other parts of China including joining a tour up the Yangtze from Ichang
through the Three Gorges to Chung King. Knowing what I did about the part that
the river had played in the journeys of my forebears I found it almost eerie to be
sailing on water metres above those dangerous rocks and rapids. I was acutely
aware that our journey of three days would have taken six weeks to accomplish
in my grandfather's day. It is an interesting fact that at the end of the nineteenth
century it took as long to travel from Hankow to Chung King as it did to make the
journey from London to Hankow. This was one reason why a posting to Chung
King was not regarded favourably by missionaries of the time.

The early days in Hankow for Griffith John and his wife Margaret were
hazardous and hard. They lost four of their children through diseases such as
smallpox, cholera and dysentery, but three survived – two sons, Griffith and David,
and a daughter, Mary. In 1860 the Johns decided that China was no place for the
education and health of young children and their son Griffith was sent home to

live with friends in Wales. In due course David and Mary followed their brother back to England and the two boys were sent to Eltham College in Blackheath, the school for the sons of missionaries.

This excerpt from Rev. Wardlaw Thompson's definitive biography of Dr Griffith John (1906) struck a chord with me. Griffith John, the elder of the two John brothers, had been sent home to England at the age of five; I was left in England at the age of six. I can well understand the mixture of emotions he must have had on seeing his parents at that reunion. In 1870 after fifteen years of continuous service in China the Johns returned to Britain. Wardlaw Thompson writes:

> *As they passed through London they naturally made their way*
> *at once to Blackheath where their two sons were in the School for the*
> *Sons of Missionaries. It was not surprising to learn that the boys did not*
> *recognize their father; the elder had not seen him for nearly ten years. The*
> *fact however suggests one of the great trials of missionary life, the necessity*
> *for the separation of parents and children during the years which are most*
> *critical for the formation of character. The facilities for frequent correspondence*
> *have greatly increased and the kindness of many friends is very great, but*
> *nothing can quite compensate for the loss of the personal intercourse and the*
> *influence of the personal oversight and guidance of the father and mother.*

Margaret John had been in very poor health for some time before they left China and because of this their leave in Britain was extended. Griffith filled his time with a great deal of deputation work; such was his reputation as a preacher that he was invited to address a great many major religious events. Although tempted to remain in England and give up his missionary work entirely for the sake of his delicate wife and his children, in 1873 Griffith decided that it was his duty to return to China. His wife insisted on going with him although still far from well and she became seriously ill on the voyage. She died as the ship came into the harbour at Singapore.

Griffith John was deeply affected by her death but characteristically, he threw all his energies into his work when he returned to Hankow. His daughter Mary wrote to him on hearing of the death of her mother:

> *I am very sorry for you, dear Papa; I wish that I was near you that I might comfort you. I must make haste and learn, and come out to you, and keep your house. Dear Mama is quite happy and has no pain. Jesus is comforting you, and grandma and brothers and myself. He won't let us stop still and feel sad, but He stirs us up like He did Abraham.*

During the course of the next few months Griffith John renewed his friendship with Mrs Jeannette Jenkins, an American missionary, the widow of Dr Jenkins of the Methodist Episcopal Mission in Shanghai. She had remained in Shanghai after the death of her husband three years earlier continuing her Christian ministry, not only to the Chinese but also to the foreign sailors from the gunboats, tea ships and other vessels which came to the great ports of China. They married in 1874 and the new Mrs John brought the same enthusiasm to her work among the sailors in Hankow as she had with those in Shanghai. The Johns' home was 'open house' for sailors who were offered food for both body and soul in a very different atmosphere from that on board ship. When the Johns' home became too small for the numbers of men who visited it larger premises were found. A spacious new building was erected in 1884 by private contributions and became known as 'The Sailor's Rest' and there services were held and the men could relax away from the 'temptations' of the outside world.

Eighteen months after the opening of the new building the second Mrs John developed peritonitis and died. Griffith John wrote to my grandfather from the ship which was carrying him up the Yangtze to Shanghai where he was going to bury his wife. In those days appendicitis and consequent peritonitis were fairly common causes of death and Tom had been in charge of Jeanette John's last illness.

Dec 31ˢᵗ 1885 'Kiang Kwan'

I wish I could tell you how much I feel your love, sympathy, and kindness, as shown to me and my beloved wife. I am thoroughly satisfied with all you did as a Medical Man, and I bless you for your loving help as a brother, or rather as a son. A son could not have been more tender and loving than you were to us both in this hour of deepest sorrow. God bless you for all. My precious wife loved you as a son, and often spoke of her affection for you.

I enclose a cheque for Tls. 20⁰⁰⁰ which please accept as a gift to the Hospital from her, to be devoted according to your own ideas to it for the benefit of the suffering women who may need a little extra care and attention whilst under your charge. It is not much, but it will be helpful, and it will give her joy to know that I have done this for her suffering sisters whom she has left behind.

Don't forget the Sunday class till I come back. I wish MʳˢArchibald could take it up, as it would get you a nice class of men. It would be so nice if dear Lizzie would step into this important place which Mʳˢ John occupied in regard to Sunday work. You may mention it to her. She would have to study for it a little, but she would have no special difficulty in getting up the lesson. Her husband could help her a little at first.

I am inclined to think that this dispensation is going to be blessed to Mary. She will begin to work at the language in earnest as from our return in order to qualify herself for work. I am extremely glad of this.

I had a tolerably good night last night, but I am in my Father's hands. How sweet it is to feel oneself resting calmly under the blessed shadow of His wing. Again, God bless you.

Mrs Jeannette John's death took place only three years after Tom's arrival in Hankow. By that time Griffith John and his wife had already established a firm friendship with him but in the years that followed, that relationship with Griffith deepened and it sometimes seemed that Griffith had taken the place of the father Tom had lost at the age of fourteen. When Mary John, Griffith's daughter, returned to China in 1884 on the completion of her education and following Jeannette's death she was able to look after her father, thus fulfilling the promise she had made to him twelve years earlier after the death of the first Mrs John who was also her mother. Tom developed strong feelings for Mary over the next few years and four years later there is a letter from Jane Gillison Tom's mother, suggesting that Tom had told her that he had proposed marriage to someone and been turned down. Whether he mentioned that Mary John was the lady concerned we cannot tell but the following letters must surely confirm it.

First Jane Gillison writes to her son:

August 23rd 1888

... Now as regards the trial of feeling you have gone through by 'unrequited love'. You may as the Poet says speak to me with 'naked heart' for I do sympathise with you. Still you must try and 'commit your way unto the Lord', lest haply you be found to fight against Him by seeking to 'choose your own path'. Cheer up. There are many good Christian ladies in Edin^r and elsewhere who would gladly share your lot & you won't be too old when you come home to take a young lady out with you.

Seek a Christ-like spirit in all things and in this matter particularly. Try to say 'Thy will be done'. This is the only way to obtain 'peace of mind.' A loving and perfect Saviour knows what it is to be 'rejected' infinitely more than you ever can.

You only can know whether it would be prudent to act upon the old maxim 'If at first you don't succeed try' etc. God will overrule all for the best. ...

The next two letters are in fact undated but common sense dictates that they must have been written in response to Tom's unsuccessful proposal to Mary. From Griffith John to Tom Gillison:

Many thanks for your kind and affectionate letter. I am sure your affection for me is returned with all the sincerity and depth of my nature. I have loved you, do love you & shall love you to the end. I hope you will come in and out whenever you feel inclined. Mary in some respects has a head old enough for a woman of forty, and what has passed will only deepen these feelings towards you. God bless you my dear friend.

Lizzie Archibald, a fellow missionary and a particular friend and confidante wrote to Tom:

'Trust in Him & He will bring it to pass in the best way.'

My dear Brother,

I am very sorry to hear the news you have sent me, yet we know our Father doeth all things well. He has something better in store for you for you can depend on that. This cloud will have a silver lining, & that you will soon see. She is a gem beyond doubt, but not the one your dear Father is going to give you at present. Perhaps dear brother if you had got that blessing it might have drawn you away from Him. We poor creatures do not know but He knows.

You have my deepest sympathy & prayers & you have our precious Saviour's sympathy for He feels what hurts His children.

I hope to see you soon & may we all live more for Him. Sit continually with Him in Heavenly Places.

Dinner waits, so excuse haste.

Here is Griffith John writing to Tom on his thirty-first birthday:

Hankow Oct 1ˢᵗ 1890 A.M. 5.30

You have my first thoughts this morning. Accept my best congratulations and best wishes. I join you in thanking God for His goodness to you during another year. He has not only preserved you in life, but has also enabled you to do a vast amount of work in His name. He has blessed you, and made you a blessing to many. How wonderfully you have been preserved in health during a trying summer! What we should have done without you I cannot see.

May God make this New Year one of great joy to you. What His purposes in regard to you may be, we cannot tell now; but He knows, and we who know Him do not find it hard to put our trust in His faithfulness. How good He is to us individually! How good to us as a Mission! How our love ought to kindle, as we think of His boundless affection for us!

If there was any awkwardness between Tom and Mary after she had rejected his proposal, neither of them would have allowed it to show or affect their friendship. Mary became engaged to fellow missionary Rev George Sparham in November 1890 and the two were married the following May. As it happened Tom could not attend the wedding because his passage was already booked for his first furlough just a few days before the wedding. Griffith John wrote to Tom:

Hankow April 21st 1891

You have been told probably, that we have fixed on May 12th for the Marriage. I have been writing a few letters of invitation, and my only regret is that your name is not on the list of the invited ones. But though I cannot send you a letter of invitation, I feel I must send you a line or two, to tell you how sorry I am that circumstances render it impossible for you to be present on the occasion. Your absence will be felt by us all, and especially by Miss John, Mr Sparham and myself. If you could have been present, our happiness in looking forward to the event would have been complete. Nevertheless we must believe that all is right, for we are all under the guidance of our Father in Heaven, and that He is doing all things well. I feel the deepest interest in your own movements, and earnestly pray that God may be in a special manner your guide, strength and joy during your absence from China.

Sixteen years after Mrs Margaret John's death, Griffith John felt there was a need for a separate hospital for women in Hankow. The bulk of the money for the erection of the building was generously provided by Griffith John himself in memory of his first wife. It was opened in 1891 as 'The Margaret Hospital'. This was the hospital to which the London Missionary Society appointed my grandmother, then Dr Bessie Harris, as its first woman doctor.

In 1905 Griffith John completed fifty years' service in China, an event which was widely celebrated by his friends in Hankow and beyond.

He continued his evangelistic work until 1908 when he suffered a severe stroke while preaching in Siaokan. His health deteriorated with further strokes and for a time he remained in Hankow cared for by his family but in the autumn of 1911 he was taken back to Britain where he died in a London nursing home in February 1912.

Mrs Margaret John 1830–1873

Mrs Jeannette John 1834–1885

In future years the Gillisons and the Sparhams were to become next door neighbours on the mission compound and their children grew up together. My father was always very proud of the fact that he and his sister Jean were baptized in infancy by Dr Griffith John.

Dr Griffith John with his grandson Brynmor Sparham, *circa* 1902.

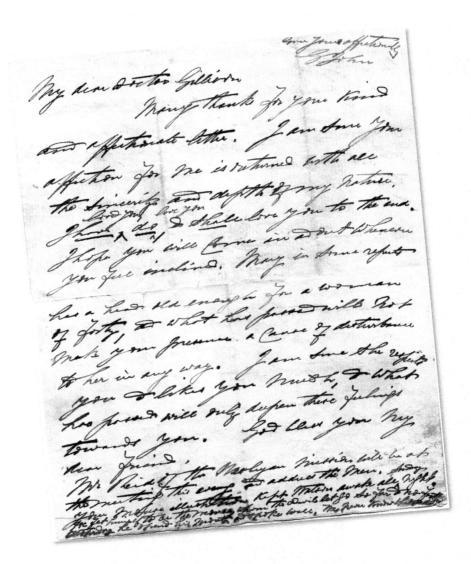

This facsimile of Griffith John's undated letter gives some indication of the difficulty of reading his handwriting.

Left Brynmor Sparham, Jean Gillison, another Sparham, and Keith Gillison in front of their next-door houses, *circa* 1907 or 1908.

When Griffith John was on furlough in England in 1881–1882 (before Tom Gillison sailed for China in October 1882) he gave an eloquent and earnest address to the Jubilee meetings of the Congregational Union of England and Wales in Manchester in October 1881. When appealing for men to come to the mission field he said:

> *We want also your best men. We want able-bodied men, because there is a good deal of physical work to be done in China. We want able-souled men. You must not send to China, nor I believe to any part of the heathen world, inferior men. We want men with the three Gs at least – grace, gumption and grit. A graceless men is a pitiful object to behold; but I have more hope of a graceless man to begin with than of a man without common sense; if a man has no grace he can get it for the asking, but if he does not bring common sense with him into the world, he cannot get it at all.*

Dr Griffith John embodied all of those attributes and many more besides.

The gloriously Gothic Barclay Church (1864)
It was the centre of the Gillison family's social life.

FOUR

Edinburgh – revisited

For much of the decade of the 1890s the Gillison family activities were taking place in four areas of the world – China, South Africa, Australia and Scotland. In a way this was not unusual for the Scots have a reputation of leaving their native land and making a name for themselves in many corners of the earth. That three of the Gillison siblings had left Scotland within the space of eighteen months must have been devastating for their mother Jane. She had a courageous spirit and bore it well – apart from a little moan in her letters to Tom from time to time. Jane's two lifelines were the letters written to and from the absent members of the family and the Barclay Church for its spiritual and social support and interest. Her letters are full of the activities of the church, comments on the ministers and guest speakers and news of individual members of the congregation. She chides Tom for not sending regular reports of his hospital and his work to the 'Supplement', the church magazine. Given the enormous amount of work he had to do he must sometimes have despaired of her ever understanding the demands being made on him. Very frequently she comments, 'Dr Wilson is exceedingly anxious to have something from you to put in the 'Supplement''. And on one occasion she criticizes his spelling, 'I did not think you did yourself credit by the writing and composition of the latter half of it, and moreover you had three superfluous 'b's' in the writing of the word baptism; I drew my pen through them before taking them to Dr Wilson'.

One little gem came in this letter from Jane to Tom in October 1885:

> Last week I received the Postal order for the third £1 and we also got the reports. Two days ago I got your letter of 31st Aug. with cheque for £2.10. and for all of which I thank you very much. The report we think you have drawn up very carefully and clearly, and at the same time very

modestly. We could not help wondering at the amount of skins which require to be rubbed with sulphur ointment!! I think if you were to erect a rubbing post, some of your patients might use it and say like the West Highlanders, 'God bless the Duke of Argyle'. Forgive this joke please. [5]

As far as the remaining members of the family were concerned – Mary Agnes was a great moral support to her mother. Although independent financially through earning her modest living as a governess in the Rev Guthrie's family for over four years, she was always there when her mother needed her. Marion, age twenty in 1885, was working as a companion and help to the Professors Stewart and Grainger's families in Edinburgh but, due to some kind of rheumatic fever in the past, her health was not robust. Apart from worrying constantly about Marion's weak constitution, Jane was also anxious because Marion and her cousin Jamie had always been close. Jamie himself, had health problems but more than that he was determined to become a Baptist Minister and Jane's Presbyterian soul disapproved of it. In January 1884 Jane wrote to Tom:

Last Thursday evening Marion and I went alone with Jamie to Dublin St. Ch. where he and seven females were baptized. Jamie gave a pretty good address, some of which I could assent to, other parts of it I could not agree to. However I felt for poor Jamie in the solemn steps he was taking. A great deal is said by Jamie and Dr Landells about the trials he had to endure in thus 'confessing Christ' – but not a word said about the grief this step caused his worthy old father. I never argue with Jamie on the subject as he is very conceited and intolerant of the views of those who differ from him.

At this time Jamie was lodging at 143 Warrender Park Road so Jane had three young students as boarders. She writes to her son:

Tom Henderson is working very hard – but I cannot say the same of either Jamie or Andrew. Tom gives the latter a little oversight when his own studies permit of it: but Andrew is too careless in his preparations for Tom's taste, and then Andrew thinks he knows more than Jamie does. Jamie however is a very agreeable inmate of the house, and we are much happier and quieter without Charlie Martin. I only miss him for any profit I might have had off his board … .

Marion has just commenced to attend a class for higher English in George's Hall, but I fear the study is not going to suit her for her headaches have again returned. She is at home today, as two of Prof. Stewart's girls have been laid down with scarlet fever and she is not to teach in the meantime, but walks with the three youngest. One of the girls was taken to a private room in the Infirmary yesterday. I trust God may so order it that Marion may escape the infection. Mary Agnes went back to Liberton on Monday as they were greatly in want of her. She enjoyed her visit to London and Newcastle very much indeed.

Tom Henderson was the most regular of Jane's boarders and Jane welcomed his influence on Andrew but was not always complimentary about him as a person. She writes, 'Tom Henderson comes back on Monday. He is much the same as he used to be only a great deal more conceited'.

Jane's concerns about Andrew's education and moral welfare were a constant worry. Andrew seems to have been a perfectly normal intelligent boy but was inclined to be lazy. He excelled however in recitation and oratory. The family letters are peppered with accounts of occasions when he publically entertained audiences with his recitations and the compliments which were showered on him as a result. To quote Mary Agnes, 'He really has a great talent for recitation and is very willing to oblige people'. It was not surprising that eventually he trained for the Ministry.

In 1886 at the age of eighteen Andrew started a degree course at Edinburgh University. Jane remarked, 'Andrew goes on very easily at the University. If he does not study harder I fear he will be a long time in taking his M.A'. He did in fact fail his first year exams in Latin and had to take both Latin and Greek a second time. Jane said, 'He is taking the tutorial in Latin and Mathematics, but he tries me with his dilatory ways'.

In 1886 both Marion and Mary Agnes's engagements were announced. The first was Marion's engagement to Jamie Gillison. In September Mary Agnes writes to Tom:

> *What do you think of her engagement? The two young cousins are extremely happy, no doubt in each other's love and of course there is nothing but the relationship to be said against it, but of course to my way of thinking that is a great deal but now that it is done they must bear the consequences. He is a good Xtian and will make a good husband, and of course for anyone that Marion loves, she will take no end of trouble to make them comfortable and happy, and she will make a splendid little wife, if her health is good. It is a pity that they are both so delicate, but fortunately Marion has been much stronger of late. I do feel so thankful for the good health which I enjoy. I scarcely ever know what it is to have an ache or pain. I have a firm belief in cold water & fresh air, and I take a cold bath every morning & very often at night and I walk as much as possible. All the four years I was at Liberton I had not half an hour's illness. Of course I was sometimes very worn out as everyone is bound to be if they have much work. I often dread the thought of being ill, but no doubt, I would get strength in my time of need, and no burden heavier than we can bear is ever laid upon us, besides when we have Someone to help us, it makes it much easier.*

There is no direct reference in any of Jane's letters to her youngest daughter's engagement and although she was critical of Jamie's Baptist views she seems to have accepted the situation fairly calmly. With Mary Agnes's engagement Jane expressed some doubts. Mary Agnes herself wrote two letters to Tom about her feelings for Andrew Henderson. The first in March 1886 reads:

> *Andrew Henderson is expected home in April. He was good enough to send me a Xmas card from the States & I sent a return one out of politeness. He came up a good deal before he went away and walked out to Liberton one evening with me and although he said nothing to me, I know*

he is devoted to me, although I have given him no encouragement, yet I have been always kind & polite, as I respect him very much. Don't think me very conceited telling you this small piece of news, but I would like to know what you think of him. He is certainly much improved of late & is decidedly good and he has passed his B.Sc. Exams. I really must confess I would not like to be a governess all my days, although there is nothing I despise more than girls marrying just for down-setting and really now-a-days you don't very well know what some men are, and I would feel quite frightened to join myself to anyone I did not know a good deal about. If you want to give me any brotherly counsels you would require to write shortly after receiving this, if I am to receive it before leaving Liberton, as I would not like any communications on the subject to be sent home, although I tell everything to Mama yet she might think it silly of me to write you anything about it.

Almost a year later in February 1887 she writes again to Tom:

If my letter is taken up with nothing but one subject, you will perhaps excuse me, as it is a most important one to me and I am sure will interest you too. I am engaged to Andrew Henderson! I tried for long to stand against anything of the kind, until I could do it no longer and had to own to myself that I loved him, and I can assure you, I'm not sorry now. For the more I know of him the more I love him. He is a decided Xtian and we both have the same aim in life, namely to live to God's glory! And besides that we have so many other things in common. He is a total-abstainer and I'm glad to say he does not smoke. Then he is very much interested in Missions, as I suppose you know that at one time in his life he had a great desire to go out to the Mission-field, but for many reasons he could not see his way clear to go, but we intend doing the next best thing we can: that is give our prayers & money, as far as we can, so we have no hope of ever becoming rich, because we don't wish to as long as we are comfortable that is all we want; but as we wish to furnish nicely and have a little to begin our married life on, we don't expect to be married for two years or about it, so we are keeping it as much a secret as we can. I can't tell you how much happiness it has been for us to be together for the last month and I only wish you were in the same happy position.

I believe it was only in answer to prayer that we are what we are to one another and I think we believe more than ever in prayer. You must not imagine that he is quite the same as when you left. He has since taken his B.Sc. degree and went to have a tour in America and since that has been in business with his father and hopes before many years are past to be made a partner. There is to be a Scientific School of Baking begun in connection with the Extra-Mural Classes at the University and he has been asked to take the lectures on Botany, but he has only promised four special ones, as he & a Dr Drinkwater are busy with some 'original research' in preparation to writing to a Scientific paper, so his time is fully occupied. He has also a good deal to do about the Y.M.C.A. this year as he is Secretary and he also teaches in the Barclay Afternoon Sabbath School. It will be a little bit of a trial to go off to Liverpool, but no doubt it will be good for both of us, and let us be thankful that we have been allowed to see & know one another in some measure, before we are separated for a time. I shall (D.V.) be in Liverpool by the time this reaches you. Now for a minor matter and very shortly, as Mama is in a hurry to get the letters off! He has given me a most beautiful ring with five large diamonds & two tiny ones between each! It is by far too gorgeous for a governess to wear, but he thought as it was to serve me for my life-time he would get me a good one, but Mama has given me a very pretty gold guard which I wear. Inside of it is 'Num. 6.24'. Inside my ring on one side there is 'A.H. & M.A.A.G.' 16.1.87. and on the other – 'The Lord reigneth'. I cannot go into details about the last sentence, but you may guess a good deal about it & the reasons why! Oh! That we might recognize His loving hand in everything – our joys and our sorrows & pray, Dear Tom, that our relationship one with another may be sanctified and that we may be the means of helping each other on our way heavenward. My heart is full of gratitude to God for giving me the prospect of such a good husband, in His *own good time! Goodnight dear old Tom, how I wish I had you here to talk to! It is dreadful how most people think of the outward man, his means, position in life etc, but why! Our lives here are only a short preparation for the life to come and we do sometimes sorely need some human friend to give us a helping hand, don't we? Although of course our chief desire is to give God the first place in our hearts. God bless you and your work, my dear Tom.*

Jane's reaction was less enthusiastic and in a letter to Tom in February 1887 she writes:

> *I do sincerely wish that I could have a talk with you instead of expressing what I have to say in a letter. How I long to unburden my heart to you about this engagement of Mary's. All things considered I am pleased with it as he possesses many of the essential good qualities every right-minded Christian girl would desire in a husband, besides he is very gentlemanly in his feelings, although he has not always mixed with such refined society as Mary has done. She however is the one to keep him 'up to the mark'.*
>
> *When speaking to me about the engagement I asked him about his means, when he said that he would furnish free of debt and insure his life for £500 or so before marriage. His income would at least be £200 a year, but if made a partner in the business he expected he would have considerably more. I said that in a case like his there ought to be a legal business arrangement with his father before the marriage. This would save any misunderstanding which might arise afterwards. I gave him to understand that Mary did not care for grandeur, but that she liked comfort, and would need a servant. This last needful he expressed to Mary as being an essential. One thing about the matter which cheers me is the thought that she will be living in town and near me, if I am spared. I often thought that Mary would never marry, as she saw so few men possessed of all the good points she thought desirable in a husband, but now she sees more of these in Andrew Henderson than any other man! Such is love.*

I hope you may approve of what she has done although 'at the first blush' of the thing you may feel a little troubled as I was. I however have got over that feeling now and think they may live a very happy life together to God's glory.

And a month later:

March 10ᵗʰ 1887

I am wearying to hear what you think of Mary's engagement. She seems very pleased herself but her mother has some thoughts she keeps to herself about it. If you were here I would tell you them, but I cannot write them. On the whole I am pleased, as I think him a good Christian man.

And in April:

14ᵗʰ April 1887

The Hendersons and Douglas were here on Tuesday evening for tea, but I did not feel very happy. I just felt as if Mary would be quite out of her element amongst them (or at least some of them). She however thinks them nice and Andrew of course nicer than any of them. The fact is I think her too good for him but would not like to vex her by saying much as he is a Christian man and she loves him. I wonder what John will say about the engagement. But then Mary says that he will forget she is a poor governess. This is in strict confidence. Excuse me as I am unburdening my mind to you dearest Tom, and it is love to her that makes me anxious about her future.

Jane Gillison's unease at Mary Agnes's engagement is clear when she states unequivocally that 'I think her too good for him'. Possibly there was an element of snobbishness in the Victorian era that considered 'trade' beneath the 'professional' classes; the family of a man of the cloth like the Reverend John Gillison's family would certainly rate as 'professional', whereas the owner of a biscuit factory –

even a flourishing one – was definitely 'trade'. However, Jane's doubts and fears must have been calmed because on July 17th 1888 a double wedding took place at 143 Warrender Park Road.

They were married by Rev. Thomas Gillison, uncle to the two sisters and father of the bridegroom Jamie. Mary Black the Gillison family's first cousin sent this account of the wedding to Tom:

19th July 1888

>*You will doubtless be wondering how the eventful seventeenth has passed off. Well all went splendidly, in spite of the fact that the day was wet and there was not even a blink of sunshine. The faces of the happy couples were as bright as the day was dull! The brides in fawn dresses, bonnets to match, carried white bouquets – Mary got hers from her S.S. girls – and did look bonny. I never saw them look better. Mary had all her usual grace and style and Marion, more than she usually possesses. The*

grooms looked jubilant and curiously both had elder brothers as best men. The ceremony took place in the dining room, the door of which was off and curtains hung instead. The brides' cakes were on the sideboard, and they as well as the mantelpiece were adorned with exquisite flowers. Aunt had got them in presents from Nanmoor, Fossoway, from friends of the Hendersons, from Kirkintilloch, & water lilies from the Castle. Forms were set around the walls but there were not seats for all the party. Fifty-six made the room pretty crowded, you may imagine.

The brides with their maids were in the drawing room and as the company finished singing the second paraphrase, the procession passed thence the dining room, in the following order – Mary and Andrew, Jane Guthrie and Bessie Henderson, Marion and Mr Reid, Bella & myself, Andrew with his best man were standing with their backs to the window, just beside the press door. Mary neatly shot off Andrew G. and took her place with her maids. Next to her stood Henry then Jamie beside whom Marion was placed, then Bella and myself. Your uncle stood just under the gasalier. He gave them a real old fashioned address on marriage and the respective duties of husband and wife. It is very nice. Then, proceeding he put the usual questions and in answer they replied 'I do' in varying intonations, but all quite calmly and firmly. A somewhat comical mistake was made by Mr Gillison at this stage as he asked, 'Do you Adam Henderson' and as he did correct himself, I am going to ask Mary when I see her if she is sure she has got the right man! Dr Wilson then prayed, and Mr Gillison pronounced them man & wife. The brides were kissed by their husbands, by the ministers, Aunt, the maids, the company generally. The grooms being also congratulated. The rings etc were attached to the favours of the cakes. [6] Miss Guthrie got the rings off Mary's & Miss Stewart the one off Marion's. Tea was handed round after the young folks had been asked to retire to the drawing room. Then those in the drawing room had some music which Annie Mackie started by playing the Wedding March. The brides slipped off to change their bonnets and don their brown cloaks, hoping to slip away, *but no, when they, conducted by the best men & closely followed by their respective grooms, reached the foot of the stairs, the lobby was laced with all young folks well armed with rice. They ducked and rushed, however so really got little rice as it went over their heads and on to the other throwers on the opposite side. After that ices were served and there was more music.*

Yesterday and today have been splendid days, so they are having nice weather for their honeymoons. Andrew and Mary are making Callander their headquarters. Jamie and Marion wrote from Greenock on Tuesday and were going to Appin beyond Oban the next morning.

It has been a very busy time for Aunt, and she has been doing too much as usual, so today I am sorry to say she is quite knocked up with indigestion. Mrs Archibald has been here today & has got away a bit of cake for you. Mr Hill from Australia has just been in bringing furs from John.

Aunt is sorry she cannot write you but sends her love & says she will write soon. After seeing Mary home, we go to Kirkintilloch to receive Marion, then go to Argyllshire for a fortnight's holiday. I hope it will quite recruit Aunt.

Andrew Henderson was one of the sons of Simon Henderson who had started the S.Henderson & Sons Bakery and Biscuit factory in Fountain Bridge, Edinburgh in the early 1860s. It was a thriving business and the enterprising Simon Henderson had even got an article in Chamber's Encyclopedia on 'Messrs S. Henderson's Perfect Food Biscuits' – a fact which was mentioned in an article about the firm in a copy of 'Edinburgh – Illustrated' in 1891. Biscuits were a moderately new form of popular 'convenience food' and the writer of the article wrote fulsomely about the benefits and advantages of this 'Perfect Food'.

About this time the firm expanded and, in addition to the Fountain Bridge Grove bakery, a new building was put up in North Merchiston – then a suburb on the west of the city – exclusively for the manufacture of biscuits which was called 'Simon Henderson & Sons Biscuit Factory'. The new factory was situated with a siding running directly into the firm's premises from the nearby North Merchiston station

Mr & Mrs Simon Henderson

Mr & Mrs Andrew Henderson

THE GROVE BAKERY.

Both sketches are from 'Edinburgh – Illustrated' of 1891.

Andrew and Mary Henderson
(Mary Agnes seemed to drop using her second name after her marriage).

of the Caledonian Co., which made transport and distribution of the biscuits to all parts of the world easier. The firm is described in the article as 'having spared no expense in installing the latest automated machinery and labour-saving appliances'.

The family recalls a story about Simon Henderson, the founder of the company, who was clearly ahead of his time in advertising ploys. In order to demonstrate the lightness of Henderson's butter puff biscuits, he displayed the biscuits in the bakery shop window, apparently floating and bobbing up and down. This was achieved by blowing a constant current of air beneath them.

The firm was eventually taken over by McVitie's Biscuits.

Bessie, Nita, Lilias and Simon Henderson, *circa* 1901.

1889 saw the arrival of three more grandchildren for Jane to add to the two little Marais girls in South Africa – Gerty and Agnes. Jane had a third child, a son Claude in January, and Mary and Andrew a son, Simon in August. Marion and Jamie's daughter Jane was born in November. Jane Gillison also made some changes to her domestic arrangements: she gave up her upstairs flat at 143 Warrender Park Road and took a five year lease on the smaller flat a floor below. She wrote:

Castlemains 24th April 1889

We came here on Mon. evening for a week's rest and change after the toil of our flitting. I was in bed for two days after I wrote you last, but I am feeling stronger now and hope to gather strength daily. I missed your help and John's but Andrew very willingly did what he could. I think we shall like the new house very well. I kept all my good furniture and Mary and Marion got what they wanted of the surplus. Marion got the mahogany table and double washstand you carried home from the sale room. You will be pleased to hear that Andrew passed his exam M.A. and was 'capped' on Thursday last. He is going to send you his photo soon. Dr Griffith John got his degree of D.D. at the same time. You will see an account of the graduation in the paper I send along with this. Give Dr John my hearty congratulations.

It was quite a coincidence that Andrew was awarded his degree at the same ceremony that the University of Edinburgh conferred an honorary title of Doctor of Divinity (in absentia) on Griffith John for his services to literature and especially as translator of the Scriptures. Rev Wardlaw Thompson, in his biography of the great man says, 'The only reference to the matter in his correspondence is in a letter to his friend Mr Jacob, replying to his congratulations, in which he says he does not feel at all home or comfortable in the new honour!'

The final piece of family news for 1889 came in November in a letter from John in Australia to Tom:

Nov 20th 1889

It is a long time since I wrote to you and I am quite ashamed to offer any apologies. This will be very short but I hope to send you a much longer epistle some day soon.

By this mail I have sent you a photo of a young lady, who will, if all goes well, be Mrs J.B.G. about the month of April next. She is a fine lassie, stout, strong and healthy and handsome as well as good – age 25 – one of

John Gillison

*eleven – mother died fifteen years ago – father alive aged 60 – only one sister
dead after the birth of her sixth child. Two brothers and two other sisters are
married and they have 14 children in all so that I shall have 20 nephews
and nieces with probably more to follow. Her name is Harriett Edginton and
she is at present in Sydney though I met her in Melbourne. But away to this
as I have a lot to do today and must write her a long letter this afternoon.
I am very well – going to Tasmania & New Zealand next week – shall be
away about six weeks – the travelling alone takes three. I hope to be able to
spend a day or two with 'the lassie' in Sydney in January.*

In 1890, Jane Gillison made a trip to South Africa to visit the Marais family.
The visit would have caused great excitement and for Jane it must have been a
tremendous undertaking. She left Edinburgh in May and returned home in mid-
October and, whilst there, she writes to Tom:

1st July 1890

    *I am very well and very happy with dear Jane and they have three
such sweet little ones. Just now Frans has gone to see a patient at a distance
and has taken Gertie and Agnes for a drive. He pets his bairns very much and
often has two on his knee at a time.*

    *This is a happy home where peace and plenty is. Food in Wellington
is good and cheap. Just now Jane gets lots of oranges and honey in presents.
On Friday we had a picnic to the mountains. Frans rode much of the way on
his bicycle. On Friday we are all going to Cape Town to spend a few days with
Mr Whitton whose little daughter boards with Jane. Whilst there Jane and the
bairns will have their photos taken.*

    *Next Sab. is 'Communion Sunday' here and I am rather sorry to be
away as I wished to see the order of the service etc, but I am likely to be at the
service in Cape Town.*

By last mail I was glad to hear from Marion that Jamie's health was improving with his stay at Castlemains. Poor Jamie needs good food and light work. I wish he had the stamina of his brother-in-law here. He is a 'stuffy' little fellow and his three bairns are like him.

I am well and very happy with dear Jane but the news of the state of Jamie's health and their decision to break up their nice little home and emigrate to a warmer climate has saddened me very much. But what can we say. It is the Lord's doing and He will order all things for the best. As I understand they are now on the sea and in less than three weeks I expect to have the joy of seeing them at Cape Town. If Jamie's health has improved by the sea voyage they will just go on in the same steamer to Melbourne, but if not he will come to Wellington for a little. John is now settled in his own home and will be glad to see them and will be very kind to them. Still he and Harriett will be moving in a much gayer circle than Jamie and Marion would care to be in, so for both parties I think that after a short time the latter would be happier in a quiet home of their own. Fortunately Marion has taken out their servant as nurse and as a gentleman in the congregation is paying her passage money the girl has engaged to stay with them for two years.

Marion is very brave and writes in good spirits. What upholds her is simple trust in God and a belief that He is leading them by a right path. Mary will write you all the particulars about them & before I left home she promised to write you all regularly.

What route do you intend travelling by on your way home? I think by this would be a roundabout way. I am sorry the L.M.S. have resolved to give only 2nd class passage money to missionaries on furlough. You must for the sake of your health and other reasons take a 1st and I shall help to make up the difference.

I had a nice letter from John and Harriett who seem very happy in their new home. I was very pleased to hear John say of his wife that she was the dearest woman in the world. This is just as it ought to be.

Jane has a busy life here with her own three little ones and Jeannie Whitton to care for. I was just saying to her this morning that she has no light task before her in the training of these four children properly. The surroundings here are not so favourable for fostering filial duties and helping in their right performance as residence in Scotland would be. Still Jane is anxious to train her dear ones in the way they ought to go if Frans would back up her efforts by being firm with them as she is, but he often neutralizes her training by overindulgence. But this must be between you and me. The children and Jane have had their photos taken and copies are to be sent you by this mail. Little Agnes has got her mother's eyes but neither she nor her sister, nor Claude in feature or disposition resemble their mother. They are all clever but self-willed. I hope however that they may by God's grace turn out fine characters in time.

There were many indications throughout the letters that all was not well with Jamie Gillison's health. In Jane's letter of the 1st July she reported that the family was to take the drastic step of leaving Scotland for the sake of Jamie's health and emigrate to a warmer climate. They travelled by way of South Africa in order to see Jane Marais and the family before sailing on to Australia and that visit happily coincided with Jane's. In that letter she also mentioned that Tom's first furlough was planned and one can well imagine her excitement at the prospect of seeing him in a year or so:

2nd August 1890

My time with our dear ones is fast passing by. I (D.V.) leave tomorrow three weeks by the Grantully Castle when a young son of Mr Richard Ross, the missionary, will be a fellow passenger to Edinr. Jamie I am glad to say is improving in health every day. Yesterday he went to Peter Marais' farm and climbed a high mountain. Today Peter is driving him to the eldest brother's farm where they are to climb another.

Marion is pretty well but neither she nor baby are as robust as Jane and her children are. Frans is busy just now – but when he has leisure he often gives

us a drive. Jane makes an excellent clever wife and, please excuse the thought, I
sometimes think that she is too good for the place she occupies. The people here
are kind in their way – but they are not like Scotch folk.

Jamie is to conduct a short service in the Goodnow Hall here next
Sab. afternoon. Frans would not hear of him taking the usual evening service
as the nights are cold just now. On Friday week Jamie and party leave for
Cape Town and as the time when their steamer may call is uncertain M^r
Whitton has kindly asked them to stay at his house. Jane and I will go into
town with them but will not be able to stay long as Jane can't be away from
the children overnight.

I am feeling the better for my change but these frequent partings take
the strength and spirit out of me. Jamie and Marion however feel that God
is leading them and whenever the Christian can say 'He leadeth me' it is all
right, so I try to say 'thy will be done'.

Jane left South Africa at the end of August 1890 for in October she writes to Tom:

16th October 1890

After a very good passage I got safely to Edin^r on the evening of
the 13th. Goodness and mercy have followed me every day since I left my
home on the 16th May last. And now I have to thank God for 'something
accomplished, something done.'

Tom Henderson is remaining in his present lodgings so Andrew and
I have the joy of being alone and I have a comfortable bedroom awaiting you.
Do try and come as soon as possible. I shall try and save £20 off what you
send me to help you to take a nice route home. What a pity you can't come
along with Philip.

I have little time for writing you today as I have been getting my house
in order and initiating my new servant into the ways of the household.

In the early part of 1891 plans and dates for Tom's first furlough were confirmed. Arthur Bonsey, a colleague wrote:

1st May 1891

> *There is so much in my heart that I should have liked to say &*
> *especially to wish you God's richest blessing both in journeying & at home.*
> *You have no need to be ashamed of your first spell of work – Apart from*
> *all the drawbacks, which your own frank nature is only too ready to suggest*
> *to your mind – you have seen a glorious work shaping itself out of the*
> *comparatively small Hospital which you took on in 1883 – Much of the*
> *blessing that has attended the Hospital work is due, first & foremost, to the*
> *healthy spiritual atmosphere of the place & that is due largely to your personal*
> *influence – The Hospital has grown in every way, & if we are willing to begin*
> *small, in our new developments, I feel sure we shall in the long run see a*
> *fine group of buildings about the present compound, representing new forces*
> *& influences for the evangelizing of the province & the building up of our*
> *churches.*

> *We shall not forget you, you may be sure & none will welcome you*
> *more heartily on your return – It is only a little break in our journey & from*
> *this time forth we must be prepared for them until the grand Consummation*
> *is reached & then we shall be 'Forever with the Lord'- Goodbye, my dear fellow,*
> *& may you prosper in all things & be in health.*

Among his many friends in Hankow there was a rising chorus of encouragement for Tom to bring back a wife and helpmate for the work:

> *For all your kindness & sympathy & generosity I cannot thank*
> *you as I ought & if you will only remember to send out to me the very best*
> *'support' for my dear wife I shall be even deeper in your debt than at present.*
> *Arthur Bonsey*

Again wishing you much happiness, & many blessings while at home – & last but not least – a fine wife & a good missionary for your companion on your outward journey. Geo Nicoll

We shall all be glad to see you back, accompanied by Mrs Gillison of course, that is to say if you can make up your mind which of the doubtless many eager suitors for yr. noble hand you will favour. Sydney Hodge

Oh what a joy to your dear mother to know that you will be with her so soon. What a happy time you will have at home & well do you deserve a happy holiday. Don't come back alone remember! Bring a Mrs G. with you, one worthy of the name. Lizzie Archibald

Tom travelled back home via the United States where he visited Griffith John's two sons, Griffith and David in Yonkers near New York and arrived back in Scotland at the end of June 1891. His first call was to his mother who had been quite seriously ill with pleurisy and we can be quite sure that her reunion with her son Tom after nine years must have given her great joy.

FIVE

The slow boat to China

T om's furlough in early 1892 was taken up with the usual busy round of deputation bookings interspersed with time spent with his relations, especially his mother. Deputation work consists of travelling up and down the country, visiting churches to take services; talking to the congregations about work in the mission field – usually on 'Missionary Sunday' ; reporting on the progress of the spread of the gospel to the 'heathen' to raise funds to facilitate this work. In addition missionaries were expected to attend conferences and meetings designed to convey the same message to any supporters of the missionary cause. The most significant of these were the 'May Meetings' held over a few days in London every year. Missionaries who were in Britain on leave were asked to address these meetings about their work; newly appointed recruits were also in attendance and all were supported by enthusiastic members of congregations from all over the country.

It is clear that Thomas met Dr Bessie Harris during his time at home and it may well have been at the May Meetings of 1892. She had just qualified in medicine having trained at The Royal Free Hospital. In those days women were not allowed to sit their final examinations at the London medical school where they had studied but the forward-thinking Edinburgh School of Medicine did not exercise the same veto so that was where she sat her Finals. She had successfully applied to the London Missionary Society to become a medical missionary and had been appointed to the Margaret Hospital for Women (built by Griffith John in memory of his first wife) in Hankow. With the frequent exhortations from his colleagues and friends in China to bring back a wife ringing in his ears Tom must have been absolutely delighted to meet Bessie – so suitable in every way – and I have no doubt he fell in love with her very rapidly. A letter dated May 1st from Bessie's mother Mrs Elizabeth Harris indicated that Tom had stayed with the family at 'South Place', the Harris family home in Calne and met other members of the Harris family there, possibly when on deputation to the Calne Congregational Church. She writes:

21st May 1892

> *It was kind of you to write us again and we are glad to know something of your movements, – I can quite believe you enjoyed the meetings, we only regretted that we could not stay to more of them. I trust you are right in thinking that we are to see greater things in the missionary world than we have seen!*
>
> *Yes, indeed our house is less full, and less lively! My boy left us very bravely, he would not let us see any emotion. I had a P.C. from him from on board the 'Labrador'.*
>
> *I have twice heard from Bessie, doubtless she is busy getting greater fitness for her life's work. We shall be happy to let you have one of our family groups, I think we must get a few more copies – it was taken just before Joe started 2 1/2 years ago.*
>
> *No doubt you will let us know about your leaving for China. I hope Mrs Gillison is in better health tho I have not the pleasure of knowing her, I should like my kind regards given her as your Mother.*
>
> *Mr Harris, Sophy & Mary join me in kind regards to you.*

Mrs Harris was referring to her son Joseph who had decided to emigrate to Canada. Joe had strong socialist views and for years had rebelled against his father's capitalist philosophy and the decision to leave his home and set up for himself in the New World was a direct response to this. He was entered into agricultural college at Guelph, Ontario by his family but then decided to leave college and moved to British Columbia acquiring some land which he farmed. In 1897 on a return visit to the U.K he met Elizabeth Raper, a young Scot whom he married. Bosun Ranch in New Denver became their home and there they started a dynasty of Harrises that flourishes to this day.

There was seldom any period in China's political history over the second half of the nineteenth and early twentieth centuries that one could say was peaceful. Friction and unrest of one sort or another happened frequently between the old ruling dynasties and the people. The internal struggle between various groups of Nationalists and Communists simmered under the surface and it took very little to stimulate anti-Christian uprisings and riots or protests against foreign business interests in the country. Britain and the West had much to answer for in the aftermath of the 1840s 'Opium Wars'.

One such period of serious unrest occurred when Tom was back in Britain on his first leave in 1891. At first it was not clear who was instigating this anti-Christian, anti-foreign feeling which was centred round the Yangtze basin. After appeals from various foreign powers an Imperial edict was issued which condemned the riots and supported the right of the Christians, both European and Chinese, to reside and pursue their calling. Although the edict was made public everywhere it only inflamed the situation and throughout Hunan, Hupeh and Kiang-Si provinces the anti-Missionary riots were very threatening. In the view of Griffith John and the missionaries on the spot the trouble was emanating from Chang-sha the capital of Hunan and Dr John discovered from documents he saw that the inflammatory literature was being printed in Chang-sha. The rumours accused missionaries, particularly Roman Catholics, of kidnapping Chinese children and using them for vivisection and lurid posters to this effect were put up in the great cities down the river inciting the riots. It is remarkable that it is acknowledged as an historical fact that it was Griffith John himself who presented the evidence he had found out about Chou Han and the printing presses responsible for the propaganda to H.M.Consul in Hankow; he in turn referred it to H.M.Government and eventually the Court of Peking was obliged to take decisive action. Chou Han the activist scholar and minor official and leader of the group was 'degraded from office' and held under house arrest and the riots died down for a time but not before the murder of two Swedish Missionaries occurred in 1893. Chou Han was eventually imprisoned for life after he returned to his publishing business in Chang-sha in 1897 when he attempted to re-ignite the anti-Christian feeling with more inflammatory publications. George Sparham, Dr Griffith John's son-in-law and a colleague of Tom, writes to Tom in July describing the horror of the murder of Argent and Green:

July 4ᵗʰ 1891

You will have heard of the disturbed times we have been having in China. I fear that very exaggerated accounts may have reached home. Various explanations are given of the riots, & it seems certain that there is a widespread dissatisfaction with the present dynasty. The only serious disturbances occurred at Wuhu, Nanking, Wu-si (near Soochow) & Wusueh – at Wuhu the Consul & Orphanage were burnt down & other Roman Catholic property, damaged. Similar work was done at Wu-si; at Nanking the foreigners had all to leave; an attack was made on the Hospital but Nicoll an American Missionary held the mob at bay till the officials arrived – I believe no damage was done there. The Wusueh affair is intensely sad. The ladies were on the Wesleyan Compound there, Mʳˢ Boden, Mʳˢ Rotheroe & Mʳˢ Warren. Boden & Rotheroe were away. A Roman Catholic was seen in the streets carrying babies in baskets which he said he was taking to Kiu Kiang – A mob gathered at once, made a rush for the Mission houses, & burnt them both. The ladies took refuge in an outhouse but were seen & chased from there. At the first Yamen⁷ that they fled to, the doors were shut in their faces. At the next the Mandarin tried to help them but was overpowered by the mob, but finally they were taken to the Go Fu's Yamen & remained there, but meanwhile Mʳˢ Warren had been knocked down & lost a good deal of blood & Mʳˢ Boden lost her baby for a long time. They finally took refuge in a pengtze ⁸ & hid there until they went to the Yamen. Mʳˢ Rotheroe had been able to get there sooner.

Argent was waiting at Nun's house for the up-steamer & the two men seeing the flames hurried off to give assistance, they only supposing that the houses had caught fire. But they were met by the mob & brutally murdered. Argent's head was battered with a huge stone till he was dead. Green took refuge in a bund but was finally persuaded to come out by a Mandarin who had arrived with a few men but no sooner was he out than the mob set in to him & when his body was found there were 50 wounds on it. The gunboat Palos (U.S.A.) was there shortly after & the Doctor said that any one of the wounds was enough to have killed him. The people in the Yang-tze Valley are infuriated against the Roman Catholics on acc' of the Orphanages & they do not always distinguish between them & us.

The higher officials have been acting well & now seem to have suppressed the rising, several men have been apprehended – & now all seems quiet. Tho' there are still gunboats at Shanghai & up the Yang-tze at all the ports – We have much to be thankful for, it is difficult now to realise how great, for a time the danger was.

It must have seemed to Tom Gillison that his period of leave passed all too quickly with the busy mixture of deputation work, attending refresher courses and missionary gatherings and also much reading to catch up with on the latest medical techniques. Most important of all was to spend time with his mother. After a full year of leave the plan was to return to China in the autumn and this time he would travel in the company of a group of new missionaries among whom were Dr Bessie Harris and her younger sister Mary.

The letters Tom had received from his colleagues in China during the year bore testimony of the high regard and affection with which he was held and the impatience of his peers to see him back in harness. Dr John wrote:

February 23rd 1892

I need not say that everywhere the beloved physician was spoken of. I was extremely pleased to find how truly and deeply you are loved by the converts. They will be glad to see you back again.

And in June he wrote:

June 6ᵗʰ 1892

>   *I hope Miss Harris will turn out to be the right man in the right place. I hear from Mrs de Selincourt that her sister is coming out with her as a nurse – but, like the doctor, self-supporting. This looks well and inspiring.*

And from Dr Sydney Hodge of the Wesleyan Mission:

May 5ᵗʰ 1892

>   *Your fame has, from time to time, by papers, periodicals, letters & vox populi been wafted to my ears & I ought to have written long ago. Rumours of what you are going to do when you come back have gone before you and already I have visions of a beautiful Operating Theatre, strictly aseptic, with bacteriological laboratory & no end of improvements I feel quite sorry for the Hankow bacilli against whom you will wage deadly warfare. We shall all be glad to see you back, accompanied by Mrs Gillison of course, that is to say if you can make up your mind which of the doubtless many eager suitors for yr. noble hand you will favour. It really must be very embarrassing for you & difficult to chose, but mind you do chose, for I foretell things worse than have befallen poor Owen if you come out alone … . Doubtless when you return the great Ji Yi Sen ⁹ will gather the clans around him once more. Shall I ever reach his fame? I am afraid not. Somebody told me the other day yr name was known all over China. Well there can only be one Sun in the heavens and I must be content to bask in yr glory & shine with reflected light.*

Yet another letter from Dr John:

June 6ᵗʰ 1892

>   *I am writing you this time not in reply to any letter received from you. You are a very good man, but not a good correspondent – that is you*

do not write often enough. I have heard of your doings at Cambridge and Liverpool, and congratulate you on the good accomplished. May God bless you & your efforts more & more. But when are you coming back? Don't stay too long. The Hospital is gone down sadly. The riots of last year will account for it in a measure but not altogether. Dr Mackay does not take with the Chinese. There is a Chinese barrier, as you know, which you must break through if you would be a successful Missionary. He has not broken through it yet; I doubt if he ever will. Anyhow the Hospital is lifeless, & it is by no means a joy to go into it as it used to be in the days of old. Chou Ki-Kwan asked permission the other day to go home till Ki' Sien Seng ¹⁰ returned, giving as the reason that there was nothing doing at the Hospital. He may have, & probably has, another reason for making the request, but I know not what it is. Don't be discouraged about the Institution. It will be as flourishing as ever when you take it in hand again.

Tom would have looked forward with keen anticipation to the very pleasant prospect of returning to his beloved hospital and at the same time escorting Dr Bessie and her sister on a journey which would last six weeks. However this enthusiasm would have been tinged with sadness at leaving his mother whose very poor health he must have realized made it unlikely that they would ever meet again.

That Jane Gillison had unlimited courage in the face of yet another separation from Tom was undeniable. There were concerns about her foot and suspicions that the diagnosis was necrosis, which was later confirmed as her condition worsened. However her sadness might have been lessened at the thought that her much loved son Tom might possibly have found a suitable wife. From the hints in her letters Tom must have confided in her about his feelings for Bessie Harris and it seems conceivable that she had even met Bessie at some stage, possibly at a 'Missionary Sunday' at her own Barclay Church in Edinburgh.

In November 1892 Jane writes:

November 17th 1892

>*I hope you are making some progress in a 'special matter', if not just 'bide your chance' knowing that there is an overruling Providence guiding you. So trust in Him at all times, and let His peace rule in your heart.*

This is followed by another letter in December:

December 1st 1892

>*My thoughts are very often about you. I hope you are not far from Hong Kong now. Now that you will be home before this reaches you, will you tell me how your house looks – if you have unpacked all your goods etc., and most important of all how you are in health, and if your lip is healed. I have sometimes thought that if you had discontinued the use of sugar as a trial it might have healed sooner. I would also like to know if you get any encouragement to hope that you may be accepted by a fair lady.*

>*Be wise I pray you, and see if you can get her to fall in love with you by showing her little kindnesses etc. If things should go against you, I get down hearted and rebel against God. Trust in Him at all times.*

Among the party of missionaries on board the S.S. Rome apart from Bessie and Mary Harris were Dr Lavington and Mrs Elsie Hart and Dr Lavington Hart's brother Walford taking up his first post as a missionary having given up an attractive legal career in London to do so. Tom, with ten years of experience of speaking Chinese, gave language lessons to the new recruits on board, and the long days at sea must have given what was described as the 'happy party' ample opportunity to get to know one another.

It might seem strange that Mary Harris, Bessie's younger sister, with no formal training either in nursing or medicine was joining her sister on this huge

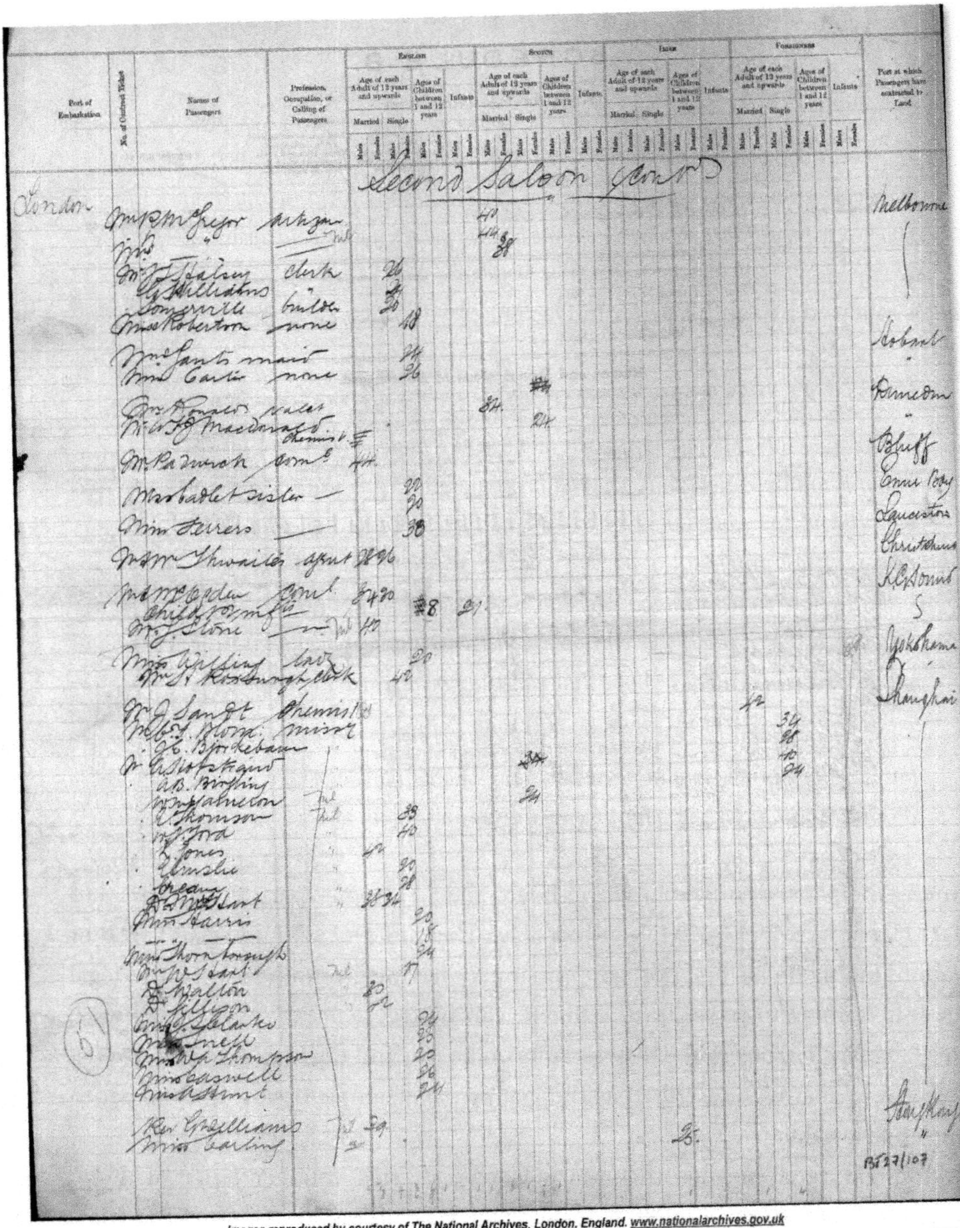
Port of Embarkation
No. of Contract Ticket
Names of Passengers
Profession, Occupation, or Calling of Passengers
English
Scotch
Irish
Foreigners
Age of each Adult of 12 years and upwards
Married
Single
Ages of Children between 1 and 12 years
Infants
Port at which Passengers have contracted to Land
Second Saloon (cont'd)
London
Melbourne
Hobart
Dunedin
Bluff
Launceston
Christchurch
Yokohama
Shanghai
Hong Kong
BT27/107

Images reproduced by courtesy of The National Archives, London, England. www.nationalarchives.gov.uk

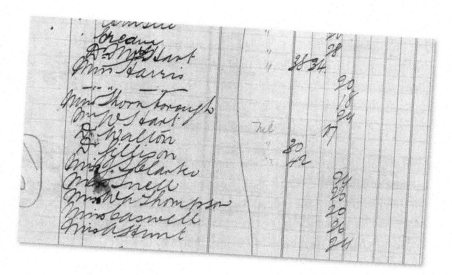

One of the pages from the passenger list for the SS Rome which sailed from London
October 27th 1892 with a large party of missionaries on board.
Mr Walford Hart, Miss Harris, Miss Mary Harris (indicated as a ditto) and
Dr Gillison seen near the bottom of the list.

adventure. The sisters had always been extremely close and when Bessie offered
her services as a missionary Mary wanted to accompany her sister. In Bessie's book
'Memories of Mary Hart' Bessie writes:

> From the time I received those letters from Hildesheim, in which Mary
> spoke of wishing to go in for training and ultimately to accompany me as
> a missionary, until my own course was finished she never again referred
> to the subject. I saw how happy and busy she was when she was at home
> and I thought she had given up the idea; so I said nothing, not wishing to
> influence her. Great, therefore, was my surprise and joy when, just before I took
> my final examination, she told me she wanted to go to China with me. The
> announcement of her wish did indeed take the family by surprise.
>
> Not knowing what Father would say, she first of all said she would like
> to go and help me in starting work, and hold herself in readiness to come back

113

at any time Father or Mother wanted her. To do this she could not of course have been connected officially with the L.M.S, and the more we all talked the matter over and consulted with Mr Thompson, the foreign secretary of the Society, the more we inclined, if Father and Mother were willing, to go out on exactly the same footing as I was going, and she therefore made a formal application to the board and was accepted as a worker.

By the phrase 'on the same footing' she confirmed that both women would have financial support from the Harris family and not be paid a salary by the L.M.S, although they would have the official backing of the Society. The important thing about Mary was that what she lacked in specialist training she more than made up for in her willingness to turn her hand to anything asked of her.

Mary was always an excellent letter writer as well as having an artistic eye and her accounts of the journey to China are beautifully descriptive. She painted with words as well as with brush or pencil, recording the colourful scenes in her sketch note pad. At Colombo the passengers had to leave the S.S.Rome and embark on the S.S. Malwa to complete the journey to Shanghai and Mary Harris writing home said that as they approached Shanghai, 'Dr Gillison quite dances a jig daily for joy to think that we are so near Hankow.'

The party then stayed for a few days in Shanghai before embarking on the river steamer that was to take them down river to Hankow where they arrived on December 16th. Dr John and the other missionaries in the city gave the newcomers the warmest of welcomes at the quay side and introduced them to their temporary hosts. The two Harris girls stayed with Mr and Mrs Terrell in the early days while they became familiar with their new surroundings and the Lavington Harts with Tom Gillison. As well as starting work in the hospital they had to continue their daily studies in Mandarin.

Although he had travelled with the missionaries as far as Hankow Walford Hart had been appointed to work in Chung King a further twelve hundred miles up the Yangtze river. The river had one hundred miles of notorious rapids where each boat had to by dragged by men through the water and many a ship was

The slow boat to China

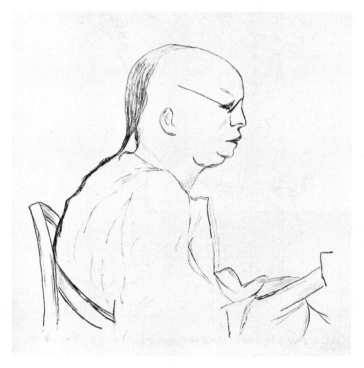

A sketch by Mary of 'Mr Hiung, our teacher'.

wrecked and many a 'tracker' drowned. After a short time spent in Hankow
Walford Hart set out on this hazardous journey which was completed safely but
not without an incident in the rapids when much of his luggage went overboard
and there was damage to his treasured magic lantern and other possessions.
Mary Harris writes in a letter home:

> They heard last week that Mr Walford Hart was wrecked on one
> of the rapids he had to go up. The towers lost control of the boat, and it
> floated backwards, but, I think, kept clear of the rocks, till one of the many
> Chinese life boats rescued them. All their things were drenched, and they
> had to encamp six days in a temple while their belongings were being

Mary's sketches of a 'Hankow policeman' and a 'Chinaman'.

'Hankow babies'.

*rescued and the boat mended. He wrote in very good spirits, although his
books, magic lantern, new concertina, clothes etc were very much hurt, if
not quite spoiled. Happily he had no further mishap, and only said he felt
'earnestly thoughtful' when in the rapids.*

Walford Hart had not apparently given Mary Harris any indication of any
particular feelings he entertained towards her before he left Hankow; it seemed
that he thought he should see what the posting at Chung King was like before
he approached her.

Meanwhile in Hankow itself the new missionaries were settling in well and
towards the end of January 1893 Tom felt it was time to propose marriage to
Bessie, which apparently came as a great surprise to her. Possibly her first reaction
was an outright refusal but there was a telling letter to Tom from Griffith John
in which he writes:

6th February 1893

*I feel that I must send you a word of sympathy, and I am sure you
will believe me when I say that it comes from the heart. I had not told Miss
Harris one word of what you revealed to me this day fortnight. When Miss
Harris showed me your letter on Saturday night, I saw clearly that the thought
of your having any such feelings towards her had never entered her mind, and
that no feelings other than that of real respect and friendship had ever been
cherished by Miss Harris towards you.*

*In the circumstances it was impossible for Miss Harris to write
otherwise than she did. The reply is a perfectly honest one, and you will
appreciate it as such. I told her distinctly that my desire was that the matter
should be left to you both & God, & that I was prepared to make any and
every personal sacrifice for your good. You & I believe in God, & we know that
what He decides must be right and best.*

Bessie was, of course, contractually and morally obliged to fulfil her agreement with the London Missionary Society to serve five years as a medical practitioner and would not lightly have overcome her scruples. However she would almost certainly have been encouraged, in the small social circle of the Hankow Mission compound, to accept Tom's proposal. On 14th February Tom made a second proposal in person because the next day she replies by letter:

February 15th 1893

My own dear Tom,

I don't want to leave you in suspense for any longer than I can help for I know how you must be feeling. Yes, I am so glad to have an answer for you. I believe God has made it quite plain to me. I believe He has meant us the one for the other.

For years I thought He meant me to live to Him alone, so I have been vexed with my-self for loving you so much as I have, but now tonight He has been showing me that He had this in store for me & that I shall best serve Him if I accept your offer. He has helped me to think about it very calmly, but from that point of view which I most feared viz. 'His Glory' I feel still the answer is the same.

I long to see you again. When can you come? We have an extra fire today so Mary & Mrs Terrell know the secret so there is no reason why you should not come. May I know when to expect you? It will be such a help to have another talk.

Will it seem very hard to you if I ask you to consider it right to wait five years. It is only because I feel that we can best glorify Christ by so doing that I ask it – you know that don't you? Will you make this sacrifice with me for our one Lord and Master?

I know there are many, very many in England who will read my action in this matter. I know that if I married soon, to very very many it would seem to mar the consecration which they believed mine to be & on the other hand if we wait so that I can render the bulk of one term's service to the L.M.S. which I came out to do; & if some know that I am denying myself in order to be faithful in this then I think they will 'Glorify God in us'. We will talk more about this when you come also about making it known or otherwise.

I will only just add to what I said above, that of course I should look forward to term upon term of service here after I was married but still in marrying one must be prepared for whatsoever married life may bring & my services to the Mission Work would then be on a different footing.

I want to see you for I feel I returned your love almost coldly yesterday, I was afraid of going too far lest I should have to retract. I am yours & I am very very happy in the thought. I feel utterly unworthy of one so good, so noble, so unselfish as you are, but I do thank God for it. It is His Spirit in you that I have learnt to love, I trust it was something of the same that drew you towards me. We shall thus have our union 'in Christ'

Yours very lovingly,

Bessie Harris

The announcement of Tom and Bessie's engagement was a cause of great rejoicing all the way down the Yangtze from Shanghai to Chung King. The news took some weeks to reach the families back home but the reactions from there when the letters came were equally favourable. First to congratulate the happy couple is Griffith John:

Year 19th, Month 1st, day 1st

I have often sent you greetings on special days, I am not sure that I have ever done so on a Chinese New Year's Day before. But I do so today with a fullness of Joy, and a strength of Faith in the future, that I have

never felt before with regard to yourself. Most heartily do I Congratulate
you, my brother, my friend, my Son, and most earnestly do I pray that our
Father's richest blessing may ever rest upon your union. The old saying is
that Marriages are made in Heaven, I am not quite sure that very many
are made there; I am convinced that not a few are concreted in that other
place. With regard to yours, however, I have not the least bit of doubt. God
has given you a woman of His own choice, and I feel sure that the relation
between you two souls will bring into your life a joy and a power which will
be an astonishment to yourself. And so it will be with her. You are worthy of
each other, and, I honestly believe, admirably fitted for each other ... .

 ... I rejoice greatly in the thought that your marriage is not going to
bring weakness into the work, for, after all, to you both this must be a vital
consideration. My own opinion is that it ought to bring nothing but strength,
and very much strength, into it. Unitedly you will be able to do more than you
could possibly do separately.

 One thing more, I want you to remember that I am your China
Father, and that you must be married out of this house, and that I am to
give the Marriage Breakfast. This is my privilege, and Mary's privilege, and
George's privilege also.

And to Bessie he writes:

Feb 16th 1893

 We have had already our quiet talk over the matter of your
engagement, and I don't know that I have anything more to add. I feel,
however, that I must send you a few lines, and put my congratulations in
writing. From the depth of my heart I congratulate you both. I am more
delighted than I can tell you, that Dr Gillison has found you, and that you
have found him. You are worthy of each other, so I am sure that the blessing
of God will rest upon this union. Dr Gillison I love as a son, and no one,

with the exception of his own Mother, can rejoice in his happiness more heartily than I do. He is one of the truest of men, and destined to be one of China's most eminent Missionaries. He has done a noble work for God already; but a still greater work is before him. With you by his side to help him and cheer him, I can see a splendid future before him.

I will not tell you what I think of you, though you have, I feel sure, divined it already, I love you as Miss Harris with something of the love of a Father; but as Mrs Gillison my love and interest in you and your work must grow and deepen. Most heartily do I congratulate him in the choice he has made, as well as you in the choice you have made.

My earnest prayer is that God's richest blessing may rest on you both, and that your united life may ever be beautiful in God's sight and strong for His service.

Remember you are to marry from our house, and the wedding breakfast is to be given by me. This is my privilege as paterfamilias.

The person who would most immediately be affected by this engagement was Bessie's sister Mary who for so many years had been her closest confidante. Mary however was not in the least put out for she writes home:

I have no fear of being an awkward third person, – I might with some people but not with these two; it will only be a help to have a brother … . Isn't it grand that this comes now to help Bess at the start of working? His ten years here will be next best to having ten years' experience in China herself; and won't it be a help to us both in learning the talk of the people? Won't it be nice too not to have to manage the Chinese servants alone? Won't it be nice for Dr Gillison? What would he say if I left his gain out? It is just wonderful how good it seems in every way. I could prolong the catalogue, but won't, except for one point. Isn't it splendid that all you home people know him?

Letters of congratulation came from friends in Shanghai, Kiu- Kiang, and Chung King as in due course did the letters from home. Tom's future mother-in-law writes:

South Place, Calne April 4th 1893

> *Yesterday we certainly had a new experience in our lives, viz, the request for one of our daughters! Such matters always come as a surprise yet, we have thought such a subject might come before us, indeed it has seemed to us that you and our daughter Bessie were most unfortunately placed! Did we not now ought to say 'fortunately', since you both seem so happy and realise God's over-ruling providence in being brought together as you have been.*

> *Dear Bessie has been very reticent about you in her letters, and we, in the matter of the hearts affection ever since our sons & daughters were of marriageable age, have, often alone sometimes together & always weekly on the Sabbath morning – unitedly as Parents, made a special request of Our Father in Heaven that He would direct all the providences, either for marriage or for single life. And doubtless dear Dr Gillison as a man of God you have felt led in the same way, and we will not doubt that this has come about in answer to prayer … .*

> *… Then there is dear Mary!! I thank you for the very kind words you say of her, and she evidently is disposed to take you at your word & believe she will not be less welcome or less needed, we must just let the unfolding of providence show what the will of God is concerning her future. We are very glad to have seen you as much as we have, and we are thankful to the friends in Hankow who in congratulating Bessie have borne witness to your Christianity, as a Man & a Missionary; to us all these letters are a very great comfort. I assure you it was very gratifying to me as step-mother to find my step-sons & their wives all flock to us to hear all about the matter and to give their glad approval, I expect Bessie will hear from the Brothers or else from their wives.*

> *I have just re-read your letter, and I must add again that we do feel happy in giving our consent to the Union. May God in his kind providence*

*make you to each other a blessing and to the Chinese both to soul & body. I
am dear Thomas the affectionate, the Mother of your dear Bessie.*

As the letters of congratulation came there are no mentions anywhere that Tom
would have to wait five years for his bride. Indeed preparations were put in
place for the ceremony to take place in early September; and meanwhile both
Tom and Bessie continued their work. Very soon after the engagement Tom
accompanied Dr John and another colleague, William Terrell, on an already
planned evangelical visit to the converts in some of the outlying country areas
of Hupeh. These trips were regarded with great importance by Dr John as very
necessary for the work of the Mission. On this occasion, Tom, writing home to
his Aunt Agnes, his mother's sister, in June that year says:

June 25ᵗʰ 1893

> *I had a nice trip to the country with Dʳ Griffith John at Chinese New
> Year time – We got mobbed in one place – but escaped unhurt – Not even a
> scar to show.*

Bessie, writing to Tom while on this journey, gave an account of all she had been
doing in his absence and described her first midwifery call:

Sunday March 4ᵗʰ 1893

> *How glad I am it will soon be time for you to be back again. I have
> often wanted you this week, not merely in a general way but for all sorts of
> special things that I have wished I could talk over with you.*
>
> *However I have had a good week & this afternoon I have ended by
> getting a call to a midwife case which I am thankful to tell you is very happily
> over. It was in a hut on the City wall. I took the Amah with me & Mary. It
> was nice to be able to walk there, the man who fetched us carrying the bag. On
> arrival I found a crowd inside & outside the hut. I went to the woman who
> was on the ground with only a bit of bamboo matting under her. I discovered*

she had been in labour since yesterday. I could understand no more except that Amah said 'Baby dead'. I then made a vex. & discovered a hand & the cord but was thankful the next minute to find a foot a little higher up. This I soon got down & by moderate traction the whole thing was soon over. The head caused a delay of some minutes, but chiefly because, as the foetus was considerably macerated I had to be very careful not to leave the head behind. The onlookers were so delighted when it was over. The woman also seemed very thankful; she was not in a bad way at all – Her pulse was good & she soon took the soup they gave her. I administered a dose of ergot & came away. Outside the hut we were indeed made much of, everybody seemed thanking us & beaming. We got back when the Chinese service was going on & we crept in at the back. The Amah came in too. We were there before the communion service began which we were glad of. Afterwards the Amah of course told people & the women I could see by their faces looked highly delighted. Mr Foster told me also that the husband was outside & wanted to tell me how thankful he was. Could I have had a better case for my first? It is just wonderful how my fears are never realised. I really was anxious when the call came.

On Tom's return to Hankow from the evangelistic journey to the country, he entrusted a commission to a colleague in Shanghai to purchase an engagement ring for Bessie on his behalf. The friend Mr Buchanan writes:

6th March 1893

It was indeed a delight to me, to learn about your engagement to Miss Harris. I can most heartily congratulate you on your choice. She is a sweet, good girl, & I am sure that she will make a most excellent wife. She quite won my heart, the few days we were together & I wondered then, who would be the lucky man to win her! Let me confess, that my suspicions did light on you, that Sunday evening you spent with us, & from all I know about you, dear Miss Harris is also to be warmly congratulated, please accept our sincere good wishes for you both, now & always, in your domestic life, your important

Christian work, in all its branches, & your helpful social life amongst your friends in Hankow.

You did entrust me with a sweet & charming commission! I wish that I could have filled it better, But with the most diligent search of all the shops in Shanghai, I could not get a ring at all satisfactory, near suiting your description. Pearls are not set in broad hand rings, usually. Two of the foreign jewellers offered to make the rings to any pattern, but I knew that they w^d give the job to a Chinaman, so thought I had better consult the latter for myself. I found the Chinese jewellers gave much better value for the money. I am sending tomorrow by Customs post 2 rings for your approval. The pearl one with small diamond setting, was made to my order, but I fear it looks clumsy. The other diamond one I send as a suggestion. You could have a flat guard ring made with three good diamonds, each of them a little larger than those in the sample for Tls 45. Such a ring would not be 'showy' & it would be much more serviceable than any kind of pearl ring. The latter is so perishable, & needs to be taken such care of. But if you & Miss Harris prefer it, I can have a band ring made with three pearls set in it, the band a little less heavy than the one I now send. I am at a loss about the size, your measurement of $2^{1}/_{4}$ the jeweller declares is too large. You might twist a piece of wire into a ring the exact size, then there w^d be no mistake. If you should happen to care for the pearl ring sent, & it be not large enough the jeweller says that he can enlarge it. I am delighted to do this little commission for you, or any other, at any time, please do not think of trouble to me in connection therewith, & please do not take a ring not to your liking, I shall with pleasure, 'try try try again'. I have your cheque for Tls 35.

Tom's own family wrote warm letters of congratulation but John Gillison's letter from Australia was more revealing of his character than he realized:

Melbourne 28th August 1893

I duly received your long and interesting letter of 8th to 13th March last, telling me of your engagement. We (that is Harriett and I), wish you a *long and happy married life and send you herewith a Bank of England note for £5 with which to buy yourself a wedding present. You can get things so much cheaper in China than we can here that you will be able to do a good deal more with it than we can. Mother sent us Bessie's photo so we know what she is like. It is fortunate that Providence has arranged for you to marry some one with a little money for of one thing I am sure and it is that you would never have been able to keep a wife and family on the small income you were receiving. Bessie looks sensible and from all accounts it seems you are to be united to a treasure. You yourself no doubt think so.*

At home in Edinburgh during the months of Tom and Bessie's engagement Tom's mother was suffering serious pain with her foot. Various specialists had been consulted and a number of treatments tried but her condition continued to deteriorate. At the end of March Mary, Tom's sister writes:

28th March 1893

> *I have not very good news to give you of Mother this week. Her foot has been getting very gradually worse & has developed very rapidly within the last few weeks. Dr Darling told us last week that there was no doubt now – it was – Necrosis – and she has been suffering intense pain, but with great patience. Prof Chiene is out of town just now, so Dr D. brought Dr Caird today to see it.*

> *He thought it very bad & that something must be done very soon or she could not stand it much longer – it is wearing her out so. They really think that nothing short of amputation will do any good and she herself is very anxious for this. She is a perfect marvel to me of resignation & patience & cheerful willingness to do whatever the D^{rs} think best. She is to go to bed now & have a Boracic Lint Poultice on & on Monday they are to give their final decision and we know that our Heavenly Father, who doeth all things well – is sure to give the sought-for guidance & we must just ask for the needed strength. Dr Darling does not fear the giving of the chloroform, but*

the shock, seeing she is so weak. It is an anxious time for us, but oh! that we might have simple, child-like trust in our God.

By the 6th April it was decided that amputation of Jane Gillison's foot was the only possible course of action and Andrew, Tom's younger brother, sent this account of the operation which took place in the drawing room of her flat – which seems an incredible venue considering our present day standards of surgical practice:

April 6th 1893

> *You will be anxious to hear all about Mother & I shall tell you as fully & concisely as I can. First of all you will be glad to know that everything has gone splendidly. After Mr Cairds first visit of which you have heard, Dr Darling found that Prof Chiene was away from home, (& between us he was not sorry) so the only thing they could do in that quarter was to show the courtesy of asking his consent to an operation, providing that Grainger Stewart did not forbid it on account of the heart & lungs. The latter came on Friday afternoon & examined mother's chest & heart & said that if she were his own mother he would have the source of disease removed. Her heart was pretty good but of course lungs weak. He rather annoyed Mother with his blustering way & talking against Laing of Kirkcaldy who was so kind to her, & other things that I need not say anything about. However that is not worth mentioning except in so far as it gave Mother a restless night.*
>
> *Darling found that Caird was away from home & would not be back till 9.30 p.m. on Saturday night. Andrew H. was to meet the former at Caird's house at 10 p.m.; but I went in his place. Caird had received word from Chiene giving consent to operation & suggesting a modification of Syme's operation. Darling & Caird therefore arranged to come on Sunday morning instead of Monday as before intended. We were very thankful as it saved an anxious day. I gave Mother a good spoonful of Castor oil that night & she got some beef tea in the morning. She was quite content that even amputation should be performed, the pain of the foot was so*

*great. After breakfast there was little time for waiting. Mary came in &
has remained ever since, Mary Black was here too. Dr Darling came in just
after everything was put in order. Mother was not put about much at all.
When Caird with 2 assistants arrived, Darling straight away began with
the chloroform. I had Mother's hand & she was pretty hard to be put over.
When I thought she was pretty well under, I said to Darling, 'Is she quite
over yet'? and she herself answered, 'No, not quite!' We were rather amused.
When Caird had got tables & everything else he wanted, the assistants went
into the drawing-room, (which by the way we had made mother's bed-room)
with all the instruments etc. That was 10 minutes past 10 & before 20
minutes to 11 Darling came out & said it was all finished & had taken 19
min. from the time of the start till she was back in bed again. The drawing-
room was very good for the purpose as there was plenty of light. In a short
time everything was cleared up & mother was herself again tho' very sick.
She came-to very quickly. Mr Caird did as Chiene suggested & removed the
foot just above the ankle. A splendid stump has been left.*

*After the operation Mother was not prostrated nearly so much
as we expected. She could & did talk quite freely. Darling gave her an
injection of morphia in the afternoon & she was able to have some
nourishment in the shape of Chicken-tea, brandy, iced water etc. At night
she got another injection & had a quiet rest with a good pulse & no
fever. Caird called in again in the evening & found all right. Mother was
anxious to have the foot buried in the Grange Cemetery at the foot of the
grave & was rather vexed because I scouted the idea. Andrew Henderson
was much in favour because he quite agreed with her. I asked Caird, &
of course he told me it was never done & that he would bury it with the
other stuff that they had! Of course we could do what we liked. So I put
it to mother & she was quite content to let it be as Caird wished! He was
going to examine it. Poor dear Mother she has been so patient all this
while and willing to do anything that was for the best. She did not like
your saying in your last letter that she had had a hard lesson to learn, for*

she never repined or thought it hard of God to deal with her as he has.
I think she rather misunderstood you. Caird told me that the foot was
'terribly diseased, the bones of the upper just rattling together, & the heel
bone crumbled away below the knife'.

On Monday morning at 10, the leg was dressed as there was a good
deal of discharge, but everything was found to be as it should. The day was
spent pretty painfully & at night Mother had to have another injection &
thereafter had a quiet night. We took turns watching on Sunday & Monday
nights, i.e., Mary H, Maggie & myself. Mary Black was at Bruntsfield looking
after the occupants there, minus the baby which was here. Maggie has since
Monday night been sleeping on a mattress in the drawing room, & finds that
Mother needs very little. Maggie's sister is helping just now.

On Tuesday there was still a discharge & Caird dressed the leg. One
spot was rather red & probing brought away a blood clot. The rest was
beautifully healthy & uniting very regularly. Tuesday was spent more easily.
Tuesday night pretty well – & so on – gradual improvement. Last night Caird
said the leg was looking beautiful & everything was very gratifying. It has not
to be dressed for two days. Mother takes a little solid food now, fish, beef-stake
[sic] etc. Half a bottle of Champagne has passed her lips, but a great portion of
it twice, as it made her sick. I know you are joining with us in giving thanks
to God for His wonderful goodness & mercy. Many prayers were offered in
public & in private for dear Mother's life & health. Dr Wilson has been most
attentive, & lots of people have shewn great sympathy & kindness. Flowers &
fruit come in showers. Mother is full of rejoicing just now 1st in God's great
goodness, then in what she calls her devoted son & daughter!! (It would be
strange if we were not devoted to her) & lastly in the news which has just come
of your own engagement.

We all rejoice with you from the bottom of our hearts. I hope to write
to her next week. You know how highly we esteem her.

Jane recovered from this operation but her troubles were not over because a month
or so later the doctors decided that the stump was not healing; it was necessary
for a further amputation at the knee. Jane showed remarkable courage and spirit
epitomized by a sentence she writes in a letter to Tom soon after the first amputation:

> *20th April 1893*
>
> *I wish I were near you to tell you of God's great goodness to me during
> my late sore trial. The language of my heart is Bless the Lord O my soul etc.
> Love and kisses to you and dear Bessie.*

Back in China Tom received a letter from Walford in Chung King indicating his
intention to propose to Mary Harris in which he says:

> *May 25th 1893*
>
> *May I ask you to hand the enclosed to Miss Mary Harris – the
> subject I believe you know something about already.*

For Walford to have received a reply within six days Mary must have telegraphed
her acceptance of his proposal:

> *31st May 1893*
>
> *I presume you will have heard ere this that I have been hardy enough
> to propose to Miss Mary Harris, & that I have been accepted by her, – Glory
> be to God – I do rejoice & praise him for His great goodness – I wonder
> how you feel about my action – I hope you do not think that I have been
> coming too close to your heels – rather be proud that your example has been
> such a good one that it has been followed so speedily – I do hope you heartily
> approve – One's future is of course very uncertain & there will probably be for
> us both months & months of waiting – & you can readily appreciate what a
> month's journey's separation means, can you not? I hope you will sympathise
> with us in this, dear old G. You will, will you not, give all the advice that you*

can about arrangements for the future – Davenport seems to be strongly of
opinion that Miss Mary ought to be down at Hankow at least 2 years from
the time of landing to get a Chinese acclimatisation in Hankow rather than
in Chung King where there would be more strain – For my own sake too he
advises me to have two years' good study. What Mr & Mrs Harris will say
about Chung King we cannot tell, but that we must leave with God – 'My
times are in Thy hands' – I hope you are well & flourishing – God bless you
in all your work very very much.

The news of the engagement of Walford Hart and Mary Harris was everywhere received with pleasure and enthusiasm. Mary looked forward with great joy to moving to Chung King with Walford whenever that would be but she was prepared that she and Walford might have to wait some months before the marriage could take place. Missionary appointments to the various stations were highly dependent on the availability and health of those missionaries. The disadvantages of a Chung King posting were that the extra twelve hundred miles up river added a further six weeks to the journey and that the climate was even more trying than the extremes of Hankow. Walford Hart may have felt that he should not propose to Mary until he had experienced life in Chung King for a few months to assess how it would be for them.

On September 7th 1893 Tom and Bessie's wedding took place and the ceremony, conducted by Dr John, was held at the British Consulate in Hankow. The paper on which Mary Harris wrote an account of the day is very fragile, and in part indecipherable, but enough of it exists to paint a very vivid picture of the day's proceedings.

September 9th 1893

The date reminds me that it is only two days since the great event
of Bessie's wedding and yet it seems a thing of the distant past, rather
dreamlike, but little notes that arrive at breakfast time from across the
river signed, 'Bessie Gillison', wake you up to the reality. Other things are

*dreamlike too, for they seem so topsy-turvy. Your visitors arrive the day
before you get into your new house, all is confusion of course & though in
some queer way you have to order the servants, (in very broken Chinese)
you feel far more like a visitor yourself. But to events. The beginning of
this eventful week was filled with preparations for moving house & the
arrival of cases from home & presents from Chinese & foreigners here.
The days went all too fast, & were very warm. The night before the
wedding was a very hot one,*

*... When we awoke in the morning we heard the rain, and were not
sorry, for it meant at least a 10° lower temperature. In China you do not want
the sun to shine on the bride, in summer time at least.*

*That morning we arranged the presents in Mʳ Terrell's house & made
a bouquet, though we had great difficulty in getting enough white flowers.
Meanwhile Mʳˢ Sparham arranged the tables for the breakfast in Dʳ John's
house. All had to go to the Consulate in (sedan) chairs, we did manage though
to get the coolies to put on clothes of their cleanest white. The chairs are none
too big & we wondered how the bride's veil would look after the chair ride, but
it was none the worse & from the photos you will see her, I can't describe, but
we were all so glad that all her fears of being too hot were groundless owing to
the refreshing rain.*

*Dʳ John performed the ceremony, Mʳ Terrell gave the bride away, Dʳ
Mackay (of Wuchang) acted as best man, & myself bride's maid. A good
many friends were present, though the storm prevented some crossing the river
from Wuchang & some of the Chinese women, for they really can scarcely go
out when the streets are dirty.*

*As they were leaving Mʳˢ Foster's girls threw down flowers & others
rice, & chairs are not so easily got into as carriages, besides it is not quite right
to see only a coolie's head in front, on such a return journey – Still it was soon
over & when they got near the house, they were greeted by triumphant strains*

of the Wedding march, for Dr Hart had got home quickly & was playing in cathedral style.

All the members of the London Mission (Hankow, Wuchang & Hiao-Kan) were at the breakfast and besides representatives of the Wesleyan mission & the Scottish Bible Society … … … .& also unitedly with L.M.S Mis.) making altogether 20. Of course there were various speeches & many little jokes about the combination of wisdom etc. etc. When all was over (by the way the bride did all the cake cutting herself) the rain had stopped & the photo was arranged, we had to be rather crowded on the steps of the house, as the grass was far too wet. Soon they told us it promised to be a success, there are some advantages in having Chinese photographers for they will come at an hour's notice let you have the prints as soon as the sun & water have had time to print & wash them.

The presents were inspected & then we went off to the feasts, the women's was very small, for the only plan possible among so many Christians, was to keep to the universal Chinese plan of giving a feast to those only who give presents. Horrible as this seems, it answered well, & I think, none but real friends came.

The united present from the Christians is a fire screen made of 45 pieces of porcelain fitted into a wooden framework of 8 sides, all the pieces have of course different designs. Besides they got pieces of embroidery, & scrolls with characters on them suited to the occasion, 'The jade stone & the pearl are united', 'A man takes to a wife like a fish to water', 'May you go along together like the wings of a bird', I daresay there are others better, but I am not scholar enough to find them out & have had no time to make enquiries. Besides they have had from natives, leopard skin rugs, bracelets Chinese silver work, vases, & lastly, a whole young pig, looking horribly oily, which I presented afterwards to our cook. From others here they have had splendid presents. A glass book case Dr John. Lawn mower Mr Foster. Outside bamboo blinds Dr Mackay. Electric bells Mr Terrell & so on.

341pf alj

w m

The identification of those present was made many years ago by my father Dr Keith Gillison. He was certain of some, but a few were named by guess work. He was unable to identify the lady at the front on the extreme left of the picture.
(*The certain identifications are in bold*).

From left to right in the back row are Mr Archibald, Dr Walton, Dr Hodge and **Lewis Jones**.

Second from back are **Dr David Hill** (M.M.S.), Dr Mackay, **Arnold Foster**, **Mrs Foster**

Third from back, **Mr Sparham**, **Dr Griffith John**, Dr Lavington Hart.

On the step behind the bridal pair Mr William Terrell and **Mrs Sparham**.

On the right of the Bridegroom **Mrs Archibald**. **Bridegroom and Bride** with **Mary Harris**. Mrs Lavington Hart on Mary Harris' left and **Gertrude Terrell**.

But to return to the Chinese feast, our part was largely looking on, for Mrs Foster told them we had just been having an English feast, still of course we did use the chopsticks, but did not take any of their soups. We also practised the chopsticks in passing delicacies to them. One old woman remarked very truly that we liked what God made, (the fruit) not what men had made. Still even the fruits had been mostly 'improved'. We left them in the midst of the feast for it was time that Bess changed her dress to start for Wuchang. As they left in the chairs they got a second big pelting of rice and this time old slippers too. So off they went, for the first part still of course one in front & one behind & no doubt they were not sorry to exchange for a boat & have a ³/4 of an hour's sail across to Wuchang. Since Thursday the river has been very rough, waves splashing over the Bund as at the seaside so we have been very glad since that the weather was just what it was that day.

Since they have been there, little notes have arrived daily, & it seems that they think nothing could be nicer for a honeymoon than Wuchang. The servants gave them a very hearty welcome and I know that Bess at least is glad they have to do a little medical work there, for she will get a chance of rubbing up her medical Chinese before starting her own dispensary on her return, & they will be able to stay away longer, for Tom will feel that as his patients are under Dr Mackay's care, he need not return.

It had been planned that Tom and Bessie would travel to Hiao Kan for their honeymoon but there was considerable unrest in the area, a legacy from the demonstrations of July when the Swedish missionaries had been killed at Sung-Pu. Wuchang on the other side of the river was safe and so their plans were changed and an exchange of houses was made – the happy couple staying in the home of the Lavington Harts and the Harts moving in with Mary across the river in Hankow for the duration of the honeymoon. Mary was delighted to have the company of her future brother and sister-in-law.

The telegram announcing that the marriage had indeed taken place was greeted with great joy by the two families back home. Jane Gillison writes to Tom and Bessie:

Edinburgh 12th October

> *It was with joy and thankfulness, that I received the telegram that you were married. May God abundantly bless your union and spare you long to be an increasing blessing to each other, as well as to Christ's cause in China. I am so pleased to have you dear Bessie for a daughter, and I may tell you what I said to a friend just a day or two ago, on his enquiring how I was pleased with my new daughter-in-law? My answer was – if Tom had searched the United Kingdom for a wife he could not have found one that would have pleased me better. It is such a comfort to know that you are united in Christ, and heirs of life etc, 1 Peter 3.7.*
>
> *I am feeling a little stronger – but the weather is changeable and I suffer much from nerve pains in my 'phantom' leg and foot.*

After their honeymoon in Wuchang Tom and Bessie returned to continue their medical and evangelistic work in Hankow and Mary busied herself helping wherever she could, acquiring all sorts of nursing skills as she worked with her sister. She was proving to be a great asset to the Mission – not least because of her very sunny disposition and her friendly nature.

Walford Hart and Mary Harris
Probably taken during the three week residency Walford had to spend in Hankow
prior to their wedding.

SIX

Valley of shadows

t the beginning of 1894 Tom's brother Andrew wrote to report that the condition of their mother Jane was causing them some anxiety:

January 18th 1894

 Dear Mother has been suffering a good deal lately with her hand. But fortunately the pain does not keep her from sleeping. Perhaps by next week you may have news of something being done for it. Caird was in tonight, & says it is the same thing over again as was in the foot. Of course it is only at one little spot, & he seems very hopeful. Mother's general health is pretty good & her appetite wonderful.

 We are thinking of giving up the house at the term, & taking lodgings at Skelmorlie if I get the assistantship there. It is nicely situated on the west coast & the air not relaxing. Mother would furnish a bedroom at Mary's & when my time was up (6 months probably) she would go to stay at Rochester Terrace, & I would fend for myself till I was settled. Then Mother would come to stay with me!!

 I had a communication from Rev Wardlaw Thompson about a subscription that my bible class at the Dean Church wants to send to the Mongolian Mission. We have been going into Gilmour's life. [11] The New College is making a step forward this year by undertaking to collect money to send two men to Canada & one to India as Missionaries. Wilkie-Brown is going as our man to India. We have 7 men over from Canada & they are

*pleading for men. The dearth is so great. In spite of all that has been said &
in spite of the great need of the heathen I think I, if I were free, would go to the
Colonies!!!*

Andrew had trained for the Ministry and was preparing for the final stages of
qualification which involved a six-month's residency as an assistant to a church –
in this case, Skelmorlie, Ayrshire. He did indeed go to the Colonies – first briefly
to St Albans in Canada and then to Australia.

Jane, herself, writes to Bessie in January:

16ᵗʰ January 1894

> *I had a great desire to write you & Tom for next mail but I am
> scarcely able as my poor hand is very painful, and a good deal of swelling
> and hardness above the knuckle joints above my little finger. The Dʳˢ are
> coming to see me tomorrow, but what they will do I know not. God's guiding
> them aright, and gives me faith to trust Him more and more.*

> *I had your kind letter of 4ᵗʰ Deʳ. If you can call me Mother I should
> like it. If not call me 'Mother-in-law' for no one can stand in such a dear and
> tender relationship to you as can your own mother. God bless her, and long
> spare her to be a blessing to you all.*

> *Glad to hear you have so many patients coming to the Hospital. May
> God's blessing rest on this work of your hands, and may your own souls be
> blest in the doing of it. Pray for me dearest Bessie, for I am weak and weary at
> times, but what a friend we have in Jesus.*

By March it was clear that the problem with Jane's hand was a return of the necrosis
which had been the reason for the amputation of her leg in May of 1893. This
time her doctors performed a limited operation on the hand but considering her
weakened state it was not considered wise to be more radical. It is not surprising
that this would be her last illness. Andrew wrote to Tom:

April 5th 1894

I cannot begin otherwise than by stating the fact that is uppermost in all our minds at home & will be in yours when you get the mails of this week. It is that last Saturday the 31st of March, our dear Mother was called home to be with God. I know the pain & sorrow it will bring to your heart but I am sure that like us you will be able to rejoice for our dear one's sake that she has been taken away from so much trouble & pain. She felt that her work was done & was only waiting God's good time. I have written an account of the last days & hours, which to me seems very cold, but I hope to be able next week to write a different sort of letter. I was glad to be with her at the end. It was so peaceful, and one learned if never before to believe in the resurrection of the dead as one stood by the side of the loved one's remains. God bless you & Bessie and comfort you in this sore trial.

Ever since the operation on Mother's hand seemed unsuccessful, her spirits seemed to have gone down. Hope of being better seemed to pass quite away & she often spoke of the end as not far off & wished that it might not be long delayed. The hand however did not give her much pain. It seemed all along to be numb & lifeless. During the last fortnight before the end however it seemed to be improving & we were encouraging her & ourselves that no other operation would be needed & that she might gain strength & be able for a change during summer. However the attack of pleurisy which came on a little more than a week before the end gave us some cause for anxiety. Dr Darling told me she was in a critical condition, having nothing to fall back upon should that lung (the left) be rendered powerless. There was a good deal of friction in the lung from the beginning of the week until Thursday 29th, when Prof Grainger Stewart examined her. He found that it had very much disappeared. There was just a suspicion of fluid at the bottom of the lung, but there could be no certainty.

After prayers that morning, I had gone off to my exit exam from 10.00 a.m. to 5.30 p.m. & was thus away when the consultation was held. However the Professor's words were, 'I think she will weather the storm'. In the evening Agnes (the maid) was out & Mary Black stayed with mother reading a little aloud. I had to be out at the last class supper at the New College & was not in till very late. When I did get in I gave Mother a little beef tea. This seemed to help her a little & reduce the headache of which she complained.

At 3.30 a.m. I was up again & helped her to the side of the bed. She was so weak that before getting back, she had to get spirits, very little food sufficed at these times ; a quarter of a cup of milk with a very little whiskey being a common thing. In the morning we had prayers in mother's room very shortly. She did not seem to be so well; the pain had gone more to the back. There was no fever however, but the pulse was very fast. When the doctor called in the forenoon he made a careful examination & found a good deal of dullness indicating fluid; & he told me that this was what was to be feared. The hand shewed if anything better, there being no discharge of matter. Mother had been taking digitalis for her heart & thought it sickened her so we got strephanthus instead to see if the change would make any difference.

Her appetite was quite gone & Cousin Mary tried her best, by giving her calf's foot jelly with white of egg & whiskey very frequently, as well as other little dainties. On this evening (Friday) Andrew & Mary were over. Mary sat with Mother for a good while. She was pretty low and felt very weak & said she would be glad 'if it would please the Lord to take her soon'. 'I am only waiting,' she said. One of the things that Mary was told was 'not to forget Aunt Martha.'!! Cousin Mary gave Mother just two verses that night the first 2 of the 91st Psalm, before she went off to bed. I made mother promise to touch the electric bell between 12 & 1 & so she did. Unfortunately she could take no food. I gave her however a little spirits & water & after doing anything I could went back to bed till 3.30. At that time she took only a mouthful of milk. I think she felt weak & lonely so allowed me to stay with

141

her. I put my feet up on a chair & she was quite quiet, sleeping some of the time. We did not speak much, and I don't remember what exactly she said; it was in the line of her words to Mary about being taken soon.

When the servant was up she would not let me stay longer and said, 'No, go & get 2 good hours in your bed. It has been a great comfort to have you with me. I'm not afraid now. Agnes will bring me a cup of tea.' She would not let me stay so I went off. About a quarter to eight Mary went in & read a letter she had got from Castlemains (we were all anxious about Aunt Agnes's health) and then gave her her porridge. This she could always take during her illness. After she was done up a little & freshened with a wash we had prayers together. This she always liked if it was not too long. The doctor came in about 11.30 & after examining her chest dressed the hand from which there was no discharge. He wanted to go away for a holiday & asked her if he might & she said, 'Oh Yes!' He was to be back on the Monday & thought she might do without anyone till that time, but after all he arranged Dr Lundie in Glengyle Terrace should come up to see her. When he said, 'Well, we'll hope to see you better on Monday.' 'I'll be no better,' said she; & even when the doctor tried to cheer her up a bit she just said simply she, 'was no better & was not likely to be'. Darling told me, before he went, that there was not much change, the fluid did not seem to have increased much; but we were not to leave her alone. He asked if I thought she would be better with a nurse, & I said, 'No! I thought she would not like it at all'. The hand he said was better, but he did not like the look of it. It was far too blue. Immediately after the doctor left she had some beef tea. She had said to Mary in the morning, 'Now Mary, I think you have been keeping the truth back from the Castlemains people, because of Aunt being ill; but you must write & tell them today exactly how I am'.

Mary read to her a little, & she went off to sleep. I had had to go out & she wanted me to get a piece of water proof sheet for the bed in case it might be needed, so I was not in till 1.30 p.m.; when I found that she had had a complete collapse. Mary said that at one o'clock she had a very little beef juice & just a minute after she had taken away the cup, the bedroom bell rang & she found mother suffering a good deal of pain & having great difficulty in breathing. She was very sick. Spirits gave no relief. 'I think it is bile,' she more than once said & seemed to think it would pass off. Mary got her hot water & a very little soda, but it was of no use. She asked Agnes to open the drawing room windows & the doors between so as to have more air. In her pain she said before I came in, 'Oh! if God would only take me soon.'

I saw the moment I entered that the end could not be far away. The hands were blue with cold & she had lost control of her face & mouth. I put my hand on her forehead but she said, 'It's too hot, give me room.' Her breathing was so difficult. I asked Mary if she had sent for the doctor & as she had not yet we sent Agnes, mother saying, 'Send for Dr Thompson (of Hong Kong) if Dr Darling is not in!' She did not wish Dr Lundie I think. Then she said, 'Go away you two & get your dinner.' It was so like her. She wanted a slight enema & that gave her a little ease. She was herself arranging & directing everything up to the very last. The pillows got a good shake up & we raised her up a bit. This was some relief & she was able to speak more easily. Her arms naturally went up to give the heart & lungs more play & we supported them. 'Surely,' she said, 'the furnace has been heated 7 times.'. I prayed with her as I saw her turning weaker & she repeated, 'I will never leave thee, nor forsake thee,' & uttered a fervent, 'Amen.' Then as I went on to pray again she sat upright in bed without any help & tried to pray, but could only say, 'O God', then she lay back. I saw that the breathing had changed & that the pulse had become feebler so I asked her if she had any message for her dear ones. She tried to speak, the lips moved but that was all. Then I repeated one or two texts & the never failing, 'Though I walk through the valley of the shadow of death,' – & said, 'He is with you, dear mother.' Then I asked her if she had a message of love for her dear ones. 'Is it love?' I said. She just turned on the pillow & looked straight at me, but just as she looked the eyes fixed & the pulse ceased to beat. I put my hand upon her heart, but it was all over. Her spirit had gone to be with God. Cousin Mary was *by me all the time, & she immediately went over to Mary Agnes to break the news as gently as possible. Just at the last moment Dr Lundie had come in, but only to say that all was over. I put a handkerchief round the dear face & put everything to rights before Mary Agnes came over.*

Mrs Henderson of Merchiston Park gave us much help in the afternoon, & by Sunday at 4 o'clock all the intimations of death & invitations to the funeral were away. Dr Wilson I saw the Saturday afternoon & he came up to see us. He was most sympathetic. On Sunday when intimating that I would take part the next Sunday in pleading for the New College Mission Society, he tried to tell the people that dear mother had passed away the previous afternoon. After saying so he sat down in the pulpit quite overcome.

The funeral was on Tuesday at 1 o'clock. We got a plain oak coffin with brass mountings & I laid my dear mother's head in the grave. There were some nice wreaths & sprays of flowers. We enclose a slip which I had printed with 3 verses of one of mother's favourite hymns. It was sung in the drawing room. Uncle read & Dr Wilson prayed most beautifully. We were all wonderfully sustained, & have to thank God for his great goodness.

A small printed card with the letter reads: 'If we do what we can, God will not be wanting to do that for us which we cannot'.

The many letters of condolence sent to the family after Jane's death expressed a great admiration for her character summed up in this letter to Tom from Professor Grainger who knew the family very well over many years:

I beg to express my deepest sympathy with you and your sister as well as with the other members of your family under the irreparable loss that you have sustained. Your mother was one of the best and most worthy women I have ever known & I feel the world poorer for her loss.

Andrew Henderson, Jane's son-in-law and the husband of Mary Agnes wrote to Tom and Bessie:

12ᵗʰ April 1894

> *Although it was apparent to us all that the frail and sorely tried body*
> *could not for very much longer resist the severe strain it was so continuously*
> *subjected to yet we did not expect that she would be cut off so suddenly. But now*
> *that it is over I think that we should rather be thankful that she should have a*
> *blessed release at the beginning of the new trouble that had already taken hold of*
> *her, rather than that she should have been spared longer perhaps to suffer more*
> *than ever. I cannot adequately express to you the admiration which her noble*
> *patience & perfect resignation inspired in all who witnessed it. Her true courage*
> *& cheerfulness in the midst of it all was wonderful. For myself I feel I have lost*
> *one of the dearest friends I ever had & will cherish her memory as long as I*
> *live. We are just beginning to realise what a stroke it is that has come upon us,*
> *& that the central figure of our little circle has been taken from us. She was the*
> *medium through which communications from all the members of her family*
> *were conveyed to one another and it will be difficult to get her place in this respect*
> *re-filled but it is most desirable that something shᵈ be done in a systematic way*
> *to keep the various members in touch with one another.*

March 1894 was to be a month of great sadness and indeed of tragedy for the family. Jane Gillison's death in Edinburgh was a welcome release from her suffering but in Hankow a joyful occasion was to about to end in even deeper sorrow.

Mary Harris and Walford Hart had accepted that their wedding could not take place for various good reasons until November of that year. However in February a telegram was sent to Chung King which said:

> DAVENPORT, *Chung King — Your letter received. All here advise*
> *Hart start instantly; reside in Hankow three weeks. Wire when starting.*
> GILLISON

The reason for this hurried change of plan was because the Davenports in Chung King were badly in need of a long holiday after Mrs Davenport's difficult pregnancy. Dr John in Hankow who as the senior member of the Mission and organizer of the staff realized that if they were to go on furlough Walford Hart would be left on his own in Chung King for many months and his marriage to Mary would be seriously delayed. The Hart/Harris wedding had to take place as soon as possible so that Mary could accompany her new husband to Chung King before the Davenports left in May. In a letter home Mary said:

February 19th 1894

On Friday evening Tom went to consult Dr John; the result of their talk was this, that at 11pm, after I was in bed and, I think had been asleep, Tom told me from outside the door, that Dr John advised Walford be telegraphed to start at once for Hankow, so that we might be married and get to Chung King in time for the Davenports to leave for their holiday in May. To go to bed thinking that our wedding was to be prolonged till November, then, an hour later, to hear that Walford might be here in a fortnight (you come down the river so much quicker than you go up), was pretty nearly as great a surprise as Queen Victoria's when they woke her up to tell her she was Queen of England!

By March 5th Walford had arrived to begin the three week residency in Hankow required by law before the marriage could take place. Those weeks must have been idyllic for the young couple. Although they were busy with preparations for the wedding and packing for their new life in Chung King they had an opportunity to spend time together and get to know each other.

The wedding was fixed for 27th March and on the day before the wedding Mary writes to her parents:

26th March 1894

I paid my last visit to the hospital for morning prayers today. I can hardly believe that I am really going away. It is nice, though, to have such very happy memories of everybody in Hankow.

On the day before the wedding Walford had been unwell with a high temperature but seemed sufficiently recovered the next day for the wedding to take place. The wedding party was obliged to go to the Consulate for the legal formalities but they returned to the Gillison's house for the religious ceremony. Bessie writes home:

> *Dr John married them. Walford got through it splendidly, but was glad to rest afterwards. We made him lie on the sofa most of the rest of the day. While we, the L.M.S. party, were at the breakfast, he was lying on the sofa in view of us all, just the other side of the folding doors, between the drawing-room and dining-room. Mary was at his side and had a little table to herself. The doorway was festooned, so they made quite a picture. They looked so happy thus. Her dress seemed just the thing. After the breakfast we had five short informal speeches – no proposing of healths, so that Walford did not have to make a reply. Dr John said Chung King had been regarded as a dismal, dull, depressing place; but he was sure we were going to send a bright sunbeam there, and he thought we should not hear so much about the depressing atmosphere afterwards. (Mary is a prime favourite of Dr John's. I am sure, if I may use the expression, 'he thinks the world of her,' so his speech was a warm, almost fatherly, one.)*

A steam tug was found to take Mary and Walford over the river to Wuchang for the honeymoon so that Walford could lie flat. Mary wrote, 'It was a beautiful evening; the old Yangtze can look fine!'.

Walford continued to require careful nursing but after three days Tom diagnosed acute dysentery and although his condition fluctuated five days later on April 14th, Walford died. Mary had been a wife for only nineteen days before she became a widow.

The effect of his death devastated the Missions in Hankow and Chung King. In less than two years since his arrival in China, Walford had made a valuable contribution to the work and was held in great affection by those who knew him. The Davenports in Chung King sent a telegram saying:

> *Unutterable sorrow; deepest sympathy; God reigns.*

Mary, herself, found great consolation in her faith and her many letters home to family and friends reiterated her still firm belief in the goodness of God:

> *All the memories I have are so beautiful. It seems natural that he should be the one God saw ready to be promoted to higher service. In this light one seems to be able to understand a little of what would otherwise be all a mystery. I found such nice lines the other day – 'Can grief be bitter when we know It is but joy delayed?'*
>
> *These hopes do make such a difference. I came back at once to live with Bessie, and, as soon as I could went to hospital and to work again; and God has been very good in giving me encouragement among some of the women there. Perhaps Chinese is getting easier; but I never had such nice times there before.*

Many of the letters Mary wrote immediately after Walford's death express a characteristically simple acceptance of what had happened and the many tributes paid to him from old friends and new colleagues seemed to console her.

In June Bessie's first child was born – a son they named Edwin Walford but out of consideration for Mary they only used his first name. Although the baby had an Amah, Mary loved her little nephew and spent many hours with him supervising his diet and clothes so that Bessie could concentrate on getting back to her dispensary and hospital work after her confinement.

It was a long hot summer and life was very uncomfortable in Hankow with temperatures exceeding 38° by day and 33° by night. Mary was invited by one of the other missionary wives to accompany her and her baby boy who had been seriously ill and still needed nursing to stay at the Society's bungalow in the Kiu Kiang hills. At first she was reluctant but changed her mind and the ten days she spent there did her a great deal of good in coming to terms with her tragic loss.

Even before Bessie and Mary had come to China there had been much discussion about a possible visit from their sister Sophy and their brothers Alick and Joe. The autumn of 1894 seemed the right moment for the Harris family at home to put the plan into action. Alick had just come down from Cambridge; Joe although living in Canada could get away and Mr and Mrs Harris made sure that Sophy would be free of home duties to join her brothers. Sophy and Alick travelled first to Vancouver Island where they stayed briefly to see Joe's chosen home and then the three of them sailed for Japan.

It was while the Harris party was in Japan that Bessie was taken ill with typhoid fever. Sophy received a telegram asking her to come at once to help Mary with nursing her sister as Tom too had the disease and was in an even more serious condition than Bessie. She left immediately, Alick and Joe joining her in Hankow more than two weeks later. As soon as Tom and Bessie were well enough to withstand the journey the two invalids were sent to Japan to convalesce while Sophy and her brothers remained in Hankow making themselves useful in various ways. At Christmastime the family gathered in Shanghai to spend a few days together before they went their separate ways – Joe to Canada, Sophy and Alick home via India and Mary and the Gillisons with the baby and their Amah returned to Hankow.

In the months that followed, the work of the hospital and the accompanying Christian witness and teaching filled the hours. The anniversary of Mary's wedding day came and Bessie wrote that 'she seemed determined to be bright, and said enough to me that she had resolved always to keep that day as one she would be ever thankful for'.

Sickness was never very far away and in early July Bessie was once more ill with dysentery. Mary took her fair share of nursing as well as looking after the baby who was now one year old but it was generally felt that Bessie and Tom needed a change and they were offered the loan of the Kiu Kiang bungalow. Sadly, in the few days before they could leave, Mary also fell ill (or 'failed', as Bessie expresses it) and this was the letter she sent to her parents with the tragic news of Mary's death:

July 30th 1895

How shall I tell you the sad, sad news that this week's letters have to convey, our hearts at times are almost breaking, and so will yours be when you get this. Our darling Mary she, the healthiest of us all, who has nursed me so lovingly through my illnesses, is no longer with us. She died of dysentery Sunday morning July 28th at 7 o'clock. I have so much to tell you, so many loving farewell words of hers to give, that after a time I am sure will give you comfort, but oh, how I do feel for you, hearing this all at once without knowing first of her illness. We decided not to telegraph because we could see no good to be gained, but on the other hand six weeks of anxious waiting for details. Darling Mary herself when she knew she was dying said, 'I do wish you need not send a telegram, it would be such a shock to them all', but she added, 'You must do what you think best.' – First let me tell you of her illness. Monday a week ago yesterday, she told me she had a little pain which she could not quite make out, but hoped it was nothing. I replied, 'We must look out and not let you get ill too.' She was seeming as bright and jolly as could be, and told me she had invited the hospital patients to come to see me, and baby and the house. I said, 'Why on mail day?' She said, 'Because one will be leaving tomorrow, and I have promised she should come before leaving.' This was just like her, she always tried to let every woman going away, come first to see what our house was like, she thought it made them know us better, and feel more friendly. The patients came and dearest Mary was going into all the rooms with them, energetically shewing them baby, and his belongings etc. That same evening after 7 o'clock tea she called me upstairs, and told me she was afraid she had dysentery, & I saw that it was so. – She was so disappointed, because she had been talking so much (and writing in last week's letter that same day) about packing up for me, to go to the hills, she wanted to do everything, and let me rest and do nothing. She tried to think however that one dose or two of Ipecacuhana would cure her. (I expect you remember from Walford's illness that Ipecac. is the chief remedy used in dysentery.) She had a dose that night, and next when the vomiting had passed off was very much better. We kept her in bed all the morning. In the afternoon I went upstairs, and found she had got out of her bedroom on to a long chair in the passage for coolness and was actually writing to you. I told her I was a bit surprised to see her writing, but really she appeared to be doing it so comfortably lying down that I could not say much. Wednesday morning we found the symptoms shewed she was not quite cured, so she had another dose of Ipecac. That dose made her feel heavy and weary all day, she did not have so much vomiting as the day before, but she seemed depressed. Wednesday night she became a great deal worse, she came into our bedroom in distress, saying she was not able to be in bed at all scarcely. Tom made me lie in bed while he doctored her, giving more medicine, and she became easier. She then sent for me and said she wanted me to write down her 'Will' at her dictation, because she wanted to make a fresh one, and especially to mention what she wanted done with the money that came from Walford. She said, 'I quite expect to get better, but with dysentery one never knows, and I should feel happier if I had got my Will made as I should like.' That day, Thursday, Tom moved her into our bedroom, where she could have the punkah, all day long, and we engaged a Chinese Amah to attend her, and when night came we got another. Tom wanted me to do none of the hard nursing, as I am not quite strong, so my part was often to lie on the couch, and see the Amah do what was needed, but Tom devoted himself to her a great part of the time, and Dr Walton fortunately came in from Hiau Kan and relieved Tom of his hospital work. Tom was often on duty at night too. In one way it was hard for me, not to do for Mary, as much as she used to do for me, but I saw it troubled her, if I exerted myself much, and I also saw how satisfied she was, with the amahs, she liked them both. They were old friends she often said how good and attentive they were. Friday we found she seemed no better, and we got very anxious. We had given her the Ipecac. in full doses, and she had been so good in swallowing it, and lying still afterwards, for two hours without moving, but oh dear! oh dear! my heart sank, as I saw she was weaker, and the dysentery not stopped. We agreed to consult Dr Thompson and when he came and was very good & cheered us up a bit. He suggested one or two little additions to treatment. We had already, before he came been using fomentations and these helped dear Mary a great deal. It was wonderful how well she took food, and how strong her voice kept, and how she seemed to know just what she wanted, and tell the Amahs. All through there was no acute pain one may say, but the days were very, very wearisome and the nights too I am sure. She was so thoughtful for others – One morning at six a.m. I came into her room, with a cup of tea the boy had brought me, she said, 'Bessie tell the boy to bring you a piece of toast, I am sure you need it.' Another time she said, 'Please write and tell Miss Davies C.I.M. to go to see my woman for me at the hospital.' At other times she would inquire if the amah had had rice etc; as she seldom spoke much, these sentences relating to others were very much a testimony to her lovely unselfish nature.

Ah I wish I could remember more to tell you. The dear, dear girl, was such a good brave patient & so grateful – Saturday she seemed better in every way, we all took hope, and she herself looked so bright especially about mid-day, I said to her, 'I do believe you are going to be spared to us dearest' & she said, 'I am so glad I do want to help you' Saturday evening Tom thought her rather excited, and he felt just a little anxious again, then in the night it seemed as if a fresh onset of the disease had begun. She again had a big dose of Ipecac and from that time onward, her pulse became very very weak, it seemed as if all strength had gone. I went into her room at five o'clock on Sunday. She seemed so glad to see me, she said the night had been terribly long, and she was so weary she longed for morning (Tom had gone to bed at 3 o'clock.) She was troubled too, because the Amah said she was not quite well, so when I went she began to discuss who we should get to take the Amah's place. I got the Amah to lie down a little, while I watched. During the next two hours I discovered how very, very low she was, her pulse could hardly be felt. She had had brandy through the night, but I pushed it, and did all I could to get the pulse better. I noticed she was occasionally wandering a little also. My heart sank again, and I went to Tom who had just awaked, and I told him I feared she was slipping away from our hands. Tom soon came he agreed she was very much weaker, we sent for Dr Thompson, he came but agreed with us that nothing could be done with any real hope of saving her.

Now dearest Mother & Father comes the part, that I rejoice to tell you about. Dear, dear Mary had strength given her, to gain such a victory over death, a triumphant death it was. About 10.30, a.m. she seemed to come round all at once, to a state of absolute clearness of mind. She said, 'Am I ill?' 'What is happening?' I said to her, 'I am afraid darling you are going to leave us you are very, very ill' she said, 'Am I really? I thought I was better.' Then she said, 'I am not afraid,' and then she quoted several verses of what she called Walford's favourite hymn, as she knew it first from his choosing it one evening here, 'Jesus is the same for ever; We may change but Jesus never; Jesus never. Ah how sweet in Him abiding, In His love and care confiding, Still confiding.' Right on with it she went. (You will see it on the printed sheet, we had for the funeral.) And then she said, 'Shall we sing it together?' and we sang it. I think afterwards she said, 'I am so sorry for you Bessie dear, and Mother, poor dear Mother, and Father and Soph, perhaps I ought to have prayed more to get better. I should like to pray now.' Then at once she began, 'Oh God for Bessie's sake and Father and Mother's sake and the work's sake if it be Thy Will make me well again even now, it would not be for long I know, very little compared with eternity, but a little while would give me time to do more work for Thee, yet I am willing for whatever Thou seest best.' Then I asked her what messages she had for you. And she said, 'Tell Father and Mother I am so glad I came to China, tell them I hope more will come out to go on with my work, for I do pity the poor Chinese women so, and some of them are so nice.' Then looking up at me she said, 'Haven't we had lot of nice women at the hospital?' The boys, her brothers, she mentioned by name, and said, she did hope to see them all in Heaven, and she doesn't want them to think it was a mistake her coming out to China. She said, 'Isn't it strange that nearly all the great heathen nations have these unhealthy climates? – if it were the other way about, it would not require much self-sacrifice to be a Missionary, we have to take our lives in our hands haven't we?' – Another time she said, 'I do thank God so much, that it is me He is taking and not you. You have Tom and Baby, my husband is in Heaven

*already.' She said, 'I shall know Walford now, as I never knew him before',
then she thought of Baby and said, 'Bessie you can call Baby Walford now
can't you?' I said, 'Yes darling, I should like to very much.' We had Baby in to
see her, she said, 'Oh the dear Baby, how sweet he is,' she said, 'I believe he will
grow up to be good' then she said, 'Perhaps my study will be his schoolroom
bye and bye.'*

*We got all the servants in to say goodbye, she mentioned each one
by name and said, 'Thank you for all you have done for me, I am going
to Heaven, my husband is there. I thank God he has spared my sister,
because her husband is here, I want you to trust my Saviour and I want to
meet you all in Heaven.' They were very much touched. We sent them out
quickly for we feared she would be tired out, she was, and panted for breath,
a good deal. Dr John came in a little later, she said, 'I have to say goodbye
to you Dr John.' Dr John said, 'You know we all love you and don't like to
lose you, don't you?' She said, 'Thank you.' Then she again said how much
better it was for her to be taken than me, and then again she again said
how glad she was she had come to China, & Dr John said, 'Shall I tell your
Father and Mother that?' – she said, 'Yes please Dr John.' Later Dr John and
Mr Bonsey came in to witness her sign her Will again as we remembered
it had not been done properly. Dearest Mary sent a goodbye to M^r & M^{rs}
Sparham, and a message to Mrs Bonsey, saying she had so looked forward
to seeing her in the Autumn. You will I am sure be surprised that the
dear, dear girl was able to say so much. It became increasingly difficult, she
seemed glad after a time not to speak – Once she said, 'Hold my hand'
and the words seemed to suggest to her the hymn 'Hold Thou my hand, so
weak I am and helpless,' and she repeated the verse. After two hours spent
thus she became very restless & longed to go, 'Come Lord Jesus', she said
once, and she complained of being so fearfully, fearfully tired. She imagined
all sorts of reasons why she was so tired, thought she was at hospital,
and had had too long a day, thus the wandering came back, until she lay*

*practically not speaking but looking as if she had some consciousness and
she would rouse a little if we said her name. About five Chinese women
came, we let them in, for they were some of her chief friends she mentioned
the names of several, and said goodbye. They wept loudly but the weeping
did not seem to disturb her. She never was delirious, she quietly sank and
died just at 7. p.m. When a hymn was being sung at the Rest, and we
could hear it. I forgot to say that Mary asked Dr John if we could have a
Chinese hymn translation of 'For ever with the Lord' at the funeral; this
had not been done so far as I knew at an English funeral before, but it
was so nice. There were such lots of Chinese Christians there. I went to
the funeral, I felt none too well able to be there, but I could not bear to be
away especially when the hymns she asked for were to be sung and oh, I
am so glad I went. I never felt so much power in a funeral service before. I
am sure many felt it. Dr John at the grave mentioned Mary's love for the
Chinese. He said, 'She loved the Chinese most deeply and they loved and
clung to her.' He says he is hearing so many testimonials to living words
and acts of hers. The grave is close beside Walford's.*

Following Mary's death, Tom writes to Mr Wardlaw Thompson the Foreign
Secretary of the London Missionary Society:

*Her brief life and sudden death have made a deep impression
on the Hankow circle. The impress left on my own mind after having
lived with her for more than eighteen months, and seen, as I did, her life
among the Chinese in the hospital and elsewhere, is, that she combined a
singularly child-like mind with an energetic will and full heart of love and
devotion. She was guileless in the extreme, but full of purposes, fraught
with a loving intelligence that saw what was needful for the work among
women of this place to be really successful; and these purposes were one
by one being carried into execution, and were receiving the approbation
of all. She did not hold herself aloof from the Chinese, but mingled with*

*them and made them feel she was one of them. She would take them by
the hand and listen patiently to their story, and they, in their turn, would
take her hand lovingly. I have scarcely ever met a more unselfish man or
woman.*

Arnold Foster, one of the missionaries in Hankow, writes to Mary's parents about
her funeral:

30th July 1895

*The scene at the cemetery last evening was most impressive. I do not
know that I ever before saw so many Chinese Christians attending a European
funeral. The number of Europeans, too, was large, and one felt, as one looked
round upon the company, that the great majority were not mere spectators, but
mourners. Mrs Walford is now with the Lord, and her blessedness is complete;
but her work here, or rather the effects of it, will live on, and she, being dead
will speak.*

Tom and Bessie with Walford and his amah went to the Kiu Kiang bungalow
after the funeral. While they were at Kiu Kiang Tom wrote this letter to his cousin
Andrew Gillison who lived in the U.S.A telling him about a little Chinese slave girl
befriended by Mary:

*Mary loved the poor & worked for them. The Hospital patients wept
bitterly when she died & among them was a little girl of 14 – a slave sold
by her relatives to a Cantonese & being kept as a slave now, but to be sold
into a worse slavery when she grew up. Evidently the little thing was badly
treated by her mistress & Mary had taken to this little girl & the little one
used to cling to Mary. Mary used to bring her to the house & was teaching
her a little simple prayer. Mary yearned over her and longed to be able
to save her from the sad life that seemed to lie before her. She thought of
buying her & talked to Dr John about it, but the difficulties appeared to be*

156

too great – how to get her – how to keep her from their clutches afterwards – where to put her. Such questions seemed too hard to solve.

    With Mary's removal we felt our hearts still more drawn out to this little one & talked the matter over again with Dr John & talked too, to one or two of our leading native Xtians. At last it was suggested that she might be bought through our Cantonese contractor – very good – but who was to keep her. Dr John took the matter up & saw our chief native preacher – Mr Tsien. At last Mr Tsien said, 'I see nothing for it, but to take her myself.' 'Just what I wanted,' said Dr John, 'but I did not like to suggest it.' He went home and saw his wife – a dear old Xtian she is & she said she would take the child for Mary's sake. I saw the contractor & found they were willing to sell her for $100. Mr Tsien got the deed written out & came to our house where the little girl had been, & after prayers in Chinese by Dr John, the preacher took her off to her new home both rejoicing. Bessie too, had prayed with her alone, upstairs – You will rejoice & praise God with us in this – pray for dear little Hsiu Shee (Obedience & Happiness) that she may live to serve God in China, as Mary would have done had she lived. We pay for her clothes & board, but that we do most willingly.

It was felt that the two weeks spent in Kiu Kiang was not enough for Tom and Bessie to regain their strength and the decision was taken to send the family back to England for a few months. Meanwhile the sad news that Jamie Gillison, Marion's husband, had died on September 5th in Australia reached Mary Henderson in Edinburgh and she in turn reported it to Tom and Bessie in a letter sent to one of the ports on their voyage home:

2nd October 1895

    We got the sad news from Australia last night that Jamie died on the morning of 5th Sept – there are no details as yet, as John had just got the telegram when he wrote. Poor Jamie, it would be a glad release to him to be at rest in the

Home Above free from all suffering, for he seems to have had a very hard struggle for some weeks previous to the end. Poor wee Marion! One's heart goes out to her – We shall talk over what is to be done for her when you are in Edin: We are sending her £20 in Nov. instead of £8, as we promised & we shall continue to give her this every year & __we__ think if all the family clubbed together & guaranteed her a sum (with the interest on Jamie's insurance) say £150 or so per annum – that she might be very comfortable in a small flat here in Edin: without taking boarders, for I fear her own health will be much broken down.

John Gillison in Australia also wrote to Tom:

I have not written to you for a long time now and without entering into any long explanations, as I have so much to write about, I simply hope you will forgive me. We have always been glad to hear from you from time to time about Bessie and the baby as well as your work. Of course the baby is an important member of the family now and I have asked Marion when she arrives in England as you will learn from a later part of this letter to get you a little present from Harriett and myself to the first male descendant of the Baldernock Gillisons. Please remind her.

We were deeply grieved to hear first of Dr Hart's death and then so soon after of Mary's and we would like Bessie as well as M^r & Mrs Harris to know that although we do not know them personally they all have our deepest sympathy.

We trust Bessie as well as you yourself will be completely restored to health by the trip to and stay in England. The climate seems to be so trying that I often think we shall never meet again on earth.

Jamie, as I dare say you will have heard by the time this reaches you, died on 5th Sept last. Marion has been with us practically since then and I met her in Sydney to escort her for at least part of the way. She is very well everything considered and the children also are well. She intended to go home by sailing ship to arrive in Glasgow early in April, but on receipt of your letter from Colombo, we decided that she ought to try to see you before your return to China. She and the children therefore are arranging to leave by the P. & O. S.S. 'Rome' on Saturday next the 16th inst. due in London on 2nd January, calling at Plymouth. Marion is advised by her doctor that the children ought not to spend the first winter in Scotland and that they should stay in the South of England. Where she will go she will not decide until she arrives. Will you please ascertain from the P & O office in London, that the 'Rome' does touch at Plymouth and the date and if possible meet Marion. Also please ascertain from Uncle Thomas <u>before</u> Marion's arrival, the address of M[rs] Mowbray, Sen[r]. It is somewhere in the South of England Marion thinks. If the steamer goes to London, you might let Tom Henderson know and ask him to meet her if <u>you</u> cannot do so. Of course I am assuming that you will stay in England till after her arrival.

As to means I shall finance Marion till she leaves. Jamie's life was insured for £500 and I sent all the papers to D[r] Gordon Douglas in Edinburgh about a month ago. She ought to have that money available on or shortly after her arrival. (By the by she travels second class from choice.) Then Henry Tod has promised her £50, the last half yearly instalment of £100 a year for 2 years he agreed to allow when Jamie had to give up work. I got the £150 odd that Marion had from the trust money invested in Glasgow. Out of this I am paying her fares etc. Marion will explain the details of our money arrangements. She proposes to live in or near Lochmaben. I propose to give her £50 a year if necessary. In the first place I want to know what Uncle Thomas is willing to do for his grandchildren. Mary Agnes and Jane have I think each promised £10 a year. I intend to ask Andrew to allow her £30, expecting him to offer less or refuse altogether as he has never sent her one penny, and I fear there have been some doubtful dealings with mother's effects in which Mary Agnes is interested. I have no proof and don't want to say anything about it, so don't tell Mary Agnes. If he will agree to allow £30 a year and you £10, for he has a much larger

*salary than you, Marion will have £100 a year and the interest on £500
or £600 in addition to anything Uncle Thomas may allow.*

*In my will I have left Marion £500 and may someday make it
£1000 if I can. Marion will tell you how difficult it is for me to save any
money although I have a good salary.*

*Harrie and the children are splendid and join with me in love to you
Bessie and 'the boy.'*

A modern diagnosis of Jamie's health problems from the symptoms mentioned
in the family letters suggests that he may in childhood have had rheumatic fever
which sometimes led to mitral stenosis and eventual heart failure. On arrival in
Australia Jamie found work as Baptist minister in Kew, a suburb of Melbourne,
but his health deteriorated and after a breakdown in May 1893 he was forced to
give up work altogether. He, Marion and their two children (Allan had been born
in 1892), went to live on a half acre plot of land in Warwick near Brisbane where
Marion did her best to grow their own food and be self-supporting. However less
than a year later he died.

From the letters of the time there seemed to have been confusion about
Marion's finances and evidence of family ill-feeling in some quarters about what the
contributions from the various family members towards her keep should be. John
was convinced that his youngest brother Andrew had neither been fully honest when
dividing their mother's estate among the rest of the family nor was he contributing
anything to help subsidise Marion and her children. This disagreeable atmosphere
between the eldest and the youngest brother was to continue until Marion was
no longer dependent on family handouts and was fully supported by her second
marriage.

After a short time in Wiltshire in close contact with the Harris family Marion
spent a few months with the Scottish relations. Neither of her children were
strong or healthy and Allan was a particularly difficult child. Mary Agnes said
in a letter to Tom:

Jamie & Marion with Jane and Allan, *circa* 1895.

22nd Oct. 1895

> *Poor wee Allan cried one day for three hours – the D^r said it was*
> *nervousness & was afraid that if he was much crossed he might go into fits.*
> *He gets into most terrible states & when he is once into these – everyone is*
> <u>*powerless*</u> *– the only chance is to prevent them – He is getting laudanum*
> *& something else every day to quieten him – but Mary Black & I both fear*
> *that the trouble is going to his brain – The D^r is afraid it may, if it develops*
> *– but if he arrives safely in Australia, we do hope the good climate may work*
> *wonders for him.*

Following this advice Marion had packed up her belongings and returned to live
with John's family in Melbourne for a few months. She then settled in Warwick
Queensland where she and Jamie had lived before his death. John wrote to Tom
about the allowances he proposed the family should make to support Marion and
her two children:

May 1897

> *Marion and family are settled in Warwick again. They are well. For*
> *three months they were with me and I was pleased to have Marion for so long.*
> *Since she began her preparations for going to Warwick and since she went*
> *there I have had to give her a considerable amount of money out of the £100*
> *I held for her & this is rather a pity as I was anxious that she should keep the*
> *principal intact, but it could not be helped. She told me of your kindness to her at*
> *home and that you had told her to draw up to £50 on some money of yours*
> *in Andrew Henderson's hands. Whether or not she has written to you or not*
> *I cannot say but in any case please direct what you hope to give her to be sent*
> *to Mary Black with whom I have an account. And further I would impress*
> *upon you the desirability of allowing her a fixed sum yearly to be paid to Mary*
> *Black say on 1st January & 1st July. If you will let me know what the amount*
> *is I shall arrange to pay Marion and then charge it to Mary Black. As you*

*know I promised £50 a year which I pay to her quarterly. Jane was willing to
send something but Frans won't let her although I believe he is making £2000
a year. Mary & Andrew Henderson give her either £10 or £20 a year I
forget which. Our Andrew never answered my letter about her and as he took
advantage of us all on the signing up of Mother's accounts I don't expect he
will. If I get home he will be compelled to explain. He simply ignored my letters.
I shall of course give Marion what she requires even if I have to borrow it, but
unless I get my salary increased soon I shall find it hard to allow even the £50.
At the least she ought to have at least £60 from her brothers and sisters and
even with that she will have a struggle.*

While she was living in Queensland she met Robert Grubb, an itinerant New
Zealand Evangelical member of The Brethren. She married him in 1901 and went
with him to New Zealand and in due course had two more children, Florence and
Ronald. Marion herself had always been considered delicate because she too had
had rheumatic fever as a child, but in fact she lived a long life and died in 1964 just
short of her 100th birthday.

The Thousand Steps. Set in the Lushan Hills, Kuling (now Guling) was, from the 1890s, a favoured retreat from the oppressive summer heat of the Yangtze river basin. For many years, climbing these steps was the only way to reach the resort. The climb was quite arduous and sedan chairs were used to carry those unfit to walk (*see page 175*).

SEVEN

An unscheduled furlough

When Tom and Bessie returned to the UK in October 1895 they brought their Chinese amah with them to help with the care of Walford while they were at home. Reading the letters the first time I found it hard to imagine how the domestic life of a well-to-do English family in a totally foreign country would have struck a semi-literate Chinese woman with no experience of anything outside her native city. She had been one of the Mission's Chinese converts and was gently guided by Bessie in her observance of the Christian way of life in this strongly Christian household. Amah (as she was called) frequently worried about her son and was very pleased and grateful to be able to earn the money to send to him. Bessie mentions her from time to time in her letters to Tom:

April 6th 1896

> *On Friday Father, Mother, baby, Amah and I went to tea at Henry's. Amah enjoyed the garden and greenhouses there – when I pointed out some cucumbers just forming she said 'We have got some bigger than that'. You see that she looks upon everything at South Place as belonging to her.*

May 9th 1896

> *Amah was so delighted that you had found something for her son to do. She has been very anxious about him lately because we never heard if Mr Foster got your letter from Edinburgh and gave him money from her.*

This last comment seems to indicate that Amah was not unhappy in this strange land. Bessie even mentions taking Amah to a concert of the Orchestral Society in Calne. She wrote in a letter to Tom, 'I think she enjoyed it but she did not say much.'

Tom returned to China in February 1896 leaving Bessie and her half-sister to carry out their plan to record Mary's short life in a book using the many letters Mary had written to tell the story. They rented a cottage a few miles away from Calne where they felt they would be able to work undisturbed. Mary had always been a prolific letter writer and they needed to sort through a great many letters and documents. Bessie's

Thomas Harris
Five times Mayor of Calne & generous benefactor to the town.

general health was still not too good and she felt she would benefit from a period of quiet and rest while they were working. Amah and little Walford were left with the Harris household and so progress was made on the book without interruption in the following weeks. Nevertheless there were many calls on her time. She found herself asked to speak of her missionary work at meetings both locally and at the 'May Meetings' in London. Public speaking did not come easily to her and she confessed her lack of confidence to Tom in her letters.

On the medical side, the Harris family had a good relationship with their local medical men and Bessie was asked to assist them in minor operations; she found time to visit old patients in her old district who told her they were so delighted to be able to consult with a 'lady doctor'. By May the manuscript of 'Memories and Letters of Mary Hart' was complete; by September (just before she returned to China) the book was printed and copies were privately circulated.

The Harris family at their home 'South Place', Calne
This large Victorian house with its orangery, peachery and beautiful garden was
eventually pulled down to make way for a housing estate.
Those we can identify are – left to right standing: Joe, Mary, & Alick.
Seated from left; Bessie, Sophy, Thomas Harris, and Elizabeth, his wife.

Bessie had planned that for part of the furlough they would enjoy a sea-side holiday with the baby, Amah and Sophy. Westgate-on-Sea was chosen and through the second half of May and early June they enjoyed a wonderful spell of fine weather. Unknown to the little group enjoying the sun, sand and sea at Westgate, an epidemic of typhus occurred in Hankow and two of the missionaries, Tom and Dr Paul Turner, fell ill with the disease. Dr Turner had only arrived at the Mission in March and had immediately proved to be an ideal, popular colleague and a great asset to the community. Within a few days Dr Turner had died but Tom recovered and when he was strong enough he was sent to Japan for a few weeks to convalesce. Tom described his illness in a letter to Marion written from Japan:

Aug 16ᵗʰ 1896

> *Many thanks for your letter of 18ᵗʰ June which I got a week or two ago – I'm very sorry I've got so little writing done of late – indeed I seem to have written to no one at home, for months, except my Bessie. You will have heard all about my illness – I was taken ill June 2ⁿᵈ and so was dear Dʳ Turner & he died as you know after only about a week in bed – I was able to be up – about the 4ᵗʰ week of June – and June 27ᵗʰ I left – by order – for Japan & seemed to gain strength immediately after leaving Hankow & day by day got stronger.*

This was terrible news for the Harris family to receive in July just as plans were being made for Bessie's return but worse was to come: they heard only two or three weeks later of the death of William Terrell. Bessie's father reacted very strongly and wrote this letter to Tom:

August 17ᵗʰ 1896

> *I desire to write to you specially and on a very important subject.*

> *The news of the death of Mʳ Terrell preceded as it has been by the news of the death of Dʳ Turner, Mʳˢ Owen, David Hill, our dear daughter Mary and her husband Walford makes me and my wife and all our relatives and friends feel very concerned about Bessie and you, also Dear little Walford, we all feel that for Bessie to go to Hankow and to work there next summer is almost certain death to her, and very little less so to you, and we cannot believe that our Heavenly Father desires that such a risk of valuable lives should be run.*

> *I did intend pressing Bessie not to go next month, but on speaking to her I found her heart is set on going, and knowing you are there and should have part in any arrangement for altering your present plans, also that Amah has to be taken back, I desisted from pressing her not to go*

next month, but I write you to ask you if you consider that you do right in subjecting your Wife, yourself, and Child to the climate of Hankow another summer – we all here, who love your wife yourself and child say No, a thousand times No. I write you that you may get this before Bessie arrives, and on her arrival to consult as to the wisest course to take.

The anxieties felt by her parents did not deflect Bessie from her determination to rejoin her husband and return to her work in Hankow. She had made strenuous efforts after the Westgate holiday to spend time in London improving her medical knowledge by observing operations performed at the Chelsea Hospital for Women and attending the consultations at St John's Hospital for Skin Diseases. During this time she stayed with Miss Fletcher, the headmistress of the private school at Crouch End where she and her sister Mary had been educated before being going to the school in Germany; this gave both Bessie and Miss Fletcher immense pleasure.

Thomas Harris's wish that Bessie should not return to China did not prevail but he was nevertheless a generous man of spirit, willing and able to ease the financial burden for his family. Bessie had been worrying about the bill for Mary's headstone in the Hankow cemetery which was outstanding and which, surprisingly, Bessie had assumed would be her debt. When the matter was mentioned within the family Thomas Harris made it clear that he expected to pay for his own daughter's headstone and immediately settled the matter by giving Bessie the money to pay the £10 account on her return.

There was however a much larger project under discussion in the circle of the Hankow Mission. For many years missionaries and their families had needed a location not too far away from Hankow and on the Yangtze (for easier access) where they would be able to rest and recuperate away from the oppressive heat of summer in the city. Some of the missionaries had already discovered the beautiful area in the Lushan hills above the river port of Kiu Kiang. In this letter to Tom Dr Griffith John describes the place:

Aug 7th

Your letter from Karuisawa found me here yesterday: I am exceedingly glad to hear that you are making good progress, & that you are enjoying the change so much. I have been at Kuling over two weeks, and have enjoyed the change exceedingly. When I left Hankow I was far from well. I had a severe attack of diarrhoea, followed by my old enemy. When I left both were upon me strong. The Archibalds sent me a most pressing invitation to come & join them at their charming bungalow and Foster did all in his power to persuade me to accept. It is well I came, for the change has done me a great deal of good.

My opinion of Kuling as a Sanatorium is very high. The air is very pure, and the temperature is very cool. The Ther. has never risen above 77° in Mrs Archibald's dining room. The average since I have been here has been about 73°. The evenings are delightfully cool, and so are the mornings. I sleep every night under two blankets, a sheet, & a coverlet. Some nights have been so cool that a thick Japanese quilt (pei-wo) has had to be added on. It is almost impossible to realise that there can be such a difference between this and the plain below. There is Kiu-Kiang at our feet, we can see it distinctly from the hill behind Archibald's bungalow. The distance looks very small; but the heat there is from 15° to 20° greater than here. I find that the difference between this and Hankow is about 20°. And then you have nothing of that clammy sweltering sensation which clings to one in the valley.

The water is very sweet & pure. There are springs everywhere, & two burns, now separately & then unitedly, run through the valley. The walks in every direction are very varied and charming. The views from the tops of Mts around are extremely grand.

There are in Kuling 118 lots in all. 21 only are left. These will be taken up soon. GJ

To develop the place needed money and this was where Thomas Harris generously stepped in. His wife writes to Tom:

Sept. 11th

> *Your good wife will be sure to write you a little letter, but her hours are few now for Calne – in a sense I shall be glad for her to be on the sea – for the packing and goodbying. Also just at last the book – happily we can help in this but it has entailed work that she only can do, & it has told on her good looks indeed she scarcely seems fit to go back to China! I do hope the sea & rest (if it be quiet) will do her good, poor Amah dreads it greatly! As for dear Walford he only seems to think of the big ship & see Papa!! He is splendidly well and leaves Calne with the same good character that he brought, tho' I am sure you will be pleased with his quickened intelligence! – Father, Sophy & I go with them to S'ampton. Bessie will tell you Father has paid her for the grave stone £10 and Dr John will tell you he wishes to pay for the whole cost of the Bungalows, i.e., the two; our hearts rejoice in the joy of the Missys at Kuling & at C.King. Seldom have I had greater joy than in giving those buildings for the health of God's servants.*

Dr Griffith John was chiefly responsible for the decision to set up the Kuling estate and in so doing earned the undying gratitude of a great many of his colleagues. For all Hankow missionaries it was a haven from the oppressive climate of summer in the city. As well as rest and relaxation it was the ideal place for a sanatorium; nowhere was better for recuperation after illness and missionary wives who had summer-time babies always went up there for their confinements for the sake of the comfort of both mother and baby. Both my father and my sister, who were June babies, were born in Kuling; my brother and I, winter babies, were delivered in Hankow. Nothing in the world Bessie's father could have sponsored would have meant as much to Tom and his daughter as providing them with 15b Kuling Estate. Even though I was very young I clearly remember it as a magical place with wonderful rocky streams and pools of crystal clear mountain water – a veritable fairyland on earth.

In those days there was no metalled road to the little town of Kuling, so that everything had to be carried and everyone had either to walk or ride in a sedan chair up the mountain side. Many years later in 1932 Gerty, Gordon Gillison's wife (who was pregnant at the time) sent this description of a picnic:

December 1932

> *I don't think we'll ever forget the first picnic we had at Kuling. First of all it was a day snatched out of the busiest time and then altogether it was a glorious day; the picnic place was simply marvellous and rejoices in the name of Paradise Pools! Six of us went and we had three chairs, two for two of us who were not quite equal to the long walk and an extra one for the bundles and for any of the others when they felt like having a rest. We started off about 10 in the morning and walked along in great style thoroughly enjoying the first cool day we had had for a month, then when we began going down hill, which makes walking rather a hoppity-hop business, I and one of the other ladies got into our chairs. Gordon and Jean Gillison gave the coolies great amusement by taking a hand at carrying the extra chair; however they found it rather painful on the shoulders and soon gave it up. After a while one of the coolies carrying my chair jokingly asked Gordon to take his place, which he did, and then the wretched men began to run. As G. was so much taller than the other bearers the pole wasn't level between him and the man behind; he had a struggle to keep it on his shoulders and hold the side poles at the same time. I got a most horrible jolting and was terrified lest he should slip on the boulders with which the path was bestrewn and send me into Kingdom Come! For the next few days Gordon's shoulders ached badly, but evidently chair carrying is not so hard on the usual chair bearers, for after some practice nature provides them with a pad of flesh on which to rest the pole. This Gordon found out in the course of a routine examination of labourers at the American School.*

> *The Paradise Pools are three lovely clear, green pools in a wild, rocky gorge. The first two are connected by a pretty waterfall of about 30 feet*

*and then the water tumbles over rocks and in and out among great white
boulders till at last it is forced through a narrow cleft and forms a natural
watershoot down which adventurous bathers go shooting into a pothole
which eventually opens out into the third pool. We arrived just in time to
prepare Tiffin and in a short time the Gorge was filled with the beautiful
aroma of our fried sausages and onions! After Tiffin we got into our
bathing costumes and sunbathed on the flat rocks in the stream and then
scrambled around till we reached the watershoot where four of the party had
great fun. They would sit or lie on the slippery rocks, holding on as best
they could, and as soon as they let go the force of the water shot them into
a pothole where they disappeared in the swirling water and then came up
all gasping and spluttering! I felt horribly nervous all the time in case one
of them would get stunned or something when out of sight! After playing
about here for a bit we had a bathe and then tea and it was time to face the
long climb home.*

Bessie set sail for China grateful for the generosity of her father who was to pay, not
only for the headstone and the building of the holiday retreat, but as the letter from
Mrs Elizabeth Harris implied, for the printing of the book 'Memories and Letters
of Mary Hart'. Perhaps John Gillison's observation to Tom on his engagement to
Bessie, 'It is fortunate that Providence has arranged for you to marry someone
with a little money', had some truth in it.

In her last letter to Tom before Bessie left England she wrote:

Sept 16th 1896

*Just one last line to tell you I expect to leave Calne tomorrow. The
week has been a very busy one – what with packing & the arrival of the
books – the latter I shall bring with me of course – Friends all seem very
very pleased with it.*

Besides all this bustle & scurry I gave Chloroform the other day for Dr Campbell when he removed another cancer of breast – It went off nicely – Dr Campbell was exceedingly warm in his good wishes & good-bye to me. Dr Fergusson also treats me like a colleague and seems to like talking medical talk to me – Friends are all very very kind – we had

Inserted here is a note 'written' by Walford.

a large valedictory prayer meeting at the school-room last evening, I said a few words – Father, Mother & Soph go with us to Southampton – Letters of thanks for our book are pouring in – I am sending to all whose addresses I know among your special friends – including Mrs Richardson & Eliza Henderson & Jeannie Gillison & Mrs Talbot Wilson & Miss Kelly. I don't know Mrs Craven's address.

Bessie and her little party arrived back in Hankow safely and she soon settled in to her familiar life in Hankow. In December she wrote to Mary Black:

Dec 14th 1895

My visit home is almost dreamlike now & yet the difference it makes to me to have seen you all is very great. I can have so much more interest in Tom's letters – indeed the distinction between my relations & his seems gone now.

I am really very thankful for my visit home in every way. Tom seems well, & Walford is the very picture of health. Walford talks a great deal now & very plainly too; he has most of his meals with us & is very entertaining. Tom does enjoy having him so much. We are doing our best also to train him & teach him obedience – it is so interesting to me to see the workings of his little will, he has plenty of determination & yet is such a loving child. I think he is a beautiful child to train & we just thank God for it & seek His help & leave the result to Him. I begin to realise now that it is as definitely work given me of God to do as missionary work.

Scenes of Kuling:

the steps;

the bungalows;

the pools;

the bathers (*lower left picture – the author [left] and her sister, Meili*).

Why did I write this to you? I can hardly say except that my thoughts ran on that way.

I have got nicely settled in here again now, but a good many changes have or are taking place, and I can hardly map out my time yet. The new worker has come, Miss Wylie, who is to take my sister's place. She seems very nice – in about three weeks we expect another, Miss Cousins, a doctor and the two will live together, & by & by I hope they will manage the women's hospital. I shall still find plenty to do I am sure. Tom is extra busy because we are short-handed here again. Dr John & Mr Bonsey have gone on a country journey of a month or five weeks, so only Mr Foster & Tom are left to manage everything & Tom's hospital is pretty full if not quite. We were delighted to get news of the travellers two or three days ago, & they reported such good receptions everywhere and such numbers of baptisms – 136 I think. We shall hear much more when they return of course but it is wonderful after the animosity and opposition in these same districts some years ago.

I am glad you liked our book of memories so much. It has been such a pleasure to us to have received similar testimonies from friends everywhere. God must have helped us very much in gathering them together for when we began, we felt so unequal to doing it & now we believe God is making it a help & inspiration to many. I think many people too feel they can picture our work & surroundings better far than before. Tom has enjoyed reading the book. Of course I miss the dear girl very much, but it is so beautiful to think she is 'At Home' now & that her life is still bearing fruit on earth.

This letter is of particular interest to me because it betrays a thought which I feel sure was at the back of Bessie's mind when she first accepted Tom's proposal of marriage: that in marrying him she was reneging on the promise she had made to God to dedicate herself to missionary work. Once she became 'Mrs Gillison' and was not there as 'Dr Harris' she felt her doctor status slightly undermined and she was afraid that it would seem to 'the very many in England' that it would 'mar the consecration which they believed to be mine'. If anything I think it made her all the more determined to play her part as a medical missionary as well as a wife and mother.

Motherhood occupied the next few years as she and Tom had had a daughter, Evelyn, in February 1898 when Walford was nearly four years old, followed by a son Keith in 1900, and Jean, a second daughter, in 1901. Howard in 1904 and Gordon in 1909 completed the family.

The political situation at the time of Evelyn's birth was relatively quiet but the following year saw the start of the Boxer Rebellion which consisted mainly of violent attacks on foreign businessmen, missionaries and Chinese Christians. The crisis deepened over the summer of 1900 when Boxer bands spread over north China countryside burning missionary facilities and killing more than 250 foreigners and many thousands of Chinese Christians. In Hankow's missionary circle there was great concern over the safety of women and children – particularly those that were up in Kuling. Tom and Bessie were among those who were 'up on the hill' at the time, Bessie having given birth to Keith on June 13th. In a letter to Tom, Griffith John says:

> June 16th 1900
>
> Robertson is down from Haoshih with the bad news that our house there has been burned. Up to Thursday there was no sign whatever of ill-will on the part of the people. Robertson had gone to Tien-tien, & Mr Yeh had gone to Goh-tsze-nan. Wills was alone in Tsao-Shih. On Thursday there was the Tien-Fu-hai on, & thousands of people had come in for the occasion. They wanted to see the house, but being so many, Wills objected. They proceeded to throw stones, & smash the gate. They made a rush into the house & set it on fire. Wills took refuge in a neighbour's house, & from there sent Teng Keu to Tien-tien to request Robertson not to return to Hsao Shih, but go to H.K. & report.

> *I have just seen the Consul & he will at once communicate with the Taotai & Viceroy. We have also sent two men to Tsao Shih to investigate & report. We are exceedingly anxious about D[r] Wills as you may imagine. He may turn up tomorrow or Monday. Poor fellow! I am very sorry for him.*

> *Everything here is as usual though I am inclined to think the people are a little disposed to be rude. I have <u>seen</u> nothing of it, but I have <u>heard</u> from others that it is so.*

> *The state of things in the North is very terrible. The Consul tells me that two of the Legations have been burned down, & two of the Ministers murdered. He fears that a general massacre of the foreigners in Peking [12] may take place. It is his opinion also that the Missions in these parts would do well to call in the ladies from all the stations inland. I gave it as my opinion that everything would depend on whether the Chinese at Peking would show fight, & whether the victory would be ours. Success on our part would bring them to their senses, but a reverse would make them mad, & the evil consequences would be felt everywhere, with which he fully agreed.*

> *I ought to tell you that Warren [13] does not like the idea of there being so many ladies on the hill. Indeed he is feeling anxious about it. I sincerely trust that all will be well with you. I don't think there is danger; but the state of things in China just now is such as to make it impossible to foresee what a day may bring forth.*

In a letter to Tom on June 28th Dr Griffith John says:

> *It looks as if the Manchu dynasty's days are numbered. This is a momentous crisis & I am thankful that I am permitted to live to see it. I am beginning to hope for China once more. We shall see great things soon in China.*

As the days went by Griffith John felt that the consul's view was over-pessimistic and that they were all reasonably safe in Hankow and Kuling as the threat was

In Japan 1900 Bessie (left) with her three children;
Gerty Jones with Lilian on her lap; others unknown.

mainly in the north. He himself was determined to remain in Hankow in case he could exert influence on the Chinese authorities. For a month or so Bessie was not well enough to travel but by early August she and her three children were part of a group of women and children who went to Japan; in the event they only stayed for a few weeks before it was deemed safe to return to Hankow. Had it not been for a wave of German measles that swept through the party they would have returned even sooner.

There are no letters in the collection dated between October 1900 and June 1901. In the one letter from 1901 Tom writes to Mary Black confirming my understanding that the Gillison family had continued looking after their widowed youngest sister Marion:

Enclosed please find a Draft for £15. to be credited to John's a/c for Marion – I will send the 2nd of exchange by the next mail – I trust it will reach you safely – I am ashamed at my wretched character as correspondent. I ought to write more – and I must try & reform. I might give several excuses – any of wh w^d do – but none of which would hold good for 6 months. Well I have had 3 or 4 months' very hard work – March, April and May are my busiest months especially for surgical operations. These take it out of one – both physically & otherwise – and they consume a large amount. During these 3 months I often spend 3, 4 and even 5 hours a day in the operating room. As the hot weather sets in (as it has now) operations are fewer and fewer, dysentery etc takes up one's time – I have the head master of our High School in our house with fever just now. He has been on his back for 3 weeks & I have been doctor & nurse – assisted by his Chinese cook – a nice fellow. M^r M^cF is better now and I hope he will be able to go with us to the hills – a week hence. Bessie is well but very busy preparing for Kuling where she expects to be for 3 months. I hope to take her up there – to stay a week or 10 days. I return to Hankow for 6 weeks & then to go to Kuling for another fortnight & bring Bessie back.

The children are well – It was little Keith's first birthday yesterday – & we were so thankful he was well – for he got a touch of cold when teething & his temp. went up to 105. He had practically never been ill before & was so fat & plump & though only ill for some 10 days it pulled him down very quickly but he is picking up rapidly. I send you a copy of our last Report. Pray for us that the work may be an honour to God. I long to be more spiritual & to see more spiritual results – I am reading Müller's life by Pierson & it is doing me good – How is dear Aunt Jessie – I long to see her, perhaps as much or more than anyone in this old land – God bless her. Give her my warm love. I must off to the bank to get the draft.

Much love to yourself – I hope you are really recovered now. What a trying time you had.

PS Bessie w^d join in love if I told her I was writing.

How slowly Boer & China affairs move! T.G

On August 1901 a second daughter Jean was born but the first reference to her is in a letter written by Bessie to Mary Black.

Jan 17th 1902

Ever so many thanks to you & Aunt Jessie for your kind thoughts of us this Xmas. The little dress for Jean is very pretty & the little pinafore will be very useful.

We were so glad to get your bright letter & to hear that you & Jessie are keeping well. I can imagine what a pleasure it was to you to see Jane & her family

We don't know yet when our furlough will be – probably not for a long time. Tom wants to do a good deal of medical teaching & put some students thro' a medical course first. D^r McAll has been in Wuchang all last year, but will return to help Tom as soon as Dr Davenport returns.

I hope you got the photograph of Evelyn & Keith – Keith is a dear little fellow, now just at the interesting stage of learning to talk. Little Jean is a bonny little thing, but has a cold which is rather persistent. Evelyn is proud to call herself 'Mother's big girl'. Walford of course is the school-boy. It is very interesting to me to teach him. They are a dear little quartet & are a great joy to us.

Tom has had a very busy year – I do very little mission work now, but I trust my work is indirectly mission work. We often have visitors, next week I shall probably have three bachelors who will come in for Committee meetings. We have an extra outside room, two in fact, that my dear sister built, these enable us to take in more visitors than others can.

Keith aged 1, Evelyn aged 3 in 1901.

Later that summer this telegram was sent on June 23rd to Tom by Bessie who was in Kuling with the four children:

On the 1st of July Evelyn died of dysentery. This must have been a devastating shock for the family and sadly it was not an unusual event: many missionaries had lost young children in the past through disease. However, until the one written in 1903 from Tom to Mary Black five months after the event, there is no mention of the death in any letters:

Dec 28th 1902

    *My life is a busy one & yet I feel that if I were still more systematic
I might get much more done – especially in the way of writing letters which
I feel is a weak point with me – Let me tell you something of what I have
to do – I have of course my share of the two Hosp^{ls} & Medical School. The
Margaret Hospital (women's) is in our care. Bessie sees the out-patients – I
have charge of the in-patients & Miss Joyce has charge of the Nursing
Department – We have not a large number of patients but we have about
as many as we want for the time being as Bessie has home duties & I have
Medical School & Men's Hosp^l & Miss Joyce has her second exam in
Chinese language soon – & I am one of the examiners. That too takes not
a few hours' work. Some six or eight papers to correct (besides having to set
them) also examining in reading & so on. Then I have one day a week at
out-patients in the men's Hosp^l and some 20 to 25 patients besides – Then
operations – some of these take a good time – I have <u>four</u> to go under
chloroform tomorrow but don't often have so many in one day.*

Jan 12th 1903

    *I laid the above aside & have not got started again till today. The
Xmas season is over – We miss our dear wee girlie but we rejoice that she is
with Jesus. We had full meetings during the week of prayer in our Chinese
churches – one of which I conducted (in the Swedish Mission Chapel,
Wuchang) – The one in our chapel was packed to the door & seats in the
aisles – Perhaps 550 present – We had a splendid Tract Society meeting
– I must send you a report – My medical school 1st prof^l exam – begins
tomorrow – lasts 3 or 4 days. I will send you report of that also – Bessie is
out or I am sure w^d send her love -*

That short significant sentence, 'We miss our dear wee girlie but we rejoice that
she is with Jesus', seems to me to sum up the extraordinarily simple acceptance

of this sort of tragic event by those who suffered the loss, particularly in the case of the death of children. It was their deep conviction and unshakeable faith that carried them through. The only other reference to Evelyn in the collection of letters is over twenty years later when Tom is writing to his daughter Jean and he says:

July 1st 1923

> *Before this reaches you I fear your birthday will have passed – but altho this letter may be a day or two late – my 'cardiac wireless' will be in good time for we will be up in the morning when you are going to bed the night before – I do wish you a very happy birthday 22! – Just think of it! I came to China when I was 23. I am sending a small cheque – Get something you need with it – and accept it with much love for my only daughter – Do you know today is the anniversary of dear wee Evelyn's death. A day or two ago, when I was passing the cemetery I looked in & saw the little grave – and Aunt Mary & Walford Hart's & others. It all seems so long ago – It is like a dream of far off days. I must take two men down & get the stones cleaned up a bit & things made tidy.*

And so life went on as usual.

The Marais family; this was probably taken on their 1901 visit to Scotland. Gertie would have been about 15, Jessie 9, Agnes 13 and Claude 12.

EIGHT

The South African Connection

T he Marais family have figured little in this story since Jane's arrival in Cape Town and her marriage to Frans in 1884. There are some forty of her letters to various members of the family written over a period of twenty years and while they paint a portrait of a successful marriage and a happy family there is sometimes a hint of the isolation she feels at being so far away from her Scottish roots. Several times she betrays a longing to go back to Edinburgh.

> *August 2ⁿᵈ 1896*
>
> *Marion says something in her letter about John – probably getting home (D.V.) next year for a visit – I do wish I could get home at the same time – Of course Frans will not readily agree, but we'll see! I won't say anything about it yet – It would be a great undertaking with the four children but I do long to see you all, & naturally too!*

We know from a single sentence in one of Bessie's letters and the evidence of Jane's daughter Jessie that on one occasion sometime in 1901 the family did come home on a visit. Bessie said in a letter to Mary Black dated January 1902, 'We were so glad to get your bright letter & to hear that you & Jessie are keeping well. I can imagine what a pleasure it was to you to see Jane & her family'.

Jane Marais was a truly remarkable woman. Throughout the years that we spent transcribing the Gillison letters she was perhaps the person who commanded my greatest admiration and respect. Modest, sensitive, well-brought up, she was a girl with no experience of life outside her family, her work as a governess and teacher, and her church; on her marriage she had to adjust to a completely new life, a different language, religion and culture. She was socially isolated and thousands of miles away from her old home. Undoubtedly Jane accepted that this was what she had chosen and therefore, with her trust in God, she was prepared to face her new life with courage and enthusiasm.

Frans was a busy and successful doctor and the family enjoyed a comfortable standard of living. According to John Gillison, Frans was earning about £2000 a year – a substantial sum by any standards. After nine years in Wellington the family had moved to Fordsburg, a suburb of Johannesburg in 1893 and Jane sent this description of the place to Tom and Bessie:

December 10th 1893

> *We left Wellington on your Wedding Day – Sep 7th – then we stayed in Pretoria – the capital of the Transvaal – for a month – until Frans finally decided where he would settle – then we came to Fordsburg, a suburb of the wonderful Johannesburgh – Eight years ago there was not a house in all this vast district – & now it is one of the largest towns in Sth Africa – You have perhaps read about the great gold discoveries in the Transvaal – We are surrounded by gold mines & of course the place is in consequence very lively and prosperous – Frans thought there was a better chance for him here than in Wellington – seeing that the Colony is getting over crowded with Doctors. In Wellington there were 4 Medical men when we left & all of them born & brought up in the place & in consequence each had his share of the work – We have not had any reason to regret our change, as Frans is already in a good Practice here – As for me – I am at home anywhere, & so are the children – I spend most of my time with the bairns or in working for them – We cannot be too careful of them in this place – with such a mixture of people and creeds – There are, however, many good people – We still belong to the Dutch Reformed Church – but we go often to the Wesleyan Chapel, & the children attend Sunday School there – we left Gertie and Agnes in Wellington for two months until we got settled & now we are all together again.*

Jessie, the youngest child, was born in 1892 just before the move to Fordsburg and the family enjoyed a good life in their new home. It is interesting that rather than use local domestic help Jane asked her sister Mary in Edinburgh to find and send out a suitable Scottish servant girl. Mary obliged and a Scottish girl called Helen arrived to work for the Marais; it was an arrangement which suited all parties:

Jan 26th 1896

I did not write to you last week or enclose the draft as promised, as Frans was away from home for two days – however, it is enclosed in this (viz £36-10-0) the 10/- for interest, and we thank you again for all the trouble you took on our behalf. Helen is suiting me splendidly, and I do not think you could have made a better choice – She is beginning to feel more at home now – She came out in the steamer and in the train from Cape Town to Johannesburg with two American gentlemen, one of whom has been here twice to see her – But of course it only seems natural after all, for her to have friends as well as other folks!

In March 1899 John Gillison was sent from Australia to South Africa to work in the Cape Town office of his insurance company for three months and while he was there he took the opportunity of seeing something of the countryside and visiting his sister and her family. It must have been the first time they had met since 1882 when he had sailed for Australia and Jane had left home to marry Frans Marais. This is his long but interesting account of his impressions of South Africa:

I left Melbourne towards the end of March and had an unpleasant passage to Durban, not that the weather was very rough except crossing the Great Australian Bight, but because all the way from Cape Leuwin there was a heavy roll from the South West necessitating the daily use of the 'fiddles'. As usual I was not sick, excepting two days from Durban, when I must have

eaten something that disagreed with me. We had time to land at Durban
for a few hours. Steamers lie off the bar and passengers are hoisted into a
large basket on board a tug which takes them to the wharf. Sometimes it is
so rough that cargo cannot be landed. The open roadstead is dangerous. It
is a picturesque town, not so much the town itself as the inhabitants. The
principal suburb the Berea is prettily situated overlooking the ocean and
benefits by the sea breezes. The climate is much the same as that of Brisbane,
sugar cane, bananas and pineapples growing in the neighbourhood. The
feature which strikes a visitor most is the number of rickshaws, which are
pulled by the Zulus, whom the British defeated in the great Zulu war – the
rickshaw is a two wheeled spring cart, a sort of large go-cart with rubber tired
wheels, more comfortable, cooler and cheaper than a hansom and the men
run along pulling them at a rate of about eight miles an hour. Their costume
generally consists of a suit of pyjamas, the trousers not going below the knee,
and sometimes they adorn their heads with bunches of feathers and cow's
horns and sometimes their shoulders with wings. They often wear round
their ankles some sort of native-made rattles – Many are fine, jolly, laughing,
stalwart fellows, who spend about six months of the year in earning enough
money to go back to their kraals and buy a wife–They are polygamous and
a Zulu's wealth generally consists of wives and cattle – a wife can generally
be bought for about five cows and if the husband does not behave himself the
wife threatens to leave him and he may have to give her father another cow
or two to compel her to stay. The Zulus before the introduction of missionaries
and the so-called civilization were the most moral people in the world. There
was only one penalty for a lapse – death to both. Other striking men are
the native police, who are great dandies – I saw two later on in Maritzburg
walking down the street dressed in blue serge knickerbockers and a tight reefer
jacket with leather belt round the waist, a little round blue cap, military style,
cocked jauntily on one side, earings of red, white and blue beads and similar
beads worked into their hair or wool, which looked crisp and curly. Round their
calves and ankles they wore bangles made of brass or copper wire–each carried

a knob stick, handcuffs and a large silk handkerchief. There are many Coolies in Natal, who have been imported from Ceylon and other parts of India to work in the plantations. When their time is up some return, but others remain and act as waiters, cooks and general servants. The Coolie women are very picturesque and wear the nose rings so common in the East. They are very fond of jewelry and bright colours.

We left Durban and had a quiet passage to Cape Town, where I stayed about two months taking charge of the office, the voyage lasting twenty-six days in all from Melbourne. I had two or three days at one of the leading hotels 'The Royal', but the cooking was horrible and I was fortunate in being able to get into the 'City Club', where I was very comfortable indeed and the charges were reasonable. There is only one decent hotel in Cape Town the 'Mount Nelson', where the charge is £1. a day.

Jane wrote me to call on Mr Whitton the Principal of the Normal College, who looked after her when she was married and I spent several pleasant evenings with him. I hired a bicycle and had a number of charming rides, as the weather during the whole of the two months was exceedingly good. I went to the Dutch Reformed Church, the doctrines and government of which are much the same as the Established and Free Churches in Scotland. A Dutch service is held in the morning and an English one in the afternoon. There is a decent Church of England Cathedral, where the music is good. I took a shooting trip for three days out towards the West and made the acquaintance of Cape carts, Cape boys, Dutch farmers and their wives and families. I stayed with one farmer 'an elder of the kirk', who delivered a long grace before and after meals in Dutch, likewise conducted lengthy family worship morning and evening. He was better educated than most, but I should not care to trust him very far. These farmers live very plainly and have little discourse with the world. I did not get much game as there was little about. On another occasion I paid a visit to Franz's family at Wellington, the old people were very pleased to see me and the sons with their wives and the daughters with their husbands and different members of the family turned up to welcome me — I found the ordeal rather trying as many of them could not speak English and I knew precious little Dutch. On another occasion I spent a few hours with Franz's brother Koos, the Principal of the Boy's Gymnasium or Preparatory School at Stellenbosch. He is a great chemist, but I did not like him and I gather from one of the recent Cape papers, that his sympathies are very much with the Transvaal: in fact he as well as many other 'Africanders' in the Cape Colony are traitors and think there is no harm in it. The Dutch are very sly and most untrustworthy as a class. I often dined alongside Jan Hofmeyr [14], better known as 'the mole' by the English, or 'Onze Jan' by the Dutch, the man who practically controls the policy of South Africa. I have no doubt he is an arch-plotter.

I climbed one day to the top of Table Mountain, which is over 3,500 feet above the level of the sea. The top is a plateau with a peak rising from one end of it and on the plateau are extensive water works, which supply Cape Town. The face of the mountain overlooking Cape Town is a sheer drop of over 1,000 feet and standing on the edge, I thought I could have thrown a stone right into the heart of the city, and put a shot from a rifle into Robben Island, which is twelve mile away. From the back of the mountain I had the most magnificent panoramic view of my life looking right over the Cape Flats, with the little towns in the distance up to thirty five miles away, backed up by ranges of mountains from fifty to one hundred miles away. The Cape of Good Hope is not the most southern point of Africa, Cape Agulhas is. Cape Town lies on the southern side of a little bay called Table Bay, to the North of the Cape of Good Hope and the mountain lies on the South side. I saw the 'table cloth' frequently, that is to say the mist hanging about the top of the mountain. I visited Simons Town and other places of interest within twenty miles or so of Cape Town by means of a bicycle.

When my work in Cape Town was nearly finished I left by train for Kimberley, where I spent three days and had a good look over the principal diamond mines. I saw the old workings of the Kimberley mine, that is to say, the hole 500 feet deep from which the ground containing the diamonds was hoisted before the diamonds were washed out of it. It is said to be the largest hole in the world made by man. It is now worked from underground and the stone is hoisted up a shaft as in an ordinary mine. The great De Beer's mine is worked in conjunction with the Kimberley mine, the blue ground, as it is called, containing the diamonds is hoisted up from below, spread out over flat fields called 'floors', so that it may become disintegrated by the action of sun and rain, harrowing, watering etc. The largest diamonds are generally found here by the Kafirs. In the course of four or six months the ground is taken to the washing machines–great circular pans in which immense revolving arms stir it up until the water washes all the clay away leaving stones of more or less value. These stones are taken by train to what is known as the pulsator house, run through sieves, so that they may be sorted into various sizes, put into boxes with wire gauze at the bottom, covered with a layer of lead bullets – these boxes of bullets are constantly shaken by machinery, water running through them all the time and the motion causes the diamonds, which are the heaviest of the stones to pass to the bottom and between the lead bullets, for they are heavier than the bullets also, while the garnets and lighter crystals remain above the bullets. Underneath the pulsators run endless canvas screens which catch the diamonds and a few of the other stones, which have fallen through, and carry them to the top of the inclined planes covered with a thick sort of grease to which the diamonds stick, but to which the other stones do not stick as a rule. All the stones are picked off the grease and carried away to be sorted. I saw, what is called 'a day's wash' of diamonds, worth about £5,000. The three largest diamonds in the world have been found in this neighbourhood. The work is done by Kafirs, supervised by white men. The Kafirs are generally engaged for four or six months and are confined to what is known as the 'Compound' until their term is up, and before leaving they are kept under observation for a week in a special place, so that they may not take away with them any of the diamonds. In the West End Compound there were *about 4,000 'boys'. Illicit diamond buying still exists, but to a very small extent since the institution of the Compound system.*

From Kimberley I went to Bloemfontein, which has a white population of about six or eight thousand in addition to coloured people. I visited the 'Raadsaal' and heard the members debate – had a look at the President's house – was kindly shown over the fort by one of the soldiers, but they would not let me see the guns. Then on to Johannesburg, the finest city in South Africa and marvellous considering that fifteen years ago there was not a building worth speaking of.

Jane and Franz with two of the children met me at the station, we drove out to their home in Fordsburg, which is a suburb of the town little more than a mile away from the Post Office. They live in a small brick villa, which is their own property. Franz makes a very good income – pretty well £2,000 a year – but they are not spending half of it, because his idea was to save as much as would enable him to retire in about five years. He had saved about £15,000, which was invested in property in Johannesburg and he did not want any war, because he did not know what might happen to him and to his savings. I have no doubt all will come right in the end. His practice is a peculiar one, generally among coloured people – Kafirs Coolies etc., who pay their ten and sixpence down on the nail, before they get their advice. He used to keep a 'cart' (sort of dog-cart) and horses but has given them up for a bicycle, which he finds much less expensive and more convenient. He can hardly do without Jane, as they have only black servants, <u>when they can get them</u>, and she has to answer the door, speaking Dutch, German, French, Kafir or any other language that the patient may think he can speak. Many of the patients cannot write. All the family splendid – each had a bicycle–and I had a really good time for eleven days. I was specially taken with the children–such fine specimens, and so well behaved, much more so than the average Australian family. Gerty is an intelligent, studious, clever girl of fourteen, not over-robust. Aggie is a jolly 'mischief' of twelve to whom lessons are a great trouble. Claude is a clever smart boy of ten and a half, very small for his age, rather like Franz' father. His specialty is bicycle trick-riding. Jessie was seven, just started to go to school a pretty girl, very fond of her Uncle Jack as they all were. They said they liked me much better than their Wellington uncles!! Jane was talking of getting home to Scotland next year, but I fancy it will be <u>several</u> years before Franz will let her go. When all is settled again he will feel so annoyed at the loss of time in making up what he wants to retire on and at the English beating the Boers and taking from them <u>their country</u> of which curiously enough, they have already sold one third, and that the most valuable part of it – that he may not let her leave for years to come. But Jane will do her best to pay a visit to Scotland, as soon as she can manage it.

I went out one day with Franz to Doornkop, where Jamieson's troops surrendered, and no wonder they surrendered for they must have been very badly led to get into the position they did. 'The Jamieson Raid' as it has been called, has been given credit for a lot of hatred, which is borne to the English by many of the Dutch. My own opinion, in view of recent events, is that it was a very good thing for England and Englishmen, that the raid took place. I heard one peculiar explanation of it which Mr. Jeffray may know more, that it was promoted by the mining magnates of the Rand as an excuse for the sale of Chartered Company shares at very high prices by which they made, it is said, eight millions. This may or may not be true. On another occasion I went with Jane and Claude to Pretoria to spend the day with the family of a Mr. Cellier (pronounced Selyes) generally known as the 'Donkey and Forage Contract Man', that is to say, he made a lot of money out of a contract with the Transvaal Government to supply them with donkeys and forage. He has a very nice house, a nice wife and family, gave us a very good dinner, and we drove about the town in his landau, behind a fine spanking pair of horses. He took me over to the Raadsaal and I saw old Kruger at about a yard's distance. He looks very fat, pasty and flabby, but at the same time, he must be a wonderful old man. I also saw at a distance that old villain Cronje. Cellier said it would take 150,000 British soldiers to beat the

Transvaal, and he must have known something for he said that they had only 35,000 Burghers in the Transvaal and expected 15,000 from the Orange River Free State. Of course as we know now, the rest were to come from Natal, Cape Colony and Rhodesia. From a recent pamphlet, I noticed that he was probably in receipt of a subsidy from the Secret Service Fund, and I should not be at all astonished, if Franz and his brother Koos, knew a great deal more about what was coming than most people. There has no doubt been a gigantic conspiracy to overthrow the English power in South Africa and to convert the whole into a Dutch republic under which they would be able to enslave and ill treat the natives to their heart's content. It is a common saying in Cape Town that only a Dutchman can manage the black servants, because, if they do not do as they are told the sjambok or rhinocerous hide whip, which is heavier and nearly as supple as a carpet beater, is brought into requisition. Franz and I got on very well together in spite of our heated arguments. He of course took the view of the civilized Boer, that Britain would never be so unfair as to take their country from them. My reply always was, that if they taxed the Uitlanders (pronounced Eightlanders) they <u>must</u> *give them representation, and to show how absurdly the taxes were imposed, I may mention, that Mr Cellier said, he was worth about seventy or eighty thousand pounds and in the previous year he had paid £4 :1 : 6 in taxes!! Even he admitted that it was not right. Franz idea also was, that if Britain obtained control of the Transvaal, he would not be able to make nearly so much money. I think he is quite wrong, for where money is plentiful, Englishmen or not Englishmen, remuneration will be higher. In Government circles bribery was rife and even old Kruger himself could be bribed by buying a farm from him for about ten times as much as it was worth. He is said to have amassed within the last ten years or so three or four millions sterling, believed to be invested principally in British Consols through Lloyds in Germany. Deeds could not be got through the Titles Office without bribery. It is said that there is no more corrupt administration on the face of the earth.*

Jane of course held views very similar to those held by Franz, because she came more into contact with Dutch people than the educated English people. They do not go out to society, and working as they are to make enough to retire on, I think she is right. It would be no attraction for her to move in such a society as exists in Johannesburg, and in any case it would be very expensive.

After mature consideration of the subject and discussion with all classes of the community, I came to the conclusion, even without the knowledge which we have gained from recent events, that the best thing that could happen in South Africa would be war. An Englishman does not like to be taunted with the white flag business, nor to be told that all British soldiers are cowards, and the sayings and doings of the young Dutch students at Stellenbosch, as full of conceit as they could hold, were simply unbearable to a man of English ideas. When the Boers are beaten, as they will undoubtedly be in the long run, there is a great future ahead of South Africa, which will be due almost entirely to the production of gold on the Rand and in Rhodesia and it will be a decent country for an Englishman to live in. I do not think that the racial hatred will last very long nor be of much consequence for when the Dutch are beaten they will sullenly submit and their children will be so satisfied with English rule that past differences will quietly fade from the memory of the people.

One piece of advice I have to give to those with marriageable daughters is don't allow them on any account to marry a Dutchman, or Africander, or 'Caper' no matter how nice he may be for a 'Caper' in Edinburgh and a Dutchman in South Africa are two different men. And an Englishman should never marry a Dutch girl, unless he wishes to fall to her level.

After leaving Johannesburg, I passed by train near Majuba and Laingsnek at night and did not see them, arriving at Ladysmith in the morning, then on to Maritzburg, where I spent the night. It is a slow going place although it is the Capital. Then on to Durban, where I saw a good deal of Dr Campbell, who with his partner MacKenzie are the leading doctors.

The English people in Natal are not to be confounded with the Dutch or French from Cape Colony. Campbell's sympathies are all with England. MacKenzie was at Home for a trip. I returned to Cape Town by sea, touching at East London and Port Elizabeth. From the latter place I went by rail to Grahamstown, the English educational centre as Stellenbosch is the Dutch

Gertie, Claude, Jane, Jessie, Frans and Agnes Marais

Jessie, Gertie, Agnes and Claude

educational centre. I saw lots of ostriches and goats and bought a few feathers at Port Elizabeth. After two or three days in Cape Town I sailed for Melbourne in the 'Moravian' and arrived safely after a passage of 18¹/2 days – fastest on record. We saw no icebergs, but it <u>was</u> cold and miserable. Hot though the Red Sea may be, it must be preferable to the passage by the Cape. I don't want to go that way again.

There is one aspect of Jane's letters which makes this chapter particularly interesting; they give a personal view of three historical events: Jameson's Raid in early January 1896; the massive dynamite explosion in Johannesburg in February 1896; and the Battle of Elandslaagte on October 21st 1899, which was one of the first battles of the Boer War.

The Jameson Raid [15] was a coup attempt against the Transvaal government tacitly endorsed by British officials which failed. It was also mentioned by John Gillison in his account of his 1899 trip to South Africa and it is surprising that even three years after the event took place a visit to the battleground was still a tourist attraction. When I first discovered the box of family letters and opened this one from Jane, I was astonished when from the fold a dried grass fell into my lap – the very one Jane mentions in this letter written to her sister Mary just three weeks after the skirmish:

Jan 26th 1896

> *I wonder if you have been reading much about Sth. Africa politics of late – At any rate you will have heard of the Battle of 'Doornkop' and the surrender of Jameson, which took place on the 2nd of this month. – Last week we drove out to see this famous spot – and I plucked some grasses to send you – We walked for a considerable distance along the track which Jameson & his forces came by before they surrendered, & it was amongst the dead horses etc that this grass was plucked – We passed at least 40 horses lying as they had been shot. Fortunately I had a big bottle of Eau de Cologne which we used frequently! – It was very, very sad – but saddest of all was to stand beside the grave of nine of the men who had fallen on Jameson's side – What a terrible waste of human life – We do not know*

yet whether it is all over or not – An Englishman cannot bear to be beaten,
and unless the Pretoria Government is equal to the occasion – there might
be war yet – The trial of the Reform Committee men is to come off in April,
and until then, things will be very much unsettled.

After his surrender, Jameson and the other men implicated in the revolt were sentenced to death in the first instance at the trial in April 1896 in Pretoria (referred to in Jane's letter) but then the conspirators were sent to London for a further trial in July.

The grass itself remains with the original letter but this scan gives some idea of this extraordinary tangible piece of history:

The second historical event mentioned in Jane's letters was not a political one. It was the dynamite explosion at Braamfontein Station in Johannesburg which occurred on February 19th 1896, a few weeks after the Jameson debacle. An explosives train carrying between 50 and 60 tons of dynamite had been standing in searing heat for three and a half days, and was struck by a shunting train. In the same letter as the one about Doornkop Jane writes to her sister Mary in Edinburgh:

Jan 26th 1896

But I suppose you know by this time that last Wednesday afternoon,
at about 3.o'clock, we were nearly blown to atoms. The dynamite explosion
took place at a point on the railway about half a mile from our house. Just

imagine 50 tons of dynamite went off in <u>one</u> moment! Doubtless you will
read accounts of the disaster, but it will interest you to hear what our personal
experiences were. At the time Frans was in the office of the Sanitary Board
attending a meeting–Gertie, Agnes, and Claude were in school opposite our
house and Helen (the servant) Jessie and I were in this house, each of us in
separate rooms. When I heard the low rattle before the explosion took place–I
at once said–dynamite! But before I could get out of the room the whole house
was fearfully shaken–every window with the exception of two (which were
open) was smashed to atoms. The heavy front door was sent flying on to the
wall opposite (quite out) one of the drawing room windows, frame and all,
was thrown into the middle of the room–the door of Frans Consulting room
was blown into the middle of that room. Every ceiling was torn up and the
beams of the roof cracked and broken, as if they had been matchwood; only
in the kitchen, where Helen was at the time, did one of the ceiling boards come
right down at the time–the other ceilings, though torn, remained in position.
Yet we did not get one scratch! Is not it wonderful!

Poor little Jessie was dreadfully frightened, being alone in the room at
the time. As soon as I found out that Jessie was uninjured, I folded up the
half of the counterpane on our bed and replaced her on it–the only spot in
the room that was not strewn with broken glass–called to Helen to remain
with her and then flew over to the school to find my other three bairns. I
was half undressed and without shoes, but that mattered not. Even before I
thought of Jessie and myself, I thought of the school building, which is not a
strong building at best. You may imagine how relieved I was to find that it
had not given way altogether and to see Aggie amongst some other children
at the door looking wildly about. I could not find Claude and Gertie at once
and you may imagine my feelings. Oh, where are my children? I asked of
everyone I could see–very soon they appeared looking quite unconcerned;
Claude in a great state of mind because he had lost his new hat. As soon
as I had all the children safe, I felt quite calm and thankful and it was only

when people came rushing for the Doctor that we began to realize what
a terrible loss of life there was. As I said, Frans was away in town and it
seemed ages before he arrived, though it cannot have been much more than
a quarter of an hour. (His horse, which he had fastened outside where he
was, had run away and broken her bridle–fortunately a boy caught her and
brought her back.) In the meantime I had heard <u>many</u> sad tales of fathers,
mothers, brothers, sisters and children–all dead or dying. One poor man
and woman, just opposite, were bewailing the loss of two children–they had
come from that part of the town just beside where the explosion took place.
It was <u>awful, awful</u> and none of us will forget it to our dying day. Blinds
and curtains, rods and curtain poles were lying in different corners of my
rooms. Our dressing table was smashed and all my jewellery lying about
the floor. Dishes, ornaments, a chair and several other things broken. The
walls and even ceilings and furniture were sticking with broken glass, but the
most wonderful thing of all is that we were unhurt. How Jessie escaped is a
marvel for she was in one of the worst positions in the house at the time–
only a few feet from where the front door fell and all around where she
stood the glass was lying thick and sticking into the walls. Helen and I were
both in less exposed places. As you may imagine my furniture is looking
scratched and badly damaged. The sideboard and press door were forced
open, picture glass smashed etc, etc.

Many houses in our area are much more damaged, and a little
nearer to the place of the explosion the houses are almost level with the
ground–this is where most lives were lost. After the explosion pieces of bodies
were picked up–some at great distances. Also huge, heavy pieces of iron were
thrown out even further than where we are. A piece of iron, about two inches
long, came through the roof of an outhouse next door at the Brown's. The
Brown's house is more wrecked that ours was and they are all staying with
us till their place is put right. Fortunately with us the walls stood the shock
very well and already the woodwork etc is nearly repaired. We were fortunate
in getting a band of clever Swedish carpenters and they soon had the roof off

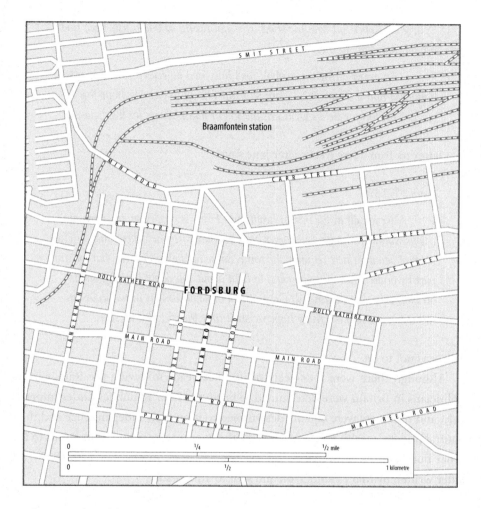

The map of Fordsburg shows the proximity of Lilian Road, where the Marais family lived, to the Braamfontein station where the explosion took place.

and on again–one night we slept without a roof over our heads! Fortunately there was no rain. A great deal is being done for the poor sufferers and the homeless–they are being well cared for and we are all <u>in hopes</u> that we will get compensation. My nice house is in an awful condition, but it might have been worse. Poor Mrs Brown–I am sorry for her– but she is very brave.

Where Dr Robertson lives the shock was not nearly so badly felt. They had no damage done to their house.

You must excuse this scribble for I have had little sleep since this affair happened and it is now 12.30 am so I must be off to bed. We hope this is our last misfortune here. Our hearts are full of thankfulness for lives spared.

In a letter to Tom a few weeks later Jane says:

April 5th 1896

We are all in the best of health and Frans is very busy just now–He enjoys wonderful health & is never happier than when he is kept busy – The political situation here remains the same. Some are talking of war–but for my part I wonder what they are going to fight about. No doubt there are faults on both sides, but the English Government or Chamberlain in particular are rather too exacting – I really hope we shall hear the end of it all soon.

This was not to be.

Although there were four years of unquiet peace following the Raid, certain politicians in Britain were determined to bring the Boer Republics under imperial rule, and the Boers were equally determined to keep their independence and their natural mineral wealth for themselves. Both governments issued ultimatums to the other but when these were ignored war was declared on October 11th 1899 [16]. A letter written by Mary Henderson and sent to Tom reads:

I am sending you extracts from a letter written by Mr McNeil to his sister in Edin: It was he who went from Johannesburg with Franz, although in sympathy with the British – but he thought he would be better helping the Boer wounded, rather than doing nothing. Well after this letter was written Franz was sent to Pietermaritzburg with the wounded & thence to Cape Town & now he will probably be back at Johannesburg working in the hospital there, but next week, I hope to send you a letter we received from him on

Sat, but I had not time to copy it & it has not returned from Andrew G. & Mary B. yet. He had seen some people from Johannesburg, & they reported everything to be quiet & he had no apprehensions about anything serious happening to Jane & the children. – but poor girl – she would have many anxious thoughts about her husband. What a terrible sacrifice of precious lives this war is causing & it seems far from coming to an end – the wonder to me always is, that anyone escapes out of these dreadful battles <u>unwounded</u> with bullets whizzing around them on all sides – Would that it were at an end! How many sad, sad hearts & homes there will be this Xmas.

Elandslaagte [17] was one of the early battles of the war. It was a small village on the railway line between Ladysmith and Dundee in Natal. Both towns were being defended by the British but the Boer troops had attacked the line and cut the telegraph wires. A young medical assistant and friend of the family in South Africa, Andrew McNeil, wrote this account to his sister, who was a friend of the Hendersons, in Edinburgh:

> *Next morning we reached Elandslaagte Railway Station, and saw the train that had been captured from the British by the Fordsburg's men under Pienaar the Veldcornet. I photographed these men beside the engine & many of these men came to me to ask that in case they were killed, a photo be sent to their wives, & sad to relate the next day some of these same men were killed. There was a concert that night at which the English captives entertained their captors & a merry night they spent together – our good friend Veldcornet Pienaar remarking – 'What a strange thing war is, that we should be singing together – Englishmen and Dutchmen'.*
>
> *Our ambulance wagons were situated alongside the railway goods shed and I pointed out to Dr Marais, 'If the English mean to re-take the captured train, we shall be in a very tight place.' The Dr. said 'Oh, we are all right, for we are simply going on at once to Ladysmith & there is no danger!' An order came from the Commandant Viljoen that we were to rejoin the main Boer camp at the Elandslaagte Ridge, but the doctor was tired of trekking & so we remained*

beside the railway shed. I was up at 6.30 on Saturday morning (the 21st) & a wretched morning it was, with a fine steady rain and no wind. There was a heavy mist all over the hills. Breakfast was late and I was still finishing in the wagon when someone remarked – 'How is it all our men are coming back?' & again – 'They are coming quick too.' I stood up on the wagon looking over the tent and saw the Boers galloping past us – all retreating to the Elandslaagte Ridge. Somebody remarked – 'I believe they are the British.' The Doctor said laughingly 'Ha! They are not such fools to come in such small numbers.'

The mist was lifting now & I could see a body of some 50 to 60 mounted men, on the ridge the Boers were retreating from – Two lines of horse swept round in a semi-circle to left & a third to the right & at once I became suspicious. Presently there was a flash & a white puff of smoke. I shouted to the Doctor – exultingly – 'Ha! They <u>are</u> the English.' With these words I fell into the wagon stunned by the concussion & feeling scorched about the face by the shell passing as it did about two feet over my head. I measured the distance afterwards and photo'd it too. Here is a sort of explanatory sketch:

The shell went thro' the goods' shed – into a railway truck & exploded with a terrific bang. Well I remember being a bit dazed & feeling my head first to make sure that that ornament had not been chipped in any way. I jumped to the ground, ran round the corner of the shed & lay behind the embankment on which the shed is built. Dr Marais was running to a place

where there was a pile of railway metal, but I yelled to him to come back,
which he did just before shell number two came roaring along. Five altogether
fell amongst our wagons or within 10 or 15 yds of them, so we had the
honour of receiving the first shots of that eventful day.

Then the Boers started to reply & the British restored all the attention
on them – it was the Natal Field Artillery who fired on us – we watched the
effects of the shooting on both sides, for the shells went careering high over our
heads, for we were in the direct line of fire and we could see the course of every
shot as it went thro' the air. Some seemed to travel very slowly, but horribly
accurately on both sides. This artillery duel did not last long, for it was only a
scouting party of the British to locate the Boer position. Some of the Imperial
Light Horse rode up to the station, but did not come to see what damage had
been done to us, altho' regret was afterwards expressed that the Red Cross flag
had been fired on unwittingly. Our flags were dripping with rain & there was
no wind. Perhaps this rough sketch will help you.

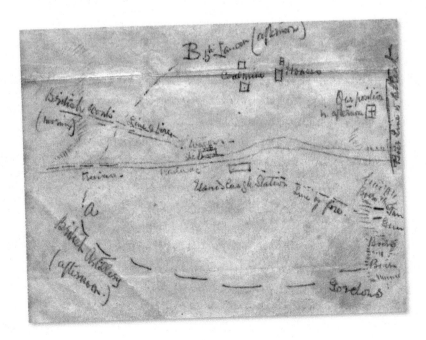

We moved our wagons to a deserted coolie store which we transformed into a temporary hospital. This store built of wood & galvanized iron, was situated on the hill to the right of the Boer position by General Kock's orders & just about a mile distant. Fighting started once more – about 2.30 by the Doctor's watch, I could see the black smoke of 4 or 5 trains – The artillery fire was awful. Shells burst on all sides of the Boers, right amongst their wagons & tents, as we could see beautifully. Sometimes three shells would explode at a time, which made me shiver. One pretty sight I saw – the Lancers, I fancy they were, crossed the open Veld from A to B (see map) & when the Boer artillery fired, off they galloped for a few yards & then at once resumed a steady trot, until the next puff of smoke warned them of what was coming. One shell went right amongst them but no horse or rider was left behind, I was glad to notice. Rain came down heavily for half an hour and under the mist which blotted out our view, the British drew nearer and general rifle firing began. It was a terrific fusillade & it lasted until dark when the British charged the hills. I shall never forget the clear ring of a bugle, which was followed by wild cheering of our men as they charged the slopes. The Boers retreated right past our tin shanty to be caught some 200 to 300 yards further on by the Lancers, who shot some & captured many. At this time we again got into danger whether from Boers or British we cannot tell, although I think the Boers – for some of them shouted out, in Dutch of course, 'You mustn't shoot. You musn't shoot.' While dressing some of the wounded, 3 bullets went thro' our tin shanty & when I went out to see what was happening, another whistled past. Then didn't the rain come down and what a night of horror followed.

Next morning at 5.30 I went over to the battlefield – Dr Costers' body lay slightly on his side &, brave man, well to the front. I picked up a Boer with _four_ shots thro' him, wandering about in the rain & led him to the wagons. All the British wounded had long ago been picked up, but the dead were left just where they fell – Such is the glory of war. Boers killed and buried the day following – 57 – and British – 41 & some have died since. The British retired to Ladysmith, & the Free State Boers again occupied these hills seven *miles nearer Ladysmith. General Kock, who was wounded & taken there, sent a message thro' the Boer lines that we were to attend the wounded, so an escort came on Monday night to travel next day with us.*

Next morning British & Boer forces were hammering away at each other, so we waited until 12 noon when firing had eased. We met a party of 35 Imperial Light Horse who were scouting. An hour later and when I was walking along the road, a stampede of Lancers took place down one of the openings from the hills & rifle shots came whistling all about me – I plunged to the ground right in front of me. Our wagon cleared but I jumped into a military wagon with 6 English soldiers on it but it too was going at the gallop & I had great difficulty in getting in to it. We had 20 minutes under fire here – this was passing … … anyone … … will find in the paper I am sending …

(The paper is fragile, damaged and illegible in places.)

Frans Marais sent a letter of his own involvement in this battle to Mary in Edinburgh. As husband and wife had no idea where the other was the whole situation must have been chaotic.

November 15th 1899

You will be surprised to hear from me from Cape Town. To be short I will give you a short account of my wanderings since 29th September '99, when Drs Shaw, Visser, Gritzke, and myself with several dressers joined the Johannesburg commando as the St John's Ambulance of Johannesburg. Everything went swimmingly till the battle of Elandslaagte, where our commando met a reverse and was cut up. The ambulance was left alone to attend to the wounded etc. The day after the battle the Imperial Authorities removed the wounded to Ladysmith as prisoners, so we were left alone altogether. On Monday we helped to bury the dead. Tuesday, we went to Ladysmith at the request of General Kock to attend to the Boer wounded there. When they (the wounded) were fit to travel, we went with them to Pietermaritzburg at the request of the Imperial Authorities. There we stayed with them for a week, and then left for Cape Town via Durban. Here we arrived Sunday evening the 12th inst. We have about 86 wounded. At present Dr Shaw and myself and 5 dressers are with them. Other Doctors etc. were left behind. We managed to get permission to go with the flying column, hence our position now. The flying column was too few and so got beaten. Now for the truth about Elandslaagte. There were only 900 Boers ! 150 never fought, because of their position, 200 scooted. Hence there were only about 550 fighting. The Boers had two small Nordenfelts. The English had sixteen guns, and numbered 5000 men. The Gordon Highlanders charged them from the centre, the Gloucesters from one side etc, etc. The Boers lost 57 killed and 110 wounded and 188 prisoners. The Gordons alone lost 150 killed, including 11 officers. The total English lost was at least 400 killed and wounded. The Gordons told us that Dargai was simply nothing compared to this charge. It was amusing to see the wounded of both sides chatting quite friendly together. Yesterday eight of the worst wounded were taken to the Military Hospital at Wynberg and we are to stay in the Bay until further orders.

The last I heard from Jane was a letter dated 21 Oct – i.e, more than a month ago. The last opportunity I had to let her know my whereabouts was Pietermaritzburg, when I sent her a cable via Laurenco Marques. I also wrote from there. Now she has no idea where I am. If I had known at Pietermaritzburg (when the communication was still open) I was to come here, I would have got her to come here also via Laurenco Marques. But Johannesburg is perfectly safe. Should the English win, they will go for Pretoria. If the Boers win, they won't bother about Johannesburg either. Some think that the Boers might wreck Johannesburg out of spite if they lose, but that is an absolute libel. They might try to damage some of the mines of the Chief Agitators, but even that I will undertake to say, they won't. As regards protection to life and prosperity, there are hundreds of volunteers.

We had a terrific passage from Durban. Friday night at about 1 am, there was a very heavy S.W. gale and the steering chain snapped. For half an hour we were at the mercy of the waves, and it is a wonder we are here to tell the tale.

At Elandslaagte we had two narrow escapes. The English set the ball rolling by sending five shells amongst the ambulance. Our flags were up and there was no wind so they could not be seen. One shell passed just over our heads, by a few inches. Mr McNeil had the closest shave. We had a good hiding place however and were quite safe after the first two shells. In the evening when we were busy dressing the wounded, bullets were flying amongst us. Dr Shaw got one just between his face and the face of the patient he was dressing.

Most of the bullet wounds are very genteel. If the bullets don't strike the heart or some other vital organ, they are very harmless. I have some cases with three bullets thro' the lungs and quite happy. One man has a bullet still in his right lung and does not feel any the worse for it. In a few cases (Dum Dums?) the entrance wounds are small and the exit wounds are terrible. The shell wounds are not so merciful. General Kock got one in his left hip, smashing the head of the femur, also one in the shoulder. He has died since, as perhaps you know.

The wounded are prisoners; but we, of course, are free and if I liked could leave the ship at once. But if I do, I will have to 'find' myself and now the English Government keeps me in a fairly big steamer. I have a first class cabin for three all to myself, with a bathroom etc off it. Being senior Doctor, I have the full control of the medical department, so have no reason to complain. Besides we are still in the service of the S.A.R. and get £3-3s a day winning or losing. So all things considered, I am well off. If I could only get Jane and the children in Cape Town, I would be perfectly happy.

When we left Ladysmith, Mr McNeil chose to stay there. Dr Currie was there and that is the reason why he decided to stay. Wrote to him from Pietermaritzburg but have not heard of him since we parted at Ladysmith.

Perhaps you would like to hear my sentiments with regard to this war. As an ambulance man I am perfectly neutral. As a private individual I am fully resigned to whatever happens, knowing that things don't happen by chance, but are directed from on high. If it is God's Will that the Boers should win, I am satisfied. If the reverse. ditto. I can get on with Boers and British alike. Nationality does not trouble me.

How happy would I be if I could send this news to Jane as well! But all communication is cut off for the present. 'All things must work together for the good of those who believe'. All will be well in the end.

The last of Jane's letters in the collection was written to Mary in Edinburgh from her Fordsburg home:

November 19th 1899

There is a possibility of this getting to Scotland by a German Steamer, which leaves Delagoa Bay in a day or two. <u>When</u> you may get it is another matter, but anyway it may ease your mind to hear a few lines from me.

We are all very well <u>here</u>, how Frans is I am sorry to say I do not know – still, have no reason to feel anxious as when I heard from him last, he had arrived safely in Maritzburg in charge of about 80 of our Boer wounded who had unfortunately been captured at the <u>only</u> defeat which we have sustained so far – I heard of his being in M.burg by wire from himself via Delagoa Bay and this wire took nearly a week to reach me. When I went to the office to reply I found that all communication between us, and the lower portion of Natal, had been stopped. I have only got to wait with as much resignation as I can command – The Lord is very near to our sorely tried people at this time & we cannot but feel His presence every day.

In Johannesburg we are quite safe and comfortable – our only anxiety is for our dear ones who are defending their community – Claude still goes to school, but I keep the girls at home as their school has closed

& they are a great use to me in the house– My servant left, as I told you, and we have only a coloured boy to do the rough work – The town is being well looked after and we have no need to be uneasy – I dare not enter into political matters or you might not get this letter– but when it is all over and if we are spared, you shall hear <u>the truth</u>.

Give my love to Tom & John & Andrew & Marion when you write – please for I don't think there is much use of my trying to get letters through to them. My love also to Aunt Jessie & Mary and to all friends. I am sure you are often thinking of us at this terrible time. Do you know that if I were only a man, nothing would keep me from fighting along with the Boers, for Justice and Freedom! – God bless you all & with much love to you & Andrew & the children.

This one from Frans to Mary was also written on November 19th:

International Hotel, Cape Town

I missed the chance last week of posting this note. Have landed yesterday. Am for the present located at the above hotel. From tomorrow I am to attend my old charges again. They have been located in a new building at the Convict Station. War news scarce here. Thousands of troops are daily going up & so I hope that it will soon be decided one way or another.

20.11.99 Some Wellington friends came to see me today & brought me your letter from there, the one C/o Mr Whitton. At the end of this week I expect news from Johsbg. An attaché from the French Consul is coming this way & so I will get a chance to let Jane know my whereabouts. If I am detained here I will try to get her through with the kids via Delagoa Bay. I met somebody from Johsbg today who told me that Johsbg is perfectly safe. So I need not worry about my dear ones unnecessarily. He left there on the 18th of Oct.

Love to all,

F.P.M

> *Wed 22ⁿᵈ My last orders are that we must return to the Frontier via Delagoa Bay, as soon as there is a Steamer ready. I will go to Johsbg & stay in the Hospital there & be with my family. F.P.M.*

It is not at all clear from the letters how the situation was resolved and exactly when the Marais family was finally reunited; neither is it easy to make out for whom Frans was working (he held British citizenship presumably from the time of his medical studies). The war did not finish until 1902 but the Marais family visited the U.K. in 1901 so Frans must have been able to clear himself of any further official medical duties in order to be free to travel. The presumption is that Frans resumed his practice in Fordsburg after the war and that the family returned to their former way of life.

Frans Marais' medical practice had always had a fair proportion of so-called 'Coloured' and ethnic Indians amongst its patients. In 1904 bubonic plague broke out in the Indian settlement in Johannesburg and it was from this quarter that it seems likely that Frans Marais contracted the disease in which, in his case, the same bacteria affected the lungs and became pneumonic [18] plague which is even more deadly than other forms of the disease. The devastating tragedy that affected this family had often been mentioned in my childhood but I had never been told any details. Frans contracted the disease and died on March 17th, his wife Jane died on March 21st, the eldest daughter Gertie on 22nd and Claude and Agnes on the 24th. It was only Jessie the youngest daughter, then aged 11, who escaped the highly contagious disease.

I once met Jessie when my uncle Howard Gillison took me to see her in a Nottingham nursing home sometime before she died but I had never met any of her family. When the project of transcribing the family letters started I was determined to discover my many unknown cousins and find out more about this particular tragedy. I knew Jessie had married Jack Hoyland, a prominent Quaker and former missionary in India, and so, with the help of the librarian at the headquarters of the Society of Friends in London, I was able to trace Rachel Gilliatt, Jessie's daughter. A subsequent visit to meet her and, through her, other previously unknown cousins has afforded me much pleasure.

The following account of the events of March 1904 was given to me by Rachel Gilliatt and is her mother Jessie's own account of that terrible week which Rachel encouraged her mother to record when she was quite an old lady.

Pneumonic Plague was carried by a kiss – by direct contact. I came home into the living room, to find Daddy lying on a couch, a most unusual sight, and Mother said to me 'Tell Daddy to go to his bed.' It was unusual but I had no idea what this meant. Daddy had caught the deadly germ from the Indians he was doctoring. It is the last moment of his life that I remember most vividly. I was in my bed when Agnes, my sister called me. She said, 'When people are dying they like to see their family around them.' As I went and stood at the end of the bed, he looked at me and said, 'Poor little Jessie.' These were his last words. He had seen enough of the plague to know that we were almost certain to get the deadly disease. All of us. (After my Father's funeral, two dear Indian women brought Mother a little bunch of flowers. When I got to know Indian women years later, I realised this was just the sweet way they had of saying 'thank you' for my Father's work amongst them.).

In a short time a tented encampment had been started outside Johannesburg. I saw a coffin in Mother's room so I knew Mother had died. My bed was used for Dad, so I slept on the drawing room floor. My two sisters and brother were all in bed. I was up, Claude called me, 'I want Mother.' With childish honesty I said 'Mother is dead.'

A nurse was packing clothes for Agnes and Gertie. I ran around the town to a friend of Mother, but she shut the door in my face. I ran to the big shop where Mother did her shopping but they took no notice when I said, 'Mother is dead.' Gertie asked me to read to her, then she said to the nurse 'You don't need to pack my clothes.' She died at home. Agnes and Claude were taken in an ambulance to the new encampment. I went in a horse drawn carriage with the nurses. When we got there the nurses were larking about in a large tent. So I escaped and went to look for Agnes and Claude. I found them, Claude was unconscious. Agnes was awake and I ran to her, she slipped two bangles off her hand and gave them to me. Immediately a nurse came and took me away. I was put in a small tent by myself. Some kind soul gave me a doll and a puppy dog that slept on the foot of my bed for one night; next day he was shot. I was told that a great friend of the family Mr MacNeil had died. I was alive and had no fear of dying. I drew a cemetery in the dust divided into sections for graves. Then I killed large black ants and buried them in graves in my cemetery. I was bewildered.

It was not long before I was rescued. My Father's brother, Oom Pieter, and his daughter came for me, and took me back to their huge fruit farm, Blou Vlei, near Wellington, our first home. You can't imagine how I loved this. My Father's brother looked a little like my beloved Dad, and his wife, Auntie Grietta, was a precious, darling Mother to me. Anna was about my age, and there were three boys, Charlie, a little older, thirteen or fourteen, Andre eleven, and Pierre about four.

The beauty of these farms beggars description with the great mountain range towering behind us. (The Drakenstein Mountains.) After the last of the plums were picked, we all went up the mountain with tents, and camped out beside the river that flowed down past the farm. (The Berg River.) We used to swing on creepers, like ropes, and plunge down into the river. This farm life was the happiest I was to experience for the rest of my long life.

Rachel heard this story from her mother over and over again and Jessie was always convinced that her reluctance to kiss her father goodbye had saved her life, although she was very much a 'Daddy's girl'. Not surprisingly throughout her life Jessie was very wary of kissing – even within the family. After her mother's death in 1978 Rachel corresponded for some time with one of the South African cousins, Pierre, who commented on Jessie's beauty. Jessie was able to pay her way from her father's estate which had been left in trust to her. By the time Jessie was seventeen some problems arose and Jessie felt that her uncle's affection for her was becoming hard to handle and there were also some financial difficulties concerning Jessie's money. On the advice of Mrs Hartley, a friend of her mother who lived in Cape Town she went to live with her mother's sister Mary Agnes Henderson and her family in Edinburgh in 1909.

It must have been a tremendous contrast for Jessie to exchange the wonderful open-air life in South Africa for the harsher climate of Scotland but in each home she was loved and made to feel part of the family. Jessie eventually trained as a teacher at Bedford College and later became a missionary being appointed to India where she met and married Jack Hoyland, a deeply respected Quaker, on 23 March 1921. Jack Hoyland was commemorated as a figure wielding a pick axe in a 'Work camp' panel F15 of the famous Quaker tapestry. It was created between 1981 and 1989 to celebrated 350 years of Quaker life and Quaker history to be found on perpetual exhibition at the Old Meeting House, Kendal.

Rachel also persuaded her mother to write down an account of the family's visit to her old homeland in 1901:

> *Two things I value are my bracelet in memory of my sister, who*
> *slipped her bangles off her hand as she was dying. Nurse only allowed me*
> *a minute as I ran round the tents looking for her and Claude when they*
> *took us away to the encampment out of the town. She did not speak; Claude*
> *was already unconscious. That was the last I saw of them. Those bangles she*
> *handed me I had always admired because they were larger than mine!*
>
> *We bought them in London when our whole family came from*
> *Johannesburg at the end of the Boer War. I remember saying 'I am not going*
> *unless Daddy comes too.' Great joy when he bought tickets for himself too.*
> *Agnes and I also each bought a large doll. Later when I was taken back to our*
> *plague stricken house it had been fumigated out of all recognition, but they let*

Page from the passenger list of the SS Briton outward bound from London to Cape Town September 14th 1901. The Marais family recorded near the base of the page.

me have my doll, turned her upside down and sprayed her all over. I kept her until I went to Scotland.

> *The precious bangles became too small for me and were left in a trunk in India. Dad and I expected to return but his ill health prevented that. This ornate bangle is a constant reminder of that very moving and awful day. I know you admire it – wear it in memory of me and the tragedy of my early life and my sweet sister.*

The family were buried in the Braamfontein cemetery just the other side of the road which runs north of the station (see map). It was said that Andrew McNeil, the young man who had written the account of the battle of Elandslaagte and was in love with Gerty, had also died of the plague and was buried in the same grave as Gerty.

Jessie made her home with her cousins in Scotland and she remained a great favourite of the Gillisons. She was frequently mentioned in their letters and they did their best to keep in touch with her as much as possible and were always concerned about her welfare.

The Gillison family in 1910.
Thomas, Bessie holding Gordon (18 months) Walford (15)
Keith (10), Jean (9), Howard (6).

NINE

The next generation

The letters are sparse between 1900 and 1905 – only eight in the first five years and none for 1903 or 1904 – so there is no indication of how the news of these tragic events in South Africa was conveyed to Tom and Bessie in China. During that time Tom and Bessie had had their own difficulties to contend with including the political turmoil of the Boxer riots. There was joy in the birth of three more children but sadness in the death of little Evelyn. From sources other than the letters it is clear that Tom and Bessie spent nine years in the field after their furlough of 1895–6 and so by 1905, a year after the deaths of the Marais family, a break was overdue. Bessie, now with four children in tow, wrote this letter to Tom from on board the S.S. Oceana on her way home:

March 27th 1905

> *I am actually beginning my Aden letter two days before we expect to reach there – & I am writing on deck – Howard is asleep & K & J are looking at books in the hammock. Since leaving Colombo, the weather has been cooler. We have had a lovely breeze & calm sea & we are all well & getting on nicely on this boat – At first we found one or two things awkward but we have managed to get over all difficulties.*
>
> *Howard is splendid & he actually goes without a midnight feed now. Last night I gave him a bottle at 9 P.M. & he slept till 6 A.M. & what do you think we saw in our cabin when we woke a dead flying fish on the floor it must have flown in in the night & we did not hear it. Of course Keith was very excited he could not believe it was dead – he thought if we put it in water*

it would swim. He took it on deck to show other boys but before breakfast, the deck steward took it away from him.

Mrs Mitchell is not very well she has a little fever & headache every day. I am glad to say that since she came into our cabin, the nights have been almost undisturbed and at 6 o'c I am sometimes able to get a bath because she is in the cabin, so it is nice for me and she says she likes being with us better than having the companions she had before. I do a little washing every day – on both steamers the stewardesses have been very good & have let me have a place to dry a few things. I do realise I have been greatly helped all the way along & shall be right thro' – I have been advised to land at Plymouth & I believe it will be best … .

On the terrace of 'South Place' during their 1905 furlough.
Tom, Keith about 5, Walford (10), Howard (18 months), Bessie and Jean (4).

It is assumed that Tom could only leave when it was convenient for the hospital and the Mission but because Walford was to be entered as a pupil at George Watson's College in Edinburgh, it was necessary for Bessie to return to Scotland to settle him in before the beginning of the September term. Andrew and Mary Henderson were to be his guardians after Tom and Bessie's return to China in December 1906. Unfortunately Bessie just missed seeing Tom's youngest brother Andrew who had accepted a call to become minister at St. Paul's Presbyterian Church in Brisbane, Australia as he with his wife and family had left the country shortly before Bessie and her children landed.

Keith (about 7yrs) and Jean (6) In fancy dress.

The period of leave was filled with the usual commitments of deputation for Tom up and down the country. Time was also spent at 'South Place' in Calne with Bessie's parents and sister.

The family returned to Hankow, without Walford, in December 1906. They must have experienced the usual heartbreak at parting from their eldest son but that does not show in their letters. In April 1907 to Tom's cousin Mary Black Bessie says, 'We are getting Walford's letters regularly – a great satisfaction to us – I hope you get news, good news of Jessie Marais'. Jessie would still have been in South Africa at the time and this reference confirms how much concern there was for the young orphan – bracketing their son and their niece all in one sentence.

For the first four years after they returned to Hankow the two elder children, Keith and Jean, were educated by one of the missionary wives on the compound; after that in 1911 the two of them were sent to the China Inland Mission school in Chefoo as boarders for two years – a journey of a week from Hankow. Bessie gave birth to her last child – a son, Gordon, in January 1909 at the age of 41 and even with plenty of domestic help she clearly found child care hard going physically. She wrote to Mary Black:

> *Thank you so much for the pretty little pinafore that has come for my new little son. It was most kind of you to send it. (Please don't trouble about the books you meant to send the other children – I know your kind intention – but it is often very difficult to buy presents and I don't want you to trouble till next Xmas). I let Jean open the little parcel – she does love to see anything that comes for baby – She goes into ecstasies over sweet little baby things – Of course she could hardly contain herself for joy when she first saw baby – She wanted to hug everyone, & now she loves to nurse the wee man but she finds him make her arms ache already.*
>
> *I am very thankful that we all are well – I feel the strain rather of the disturbed nights, but I try to go to bed very early and when I do that I keep nicely well – Tom too is well tho' the strain of his work is great. It is a great blessing he*

can always keep cheery – It is a great joy to him that the Medical School has now become a 'Union School'. I must send you his report – The Medical School is his baby. It is just beginning to get out-of-arms now, but needs much care & help yet.

It had been decided that in 1910 Walford would come out to China and spend his summer holiday with his family. This was to turn out to be an inspired idea and was probably only possible because of Harris money – the cost would have been beyond the pocket of the ordinary missionary. Bessie writes to Mary Black:

March 24th 1910

Just now Howard & Jean have mild whooping cough – This is of course rather trying, for tho' the children are not ill with it, I have to keep them from school & from other children. They were rather poorly last week when it was beginning – but now they seem very bright except in the fits of coughing occasionally. Baby Gordon is well so far – We hope to have a clean bill of health when Walford comes. Is it not good that Mary has heard of such a suitable escort for him? Of course there is no small measure of excitement among us here at the prospect of having him to spend the summer with us –

This is the only letter dated 1910 and there is no indication of where the family spent most of their time on that holiday but, judging by the stream in the background of the photograph, it could well have been Kuling.

There are a number of letters from Walford in 1911 and 1912 in which he told his parents about his life at George Watson's College. As the College was only a day school he boarded with a Mr and Mrs Allan of St Oswald's Road with a number of other boys in a similar situation.

Walford wrote:

27th March 1911

Well! I am writing on Monday this week because yesterday morning I had to go off early to Aunt Mary's for Communion Sunday at the

This charming photograph of Walford, with Howard and Gordon on his back and Jean standing behind, was probably taken in Kuling in the summer of 1910.

Barclay Church, though Mayfield only has it next Sunday. Last Wednesday night at 8.30 P.M. I paid Mr Sangster Anderson a visit at the Manse. He wanted to see each one of us, so as to know us personally. Then on Friday we were received into the church. Yesterday we had a lovely sermon from Mr Anderson on 'Except a corn of wheat fall' , etc & afterwards a very nice communion service, I am very very glad that I have at last joined, I am sure it has & will do me a lot of good. The service in the evening was conducted by a Mr Elder the new minister in the Stockbridge Church. After the service I went to a meeting really meant for Students & such like, its purpose was to get some of the fellows to form Study Circles for discussing the real situation with regard to Home & Foreign Missions & also the Social Questions. It was addressed by a Mr Stewart whose Father knows Father so well. He spoke very well, I would like to join but I feel that the others would only feel me as a sort of burden, because they are so much older than I am. The thanksgiving service is to be held on Wednesday night at 7.30 p.m. I intend to be present at it.

Please excuse the scrawliness of my writing but I feel I have no time to waste nowadays. I have taken a few more photos lately but I have no had time to develop them yet. Last Monday I went in for a football kicking competition; I kicked two out of three while another two boys kicked all three goals. Another of Mr Allan's boys got the prize; it will be given him on sport's day. Mrs Allan is a good deal better this week & indeed she is downstairs today. Aunt Mary is keeping much the same, pretty well. A tall telephone pole has been placed in the Guest's garden spoiling Aunt Mary's view also one or two houses round who are going to see whether Mr Guest has the right to allow a pole to be put in his garden without the landlord's consent, it is something fearfully ugly.

I am very pleased that you do not totally disapprove of my going to Shakespeare. I would not like to go to any others & I have no inclination to go to any more of those as yet, although I am not sorry I went both for the *education of seeing the plays & also for the knowledge of the theatre as a whole which will help me realise all that is said about & against them, much better than I otherwise would have been able to do. The Cadet Corps will have a Royal review when the King comes to Edinburgh. (By the way King George coins are out now). Then 40% of the C.C. is to go down to Winsor [sic] for a Royal Review & to be down there for about a week, expenses paid; some time after the coronation this will occur. On Saturday at 2 o'clock we assembled in the playground, whence we marched out to the other side of Corstorphine hill where we had a field day. I was the most advanced scout in the company and was situated on a road where I met a nice old man with the best pair of field glasses I have ever seen. He knew the country well & sighted the enemy about a mile away so that I was able to go back & inform my commanders. After a tramp of about 12 miles & running over ploughed fields till we were dead tired, we arrived here, 8 of us, to a supper of Bread & butter, & marmalade with tea; while enjoying this sumptuous (?) repast we were told by the matron that we were being greatly indulged by having marmalade; I forgot to mention that we also had a fairly stale bun. I realise M*r* Allan's great generosity …*

*… ..I have been talking to Uncle Andrew & Aunt Mary as to my best course if as I intend, I am going in for medicine. It is not usual to go in for MA before Medicine, & is quite out of the way. My next year at school would not help me in the slightest bit, it would be far more useful to me to spend the extra year at the end of my course for tropical Medicine, say; Uncle Andrew is going up, tomorrow I think, to M*r* Alison to ask his advice, so I will tell you the result of that next week. Aunt Mary even proposed my leaving at Easter & knocking off some of the preliminary subjects, such as botany & zoology in the summer term, so as to leave me free to start Physics in October. A lot of boys start their medical course at 17 or even before it often. More of that next week.*

I hinted to Grandmama that I intended to go to Switzerland in the summer, & she seemed disappointed that I was not going there. But I wrote

This photograph of Jessie Marais must have been taken about this time.

back to show her that there would still be 3 weeks holiday at the end of the Swiss one which I could spend at Calne with them after. Then also Jessie [19] will have to come back to England a little before the end, for her training at Bedford. She could not come back alone travelling by herself on the continent & so I could come home with her & have even more time at Calne. I don't think Grandmama realises how much education it would be to me. Not the sort you could possibly learn in schools but a far better sort. Getting a broader & fuller view of life; seeing people of other nationalities than your own at home in their familiar surroundings. I am waiting patiently & expectantly for your reply, I have thought it over & over, & am longing to know your decision; I think Aunt Mary is writing to you.

Back in Hankow Tom and Bessie were beginning to think ahead about the education of Keith and Jean. Ultimately they would be sent to school in England but that would not be until Tom and Bessie's next furlough. Bessie again writing to Mary Black said:

> *I was so glad to know you both are fairly well – it is no small mercy that you are spared to each other – we often say so when speaking of Aunt Jessie & her operation. Walford told us how he had seen you. We had a splendid letter from Walford the other day – He is making decisions & developing very nicely – We are interested in what we hear of Jessie Marais – She too is almost grown up – I wish we could see her – I am on the eve of going to Chefoo with the children – I am to stay with them there at a Missionary Boarding House during this term & the summer holidays – and in September I hope to leave them as boarders – It is a rather big separation for Tom & me – He will miss us all greatly but he hopes to join us in August. He is terribly busy – but full of hope that help in the Med. School will come ere long – One or two Societies really seem to be moving a little.*

1911 saw the beginning of the Republican Revolution which ultimately threw out the Manchu Dynasty and led to the abdication of the last Emperor of the Qing dynasty, the child Emperor Puyi on February 12th 1912. The fighting started in Wuchang – just across the river from Hankow. Walford, having read about the uprising in the press, sent this letter to his parents:

October 15th 1911

> *There are long paragraphs in the papers this week about a Republican rising, with the centre at Wuchang, Hankow & Hanyang. I hope & expect it is not nearly so bad as they make out. There is said to be a massacre of 800 Manchus, I hope this is not true, if it is things will be serious, no pardon. Of course my knowledge of Chinese politics is limited but as far as I can*

Walford Gillison

make out it w^d be good for China to have a republic though it might have been better to wait a bit. I will wait & see, leaving all in God's hands.

The following entry is part of a letter sent by Tom to Mary Black of which she made copies by hand in order to send them to various members of the family.

31 October 1911

You will not be surprised to hear that our teaching work is temporarily suspended. Many of the students have left because of the revolutionary trouble, but more have stayed & are helping in the Red Cross work in our hospital. I append a rough map of the situation below

The map may be said to be upside down, but note the directions
in the bottom of the left hand corner. The Imperialists came by rail and a
great fight took place at Railway Station A. They captured it, then fought
their way to Rail. St[n] B. & captured that. They have not yet got Rail. St[n]
C. They have fought three days and a half for the straight boundary road
D. My house is on that road marked O in the British Concession and my
hospital, similarly marked, on the other side of the road further along. These
concessions [20] are neutral and are protected by foreign sailors from men of
war lying in port. The fight has been fierce & hundreds have been killed &
over 1000 wounded have been treated in our mission hospital and elsewhere.
Bullets whistle along our street & we keep the shady side of the street. A shell
fell into the compounds where our medical school is & a barricade to stop
bullets — composed of bags of sesame seed is placed outside my hospital gate

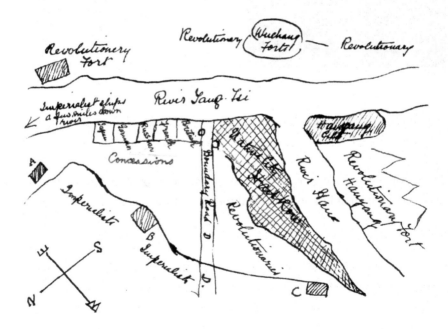

across boundary road. The sharp rattle of the Maxim guns & the crack of the shrapnel – the boom of the canon & the plop, plop of the rifles – are heard at intervals day & night. It has taken the well-trained, well-armed Imperialists with better canon & shrapnel, & with those deadly Maxims over three days to contest this one road & I do not know whether they have got it.

Nov. 1st

Yes, they have got the road now, & are setting fire to this great city of 500,000 inhabitants. It seems devilish. Of course, most of the people have left Hankow, which is almost like a city of the dead. I can see the smoke rising from the burning pile as I write. It will destroy the trade of this place for years to come & will ruin thousands of homes.

I must not stay to write more. We may have to move out our patients into the foreign concession, if the fire spreads our way. In the Wesleyan Mission Hospital they have failed to get to their 150 patients. Will they perish in the flames?

Asking your continued prayers that out of this chaos may become cosmos & glory to Him, who looks on with an infinitely pitying eye.

There are no further letters from Tom about the progress of the Revolution but from Walford's letters over the next few weeks there are glimpses of what was going on. In addition there is an account of the fighting from my father's book, 'The Cross and the Dragon' which, although he was at school in Chefoo at the time, must have been given to him by his parents who witnessed it. He remembers he envied his seven-year-old younger brother Howard, who proudly showed him a bullet he had picked up which had ricocheted off a tree in the garden. My father wrote:

......Before long fierce fighting took place between the revolutionary forces and Imperialist troops sent down by the Peking Government. On

the first day of the fighting our Hankow hospital of 60 beds received 200 wounded. Our large church adjacent to the hospital was turned into a temporary ward to help cope with the situation, and the other Wuhan mission and Red Cross hospitals were filled to overflowing with wounded soldiers and civilians. Many foreigners, chiefly missionaries volunteered for work with the Red Cross, bringing in the wounded, changing dressings and helping generally. 'For days', wrote Father, 'fire and sword, bullet and shell made the back of the Concessions a simple inferno, the sound of rifle and maxim fire was almost incessant'. Many a bullet came whizzing down Sin Sen Road that bordered the compound where Mother and Father and our missionaries lived, a road they had to cross to reach our hospital. They were grateful when a barrier made out of sacks of sesame seeds was built across the road to make the crossing safer. Two bullets came through upstairs windows of our house, one through a bathroom window pane and one through a garment that was hanging in a bedroom wardrobe; several hit some of the big trees in our garden.

By November 1st the Imperial troops had captured the north end of Hankow. Their shelling of the native city started the fires that, fanned by a strong north wind, burnt down about three quarters of that part of the city where about 40,000 of the Chinese population lived. Many had fled but the weak, the aged and the bedridden died in the ravaging sea of fire. One of our chapels, a school and a house that was Griffith John's first house in Hankow were destroyed. There was any amount of looting, and to stop it Imperial troops beheaded looters caught red-handed and hung up the heads and loot as a warning. Those troops also killed any adult male Chinese they found without a queue or pigtail. The queue had stood for loyalty to the Manchu rulers and the revolutionaries cut off their queues. Fortunately foreigners like Father were spared even if they had 'short back and sides'. The fighting waxed and waned around Wuhan for a few weeks but gradually the Revolutionaries were in the ascendant and on December 24th 1911 the fugitive Dr Sun Yat Sen arrived in Shanghai and was appointed President by the Revolutionaries.

Walford's regular letters to Tom and Bessie gave them plenty of information about his progress in school and his many interests. Here are a number of excerpts which give a good idea of the young boy:

15th October 1911

> *Thank you very much for your nice letter, I am so sorry you were so very tired. You should really not have troubled to write to me. I hope you are better now. Thank you very much for the sweet little photo, Gordon is very sweet he must be growing very fast indeed. You said that you did not understand my plan for this school year, it is that I take Science & Mathematics chiefly while still keeping up my English, to which subject the Literary Society is a great help, I also get more knowledge of French & German. You also say that you think it was a mistake for me to have dropped my Latin, i.e. changed my course. My subjects before changing were English, Mathematics, German, Latin & History & Geography. When I changed I kept on as before English, Maths & German, the two subjects then which were altered were Latin & History & Geography, the latter I w^d have dropped anyway, I had worked them into a special time table because I needed them for my Higher English, after that came off at Easter I had no more need of them & w^d have dropped them anyway. My Latin also after the Highers were over was not worth keeping up. So on the whole I thought it best to have Science for the last term & I wish I had started at the beginning of the year. You also said that my marks were barely average. That w^d partly be on account of my cut up term by all my Cadet Corps engagements, & partly owing to my taking up Science & French again. Anyway I am very pleased that this year I did get my Science & French rubbed up a bit. I hope my marks this year will be much better & even good in Science & Maths. I have been moved to the higher division in English, & since I am not good at it & also because I am devoting the most part of my time to Science & Maths my abilities in French & German are not very great. I have to read a paper in the Literary Society this next week.*

12th November 1911

Thank you very much for all the news you have sent me, cuttings letters etc. We of course hear all the general turns of the revolution in the papers but we cannot hear much about Hankow on account of the cutting of the telegraphs, so far all is satisfactory though today the papers told of contentions in the revolutionists camp but we cannot tell what is true. Last Tuesday I went out to a tea-meeting at the Augustine Church & I met Dr Somerville for the first time since China. I then heard him give his opinion of the revolution at the public meeting which followed. He has invited me out to his new house at Dalkeith sometime in December to fetch my rug. On Thursday I played in a fierce house-match it ended in a draw 6-6. The Watsonians have not lost a match since Oct.1908, next Saturday may break their record. I have a slightly sad thing to tell you I noticed that I could not always see the writing on the school black-boards nor the bull's-eye when shooting so I got my eyes tested by Dr W.G.Sym & found that I was slightly short-sighted & have to get specs not for constant use but only when I wish to see specially clearly. I will have them on Wednesday. Although I never saw the bull's-eye the other day I made $^{37}/_{60}$ but I expect I will get another shot at it yet when I get my specs (steel ones). We had a fire alarm last Monday, all the bells started suddenly to peel out & everybody proceeded out of the school in an orderly way clearing out in about $2^{1}/_{2}$ minutes everybody taking up a special place in the playground. Though it was a sham, one of the Latin Masters got one of the boys to carry out his huge dictionary. It is about half time in the chess solving tourney & so far I have 33 out of 38 points. Hoping & praying that all are well.

26th November 1911

Thank you ever so much over & over again for your lovely long letters telling all the news about this glorious revolution, at least with, I hope, glorious results. Your letter of the 4th was a lovely long interesting one. What a time *you must have been having! Shells crashing in all directions & poor father with so many wounded to look after. How anxious you must have been about Dr Booth's blind boys & patients. The fire must have been terrible. It seems so poor for me writing only these short letters & getting g^t long ones but then of course you have plenty to write about if you had only the time to write. If I had not got Sunday I would have difficulty each week in finding time. Exams! Exams! Exams! Four days last week & plenty more to look forward to. The only result I can yet give you is 32 out of 50 in an English Exam. I did fairly well in a Magnetism one last week but I have not heard the result yet. In the football line I have very sad news to tell you. The Watsonians received their first defeat in a championship match yesterday since their first match 4 seasons ago i.e. October 1908. They were beaten 3-0 by the Glasgow Academicals. They had very hard lines & should have won easily. All are well at Churchill. It is hard lines on Jean especially that we dare not send Christmas presents yet, her doll is a beauty. School Parliamentary Elections come off next Friday. Parliament is peculiar just now. I was in the chamber of death (i.e. the name all the boys know Mrs Allan's bedroom by) for an hour on Wednesday. It gets its name from the tortures you undergo there usually. It is frosty here now & has been for a week or two. Jessie is enjoying herself very much just now at Bedford. Dr Lewis Davidson has got Neuritis & will not be able to resume his duties till the New Year.*

4th February 1912

I am writing again on a Sunday & another letter came from you last night. I used to get mine on Monday's but they often come on Saturdays now. I was very pleased to hear that the medical school classes were starting again & that more order was being restored. You also told of parties galore. You were also exhorting me not to overwork myself. I will take good care of that though the week before last my <u>average</u> bedtime was 11.30 with the result that I was dead tired last Sunday night & slept nearly all evening. It was my *first absence from evening church for I don't know how long, Switzerland I suppose.*

I have got two more results of 100% in Maths this week bringing my total up to 665 out of 700 or 95% for this session. We have had a very cold week & a good deal of skating this week end, though I have not had any yet because of what you will hear of later. The snow is about two inches deep. I hope we will get a skating holiday next week if the frost holds, which I think it will.

Well! yesterday the Cadet Corps was invited out to Dalmeny to Lord Rosebery's to dinner. It was terribly cold & we were marching about in our kilts in a blizzard but we had a fine dinner, Menu:- Clear Soup, Julienne or Scotch Broth, Fillets of Sole, Roast beef, or round of beef, or Turkey & ham with potatoes & green pea salad, meringues, jellies & cream, Cream shapes, trifle, etc. sugar cakes, biscuits, butter & cheese, oranges, apples, bananas, grapes etc. coffee & cream, rusks, lemonade, soda water, kola, ginger ale, Potass water etc, etc, etc.

After dinner we strolled about the park while the snow was falling fast we then formed up & bade adieu to 'his Lordship' & ran most of the two miles back to Barnton Station.

This week has been a sad one, Grandmama will have told you of Uncle Herbert's death, also our minister Dr Lewis Davidson died yesterday at Cannes while recruiting his health, he took ill 2 months ago. A boy at school's father also died this week. Aunt Emily & Mrs Allan are not so well, & Mr Ligertwood fell & cut his brow when skating yesterday. Now I must close.

11th February 1912

I have to report another 100% this time for Analytical Geometry bringing my total up to 765 out of 800 or 95$^5/_8$%, for the year, my marks this term are 400 out of 400. I did rather worse in an English exam with only 37 out of 70. But of course I am devoting only a small fraction of my energy to English, & similar portions to my French & German, leaving me free for my six Mathematical subjects & my Science ones. This working at two subjects in particular does not mean that I am slacking, for my go-to-bed average was 10.20 last week. Now I must close, much love to all

25th February 1912

   This is the half term week-end but I am not staying at Churchill, as I usually do, because it would crush them a little, they had a friend staying there all week & were not sure whether he would be staying over this week-end or not. It is scarcely worth the trouble moving. I am starting this before breakfast because I have been invited to Aunt Mary's to breakfast & the day. I was not there, as I usually am, yesterday, Saturday & so they asked me to breakfast today. I could not go yesterday because we had a sham fight with the Cadets & I was not in till about half past six. The field day went off well, though it was fairly cold.

   Please excuse the scrawl but I am in a hurry on account of today's pleasant arrangements. I got a nice letter from you last night, but I will continue this later.

   <u>Monday</u> I did not come in till late last night so I was not able to continue this, & today I am going for a walk over the Pentlands & will not likely get another chance today of continuing so please excuse the broken nature of this letter.

   I am not doing so well in Maths just now, I only got an 84 & 80 in a fairly hard exam, I was second, one boy had 88 & 80. In the first case I lost 16 marks in mistaking what was required in a question & 80 was the top mark gained by anyone in the second. I had an algebra exam on Friday but have not heard the result. I did not do well in it. Those other marks were for

Geometry. Uncle Andrew was not very well yesterday & didn't go out, he has a bad cold. Mrs *Allan varies greatly. I am very sorry this is so disjointed. Aunt Mary was pleased to know that you had received notice of her parcel. Hoping all are well.*

It was to be his last letter for in March 1912, with no hint of a warning, Walford fell ill and died of pneumonia very suddenly. It was said that he caught a chill on his walk to the hills exactly three weeks earlier which he mentioned in the previous letter, but whatever the cause, it was an enormous shock to everyone not least his guardians Mary and Andrew Henderson. In a conversation I had with their grand daughter recently I understand they were not told of his illness until after his death and as a result they were deeply upset and felt some responsibility. It must have been a terrible ordeal to telegraph the news to Tom and Bessie. They received many letters of sympathy – amongst them was this from his Headmaster Mr Alison:

*Walford had risen to be one of the 6*th *Classical boys and he was one of the most influential among them. His influence was steadily & strongly on the side of the right. We looked forward to his doing much solid work in the world when he was fully equipped. But he has done lasting work already in the example he has set his classmates of conscientious industry, of kind helpfulness, of Christian manliness. And now when he seemed to be developing more quickly than before, he is taken home.*

And this from his Mathematics master Dr Pinkerton:

It is not often that a school finds as one of its pupils such a boy as Walford. His fine character attracted and secured my admiration from the beginning of our acquaintance about three years ago, and I have never once known him to fail in any of the qualities that are expected from a high minded Christian youth. In consequence he was held in the highest respect by his schoolmates. The demeanour of his classmates today has been a very remarkable testimony to his influence on them. I have never seen anything like it – they are silent because their feelings are beyond expression. His early death is a great loss to the world.

I have often thought of the fine life that was before him. He had great gifts of mind and indeed was the best mathematician in the school. While I recognise that he might some day win great fame, I liked best to think of him as a man who, put anywhere, would follow the path of duty in a plain and simple way and devote his powers to understanding and supplying, as far as he could, the wants of his fellows. And I am sure his courage and sympathy and public spirit would have touched their imagination. It was not to be. His work is over but it was well done and will be in the memory of many of us all our days. I do not write because I can offer you any consolation you do not already possess in the memory of his life. He has spent his later years far from you. His anxiety for you during the recent scenes in Hankow showed that you were always near his heart. To me he was very dear. In the natural course of events he would soon have left my hands but his example will always remain to guide my own steps in the future as it did in the past. Indeed I had learned to lean on him for advice about the class and its work and he took such an interest in everything that it was a daily pleasure to meet him. I shall never forget him

From his English master Mr Ligertwood:

I should like to say how much, along with the other masters and the boys at Watson's I have felt the death of Walford. I took to your boy from the beginning and have watched his career with the greatest interest. He gave promise of being a distinguished student and high hopes were entertained of his future. What was better however was that he had already given himself to Christ and was seeking to serve Him. He sometimes acted as substitute at Grove St. Sunday School for Nita and Simon and I admired

*the gentle earnest way he spoke to the boys. This year I marked a growing
thoughtfulness, uncommon in one so young and felt that here were the
makings of a fine character. With it all there was a singular unconsciousness
of self that was altogether delightful. On looking back one feels that he
was already prepared for the great change. He was buried yesterday in the
Grange, amid tributes of respect and affection seldom witnessed in the case
of a schoolboy & hundreds of old and young gathering round his grave to
testify to their sense of loss in the removal of their companion and friend.*

And from a Mr W Gordon Boxer:

*I know that anything in the nature of a testimonial must be
distressing to you but I feel that you ought to know how highly the boys
thought of Walford. He has lived the thing before the other fellows and
has been unconsciously laying foundations. Especially is this the case in
Glenbourne. I know many of the boys there, and they have told me from
time to time of the 'quiet goodness of Gillison' and these are the fellows,
who generally don't talk much about the deeper things. And his death is in
a peculiarly striking way, speaking to these boys. From what I have heard
already, it has meant something that will last. I pray God that you may be
enabled to give God hearty thanks for what he has done with the quiet life
of Walford and for what, please God, He shall accomplish by his death.*

There is no mention of this terrible family tragedy in any of the personal letters in
the collection but Tom and Bessie must have been so glad and grateful that they
had that wonderful family holiday in 1910.

In the space of two years three of Tom's siblings died. Tom's elder brother John
died in January 1913 but there are no details of where he died; I suspect he had
returned to the U.K because his wife Harriett is mentioned as being in England
in one of Bessie's letters six months after John's death. The two daughters, May
and Effie, never married and made their home together in Knebworth; they both

worked in the offices of The Hong Kong & Shanghai Bank and are said to have done pioneering work to promote the place of women in positions of authority in business. I think I met Effie only once; they were known in the family to be inordinately fond of cats.

Tom also lost his much loved sister Mary in July 1915 of natural causes and his younger brother, Andrew, was tragically killed at Galllipoli in August of the same year. He had made Australia his home and served as minister in the churches of East St Kilda, Melbourne and St Paul's Presbyterian Church, Brisbane

Andrew Henderson, Mary's husband, and their family of four children stayed in Edinburgh. Isobel, Andrew's Gillison's wife, remained in Australia after Andrew's death and brought up their four young children still maintaining close ties with the many relations at home and abroad. Chief among these was Mary Black, their mutual cousin, who became the focus of the family world-wide for news and information. So many of the letters in the collection were written to her that it must have been she to whom we are indebted for helping to keep them all together.

From The Sydney Daily Telegraph 6th March 1916:

Chaplain Captain Andrew Gillison Attached 14th Battalion, Australian Imperial Force – Mentioned in despatches.

On Hill 60 on the 21st August 1915 the intense machine-gun, rifle and shell-fire had set light to the bushes on the ground across which the allied units were attacking. The flames, reaching some of the dead and wounded, ignited their clothing and exploded their bombs and rifle-ammunition, and thus pieces of burning cloth or wood were flung to other ledges, starting more fires ... any attempt to reach, or move upon the exposed slope meant certain death ... On the following morning, while Gillison was waiting to read the burial service over the bodies of some of those who had fallen in this action, he heard someone groaning in the scrub on the ridge. ... Gillison at once called Cpl. Pittendrigh and a man named Wild (of Hinton, NSW) of the 13th Bn. The three crawled forward, reached the wounded man, and had dragged him for about a yard when a Turkish

245

Chaplain Rev. Andrew Gillison

sniper opened fire and severely wounded both Gillison and Pittendrigh. Gillison died the same day' (Cpl Pittendrigh, Clergyman of Lithgow, NSW died of his wounds on 29th August.)

Bessie came home on furlough with the children, ahead of Tom, in December 1913 returning almost two years later in October 1915. Tom also had an extended leave lasting from May 1914 to September 1915. Keith and Howard were sent to Eltham College; Jean to Walthamstow Hall – both boarding schools for the sons and daughters of missionaries. Gordon returned with them to Hankow but would be sent away to Chefoo School in September 1916. Bessie wrote to Mary Black:

Sept 12th 1916

> *I am now on a river steamer returning to Hankow after taking Gordon to Chefoo to school. I have not written to you or to Church Hill for a long time so I must gather up the news.*

> *Thanks very much for your letter of April 25th. You were hoping then to go to Moffat. I hope you & Aunt have passed the summer happily & kept well. I expect you have been saddened again & again by hearing of sad deaths in France. We certainly have out here – There are many Missionaries' sons at the front & we have heard of several being killed or wounded.*

As to ourselves the summer has been very bearable. The heat has not been so trying as it sometimes is & Gordon & I were at Kuling most of the time – Tom did not have much holiday this year, but he has kept well all through – The thought of losing Gordon in September was like a shadow over my enjoyment of Kuling. It has come to the realization now & I do miss my sonny boy very much, he was such a bit of sunshine & affection. I am glad though to have got him into the Chefoo preparatory school. It is I think the very best place for him and we shall look forward to seeing him at the beginning of December. The teachers at Chefoo after his first day in class told me they thought he would get on very nicely with other boys of his own age – He answered quite brightly. One lesson was Grammar & the teacher asked for examples of <u>common</u> nouns, she then proceeded to <u>proper</u> nouns & then to <u>abstract</u> nouns – to get these, she asked for nouns that you could not see, Gordon gave his as 'germs' – then she said that she wanted a noun that you could <u>not even see with the microscope</u> and Gordon said 'Oxygen' – It was fairly smart for a small boy seven years old wasn't it, but he told me that 'it wasn't right either' . He had one or two good cries at the thought of being left behind but at the last was very sweet & brave. There is a big girl in the girls' school who will be coming to Hankow at Xmas & will look after him on the long journey.

We get lovely news of the children, the boys reports are particularly good & dear Jean's is not at all bad – She is making some progress but goes slowly. Their letters from Calne are very bright & jolly & Keith was looking forward to going to camp at Matlock.

On my way up river I made a detour & went to Nanking. I went there once before fourteen years ago. This time I wanted to see some of our Hankow women who are now there. I had a nice time there. I arrived Saturday evening & stayed over Sunday with some American Missionaries who have a large Bible School for Women there – They can take 150 – and they give a five years course – more advanced than ours. We are now sending our young women, if promising & equal to more advanced

*study than we require, to this school. We have now sent five women there
– & they are very happy & thank us very much for giving them this
chance of further education – We often get <u>young</u> women coming to us
& the problem was what was the best we could do for them – This was
our solution. Our school was started originally for women of <u>mature</u> age
suitable for Bible women & we still like such, for they are much needed in
every mission station. I hope to give more time than before to Chinese work
as I have no bairn. I will not begin another sheet but will close – Ever so
much love to Aunt Jessie & yourself.*

A year later she writes to Mary Black:

July 31st 1917

> *Gordon is at Chefoo Preparatory School. I miss him here – this is the
first summer holiday I have had without a child. We get very bright letters
from him. The distance is too great for him to travel here in China summer
heat – He would need an escort to & fro & there is a great risk of getting ill
on the way – It is a week's journey – We get very good letters from the others.
They all seem growing up as we would wish. If the war is over, I want to go
home & see them next summer. God alone knows if it will be possible, oh, this
terrible, terrible war – I sometimes think it will go on till we get Prohibition,
it is as if we are not to see the end of the war till our country has gained <u>that</u>
victory. Oh why do we arrive at it so slowly.*

These last two sentences show Bessie's very strong and rather strange views on the
reasons for the war and the causes of war. She reiterates them later in a letter again
written to Mary Black:

January 28th 1919

> *Your letter is very interesting telling us all about people and conditions
after the war – of course our newspapers have now given us election news &*

other developments. We are thankful that Mr Lloyd George has the confidence of the country & can go ahead. May he do much for England now & may we see Prohibition come in as a crowning Victory. Poor Russia – & poor Germany – it will be long before they are happy I imagine – but the German people do not seem conscious of guilt, neither the leaders nor the masses. We need to pray for our enemies & keep out wrong feelings.

In 1917 the L.M.S. authorities decided to move Tom to the Tsinan Medical School and close the 'Union School' which he had started in Hankow. He and Bessie were to be based there for the next four or five years.

Now I must try & tell you how matters stand about the Medical School & Hospitals. A cablegram came from home saying that the combined committee with the Wesleyans advised, either the closing of the school & uniting with the one in North China, or else buying a new Union site on which to put a Union hospital and medical school to be worked by a larger staff, viz. four men from each Mission. Ultimately this last scheme was decided on because the Wesleyans seemed really keen on it – Resolutions to this effect have now gone to the Home Boards & out here a sub-committee is looking out for a suitable site. We may sell a good part of the site which we had previously bought but it is still wished to put the Women's Hospital and dwelling houses on it. Tom seems pleased & hopeful – I don't know whether D^r Wu is really coming. I have heard nothing of him for a long time. I may hear when I get to Hankow tomorrow, if so I will add a p.s.

You knew we were to have a Deputation out to consult about the Medical School, well, Mr Hawkins has been and he has decreed that the school must be closed – I don't think there really was any hope of getting help from the Wesleyan Soc^{ty} or ours for carrying it on – I am satisfied & I think Tom is, that this will very probably turn out to be the best – but now comes the hard part for us – We have been transferred to Tsinan with the Medical School – We are to go next February – i.e. after Chinese New Year. It will be *hard for us to go & all our friends seem to be up in arms against our going, but there is another side. It will perhaps be better for Tom to go on with work concerning training doctors than to continue in Hankow without his beloved Medical school. There are to be new hospitals built in Hankow – we rejoice that at last the money collected for them is to be used.*

Although at first neither Tom nor Bessie had been enthusiastic about going north to Tsinan, the move gave Tom an opportunity to spend time translating medical text books into Chinese as well as continuing his medical practices. Writing to his daughter Jean he said:

> *It is not often I write you, but I must not leave all the writing to your faithful mother. I have three nice letters of yours before me as I write – March 2, 13 and 16. The last one has come in 44 days which is a little quicker than usual. Quarantine for German measles, or French whooping-cough, English chicken pox. Dear me! How you do seem to be always quarantining for something. We don't quarantine much in China. but there would be less sickness if we did. That was a grand way of playing Eltham at hockey – when Eltham was not there. You had better play India versus China next time! You have bird meetings but we have such a funny bird here. It came on to the roof of the next door house and said Cuckoo Cuckoo – over & over again, and every time it said it, it nodded its head. It had a long beak and a tall crest on*

(The bird is, of course, a hoopoe).

its head & it was so funny to see it bobbing up and down. I think the 'Cook' should be where the 'Coo' is & vice versa. I wish I could draw like 'you three'. I wonder if the bird is a sort of woodpecker. If I were in your bird meeting I should perhaps be told – 'Of course it is not a woodpecker it is an XXX YYY ZZZ as every girl knows'.

You have a 'weekly cleaning' but in Tsinan there is so much dust, that if we left it for a week, it would fill basins & dust-pans etc! but Tsinan is a lovely place all the same. I am going to a temple in the hills on Sunday to speak to some Y.M.C.A. young men at a Conference. The scenery is lovely. Hills with winding paths, violets, goat, sheep – black & white. We have many lovely flowering trees here – Liliac, Japonica, roses, peach blossom, flowering fruit trees, apricots, apples, peaches, etc. We have nice house & garden. I have been sowing some seeds today, sent by Mr Geller from Hsiao Kan; Delphinium, Gaillardia etc. This I do in the evening after the day's work is done. I go to Med. School prayers at 8.45 in the morning then to Hospital 9–10 or 10.30, then translate with Mr Chao till near tiffin time. Then in the afternoon I see out-patients thrice a week & have operations on Tuesdays &

Tom and Mr Chao, his writer, in Tsinan.
The large book on the table is Giles English-Chinese dictionary.

Fridays. I have five operations tomorrow. Dr McAll is with me. I suppose you see my dear little Wyn & Joy. Give them both my love and say I'm so glad to have their Daddy here and I give him lots of rice to eat!

I wonder where you will all go this summer and whether Keith will go for his trip on the Continent. I rather hope he will. I think it is a great opportunity, & would be so helpful & interesting to both himself & for you to hear about it afterwards. I must close now.

Keith and Howard were at Eltham College throughout the period of the war, although Keith actually left school in July 1918. He joined the army for a very short period. Howard, then 13 years old, sent this letter to his sister Jean at Walthamstow Hall:

October 21st 1917

As you see, this is a hurried note at twenty minutes past one, in the middle of an air raid, I could hear distinctly the hum of their engines, the guns have been going fast. We were called at about 12 o'clock, and I do not know when it will end. The window by me shakes at the shells, they seem to be overhead. Thank you for your letter with Mrs Lindsay questions, I will enclose a letter to her. I imagine she is now at Seaven [sic] Oaks.

I have had a good many letters from Mother lately, two or three during the last few days, one also from father and two from Gordon, asking if Keith can swim seaven [sic] miles etc.

All I have got on is a pair of pyjamas and a dressing gown, fairly cold?

I should think it is fairly cold for the German aviators seeing at 16,000 ft on a moderate night it is 60° below freezing point. Down here the record last winter was only 22. That is why the Zepps the other day had to come down lower and consequently they were brought down.

Nothing much to say now, O I forgot. Our school tower is taken on by the Admiralty as an observation post, and we work it. I was on observation

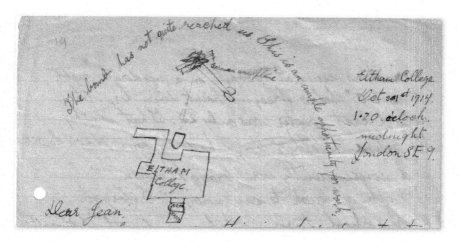

duty from 1–2 on <u>Sunday</u> and had dinner late. We have to report aircraft, guns, etc. We saw two aeroplanes flying 320–10 and heard one gun. I say 'we' because we go on two at a time from sunrise to sunset or rather 7AM–5PM only daytime you see. The government send over aeroplanes at a high altitude to test us.

At the end of the summer term 1918 Keith left school and joined the Artists' Rifles which was a popular regiment for public school and university volunteers but, as the armistice was signed in November, there was little time to complete his officer training. Keith wrote to Jean in a typically enthusiastic manner – especially for anything demanding:

Have been here $2^1/_2$ days, it is simply splendid! <u>Very</u> hard work, <u>very</u> little time, but splendid. Chaps, huts, food, drill, shower baths, wash ups, Y.M.C.A.'s, canteens, instructions, officers all splendid.

My address is
Pte. K.H.Gillison
Hut 32
B. Company
2nd Artists' Rifles

Hare Hall Camp
Romford
Essex

PS We have plenty to do, plenty to eat, plenty to polish, & plenty to be thankful for.

PPS I have just finished sewing on a hook and eye & a button, it took me about an hour.

PPPS I have no time or patience to write more now.

Gordon aged 9, Keith's younger brother writes from his school at Chefoo:

I hope you are quite well. If by the time this reaches you, you have not decided what regiment you are going to join please join the Gordon Highlanders and try to be a bag piper because I like pipers very much. I have read quite a few stories about them in a book about this war – or if you like Cavalry. Cavalry in Latin is 'equilatus' it is only used in the singular I hope you know that. Please try to get the Victoria Cross. I am getting my fingers rather inky. It is visitor's day tomorrow and Mother can come and see me in school etc, etc.

This was Keith's reply

September 15th 1918

I am hoping this will catch you just before you go back to school. Thank you very much for your letters and for the one from Gordon, I enjoyed all three immensely. To tell the truth I had really thought of the Gordon Highlanders as a possible regiment some time ago, but you are not given much option in these matters. As for the bag-piper part of it, he better go & tell that to the horse marines! I am glad he only asks me to try for the V.C. that is a bit easier than getting it, & by the way the Americans seem to be doing their best to make it impossible for me to get even a chance. I am glad you reminded me about Aunt Molly, Jean, it is high time I wrote. I heard before of Mother's new shorthand idea for Chinese, it seems very good and ought to make work much easier. I read also about it in 'News from Afar' I think.

Don't trouble to send my cycling clips, but if you like you can take them to school and give them to me when I come next Saturday. There are several things I should like if you can find any of them & take them with you. 1st. any stockings of mine. My army socks have all shrunk too small, and the khaki socks are rather thin to wear alone on a long march. 2nd My white sweater. They say we'll be here till November, and the nights are cold enough as it is sometimes here. 3rd Two pairs of pyjamas. (I have only one thin pair and it is hard to get them washed & wear them at the same time). 4th My big knife. It doesn't matter if you can't get these things, but they are what I most need and I thought if you took them I could fetch them next Saturday.

My present scheme for leave is to get my road pass next Saturday the 21st and cycle over to Eltham reaching there about 3.30. Then if Howard could get a bike, we could both go on to Sevenoaks & meet Jean at about 6.0 o'clock. We might just call in at the Shadwells on the way. Then if Miss Hare w'd allow, I shd like us to go out for tea together. Somewhere in Sevenoaks. We could start back in time for Howard to get to bed (Mr R w'd probably fix the time). I am trying to fix up my own lodging privately, and have several schemes which will do nicely. I sh'd spend most of Sunday at Eltham but have to be back here at 9.30 P.M.

P.S. Please Howard keep a look out for my football things & bike pump, as I sh'd like to fetch them also. Please Jean send on the enclosed letter & photo to Gordon, I can't send it from here as the post-mark will show where the Artist's are stationed,

P.P.S. Photo enclosed.

Private Keith Gillison – Artist's Rifles

P.P.P.S. Do try & get a bike Howard, beg, borrow, or do anything but steal, if you can't borrow try hiring & let me pay. You will need lamps too, but that's nothing. If someone has a bike which w'd do but is punctured, get Hydes to mend it & borrow on those conditions, don't worry about expense, leave that to me. I've been saving up a bit so it ought to be all right!

P.P.P.P.S. I'll let you know again when I know more definitely about the pass. You can let me know by post card if the scheme agrees with you if you like. How do you like the photo?

After Keith left school he remained in the army after the Armistice until January 1919 and then began his medical course at Edinburgh Medical School. Letters from Howard kept his parents in touch with his own progress at Eltham and in 1920 Bessie came home ahead of Tom bringing the eleven year old Gordon with her so that he could join Howard at Eltham College. The headmaster sent this letter to Bessie which she proudly forwarded to Tom having underlined the best sentences:

April 1ˢᵗ 1920

Dear Mrs Gillison,

I have been out of action this week owing to influenza or should have sent you the enclosed forms earlier. I sent a message to arrange that Howard should leave on Monday afternoon and I shall be back in school by that time. I had a message from Miss Hare asking if he might accompany his sister but in the absence of any intimation from you that you wished him to cut out the rest of the school term – including examinations on which he is 'placed' – I naturally did not let him go. But he may easily go home now and travelling late on Monday he should be quite comfortable. The train you said was at 4 p.m. from Paddington.

We are reasonably satisfied with Howard's work though he still concentrates his interest more than is discreet upon mathematics. Miss Turner is quite sure of his mathematical ability but it would keep till he specialises in it later. He has a lot of work to do in the ordinary subjects before he can reach the distinctly high standard required for Edinburgh (It is a stage <u>higher</u> than London). That's the only consideration that disturbs me about him. It always upsets a boy when he reaches the stage for University work after his heart & is held up to study some subject he dislikes. But he <u>should</u> be able to combine both ways. At present he has not enough ideas or words for literary subjects.

<u>His conduct has always been excellent in every way.</u> The forms I should have back shortly but assuming that the medical certificate is in order, they are only a formality & it is unnecessary to wait for this formal acceptance by the Governor. The new term begins on Thursday the <u>29ᵗʰ April.</u>

I hope you will be able to come down with Gordon when he comes or, if not then, sometime in summer. !!If he does as well as either of his brothers here, we shall be very happy indeed to have him.!!

With kind regards,
Yours very sincerely
George Robertson

April 12th

I find I missed last weeks' post for China so I kept this back to add a p.s. I can enclose Jean's report – we need pay no attention to the low opinion the school has of her ability. She is better than her report, in my opinion.

Saturday Keith helped to clean the Free Church after the flood had subsided – the others helped Mr Wheeler get his bathing house clean – inches of mud were taken from it. The Church had had two or three inches of water covering the floor – we could not use it yesterday for services – had Kingsbury Hall instead – today it is still wet. Gordon & Jean are writing to you – theirs will go under separate cover.

Keith has one week more, the others have two weeks, then I go to London also. Gordon gets on nicely with the others.

Howard took on his role as elder brother to the young Gordon very seriously and sent this letter to his mother:

2nd May 1920

I will not say any more about the journey as I gave you a broad outline of it in my post-card to you, which I hope you got.

When we arrived I played a short game of fives with Gordon, and since then we have had a game every day.

I showed him round most of the school and its grounds, but such places as G dorm, where no boy except G dormites are allowed to enter, he did not enter.

Then I took him to the head-master, where we had a confidential talk, and we came to the conclusion that as in the 2nd form they would be 2 terms ahead of Gordon, especially in Geometry (as he has done almost none) Algebra (where they are rather advanced), Latin (where he has been used to a different pronunciation), and in other lessons as well. Moreover he has not done any work for six months, while if he has one term in the 1st form, he will get a little nature study, and writing lessons, and his French and other lessons, will be rubbed up, and then he can start a fresh term in the 2nd form.

A school tuck shop has been started, in the part of the school called West House. It is run by a man from the village who pays for the monopoly which goes to the Games funds. He had sold out of all mineral waters, of which he had a moderate stock, in 10 minutes, on the first day.

And this was Gordon's first letter to his mother (spelling as in the original):

May 30th 1920

Miss Wilkins told me to ask you wheather I am to wear that striped blue flannel suit for Sunday or otherwise. And shall I bag a school tie I knead a tie fairly much don't I? I have bought a six d pockit comb. I will pay for it if you like I think that I have used my money rather too quickly. I have now only 2/11 or about 3/- its has been used on a fives ball (now lost) & a bottle of ink, swan ink, and three hens eggs 1 for Howie's birthday & 2 for myself – 7^d + 3$^1/_2$^{d} = 10$^1/_2$^{d}

Accounts
<u>ink</u> = 6
<u>ball</u> = 6

eggs = 10$^1/_2$
Crusaders Mags
& cards etc = 2^d

Tuck = the rest = 2/6 such as mineral waters 9$^1/_2$, one ice cream
2d = 11$^1/_2$ some was only lemonade powder, Biscuits chocolates, toffees &
Butterscotch = 1/6$^1/_2$.

    I am now saving up for a nice fountain pen which I need badly. The
want helps me not to go to tuck shop even on a hot day. Thanks also to
the swimming bath. I have been in 3 times seeing I had a bad knee. I am
supposed to be at least the 2nd best swimmer & the best diver. The other day
Mr Philips L.M.S. India, through in a half-penny and told me to dive for it. I
did so and got it about 5 times but when he threw it in the middle of the bath
and as the water was not very clear I didn't get it but I am going to try again
next baths when the water is clearer. We lost a match last Wednesday H.M.S.
Worcester 80 to 81 & Won 2 on Saturday – one away & 1 home. Cannock
House 1st XI & our 2nd Form 45 – 31. Home match Crusaders men v our
1st XI 195 to 156 our highest score was 63. Lucher, a day boy who owns a
motor-bycik and side-car £170. 4 stroke engine, made it only one out with a
duck.

It is clear from Tom's remarks in the following letter that he and Bessie had already
made a decision. This was that Bessie would stay on after the specified year of leave
in order to provide a home in Edinburgh for the children. Keith, Jean and, in due
course Howard, would be studying for their chosen careers in Edinburgh – medicine
at the University and in Jeans's case – nursing at the Royal Infirmary, Edinburgh.
Gordon was to continue as a boarder at Eltham College. Tom writes to Mary Black:

21 November 1920

    I must not let time go by too far without sending you my warm
loving good wishes for the New Year. I don't know how long it will take this

letter to get home – but it should arrive somewhere near Jan 1. Well, may you
have a real happy new year is my prayer for you. I'm so glad Keith and Jean
have got to know and love you both – It is some compensation for my not
being able to be there myself – but O how I look forward to seeing you both.
In some ways I have a greater longing to be home this time than ever – You
see I'm not so young as I once was, though I try & keep as young as I can!
I feel it is right to stick to my task till I see it safely through. It is a long pull
yet. By the time you get this – Vol I. will be out of my hands & by Jany 31, I
hope it will be available for the students, but there are still two volumes – and
they will take me the best part of next year.

I get lovely letters from Bessie – and Keith, Jean & the other two.
How much one has to thank God for. It is such an interesting thing to watch
development. Jean is developing nicely – Her letters show it very markedly –
What a glorious time Keith has had on the continent. It will be the memory of
a lifetime. I suppose you remember your trip Mary – with Marion in North
Italy. Good old Mrs Finnie! She was kind to us Gillisons.

I wonder where Bessie will get a house – She has nearly got one in
Leamington Terrace when she wrote. Isn't it strange to think of all the old
associations – Mrs Logie & many others! One's heart gives a thump as
one thinks of them. Then Keith saw Tom Henderson too! That is another
old link. Do you know that one of the streets in Hankow is called Lockerbie
Road! Of course it is on Jardine's property …

… You know there is a sad famine to the North & West of us –
Thousands are dying & without big help – millions will starve to death
during the next five months. Money is coming in though not enough –
and numbers have gone out from here – some 3 or four from our staff to
help in taking relief to the poor sufferers. I am taking 4 hours teaching of
English a week to let one of our men free – The remainder of his work is
being shared by two or three others. I also have two hours a week teaching
Therapeutics. So you see I get some variety. One reason why I am not

hurrying home (though the book is the chief one) is that I have to face the
fact that when I return to China after furlough – Bessie will probably not
return with me – therefore I would rather take my medicine now & put off
taking it later!! A rather lame metaphor perhaps!

Bessie bought 23, Leamington Terrace, Edinburgh and had moved in by October 1921. After leaving Walthamstow Hall, Jean took a short course in Domestic Science at Atholl Crecsent in Edinburgh and then embarked on her training as a nurse at the Royal Infirmary. Keith was well into his medical studies but Howard who had passed all the exams to gain entry to Edinburgh University at the age of sixteen was told that he was too young for the medical course. In the interim he took a B.Sc in Botany before starting on medicine.

At the end of 1921 Tom came home on furlough but took the opportunity to stop off in India to see his niece Jessie Hoyland (Marais) and her husband.

Those few years of the family living together in Edinburgh must have been a rare opportunity for the family to get to know each other; Gordon joined them for his school holidays and Tom was based at home for his 1922 to early 1923 furlough. On his return to China Tom was reappointed to Hankow and in this letter to Mary Black he says:

1ˢᵗ November 1922

> *In regard to my going back to Hankow – Yes! It is very nice though*
> *it is a wrench leaving Tsinan – The great thing is that I know it is the right*
> *thing to do – I have just got a pleasing appeal from Nurse Bell – I'll enclose*
> *it & you can send it back to me when you next write – You will have no*
> *doubt that I am doing the right thing when you read that letter. The District*
> *Committee by a <u>standing vote</u> unanimously asked me to go back – the*
> *China Advisory Council approved & the Board endorse their approval – So*
> *my duty & course are clear – The work will be harder & the difficulties*
> *greater but the knowledge that I am doing the right thing will more than*
> *counter balance the difficulties.*

Jean Gillison – bee keeper at Walthamstow Hall.

The quiet domestic life of the Gillisons in Leamington Terrace supporting the medical studies of the three eldest continued until the family received news of Gordon's illness at the end of the Christmas term 1924 when he was 14 years old. Bessie sent this letter to Mary Black:

December 21ˢᵗ 1924

Alas I have a fresh trouble to tell you of & it seemed at first a grievous one, but as usual no sooner did the trouble come than attendant circumstances seemed to show that God's love was at work also to ameliorate it.

It was found out at school that Gordon was losing weight – The Master tried to feed him up & gave him tonics, but he continued to lose, so the doctor was asked to overhaul him & he found out he had diabetes. Then they arranged for him to come home at once – shortly before term ended – so he came up last Tuesday – I asked Keith to find out who would be the best doctor to consult. Keith was very careful not to decide in a hurry – but soon after talking it over with a friend or two he decided on Prof. Murray Lyon, a comparatively new Professor of Medicine. Gordon arrived looking very thin & delicate but quite cheerful. It was good to get him home & give him supper & then a nice hot bath & bed – Next day Keith took him to be examined & they came back saying Prof. M.L. would like to have him in his ward in the Infirmary – if a bed could be spared, without waiting more than a day – Very soon we heard he could go in, so he went in Thurs. evening – and they gave him the first injection of insulin that night – he is to have it three times a day – It is such a relief to me that he has begun the insulin treatment – it seems to be such a wonderful thing, & I look forward soon to seeing the dear boy get fat & robust again, but probably treatment & diet will have to go on for a long time.

It is a big cloud over our Xmas, yet it has begun to show its silver lining – I saw Gordon yesterday & he seems to like being in hospital pretty well – The 'Sister' is 'topping'. She calls him 'Gordon' & is very nice to him

& to me – As soon as he can get up he will like it still better – I expect. He is only to stay in the Infirmary till the treatment gets well under way & then it can be continued at home. I expect I shall have him with me in Edin. now right on. He will not be returning to Eltham – Jean can go in & see him occasionally – It will be a blow to Tom to hear of it – I found it hard to write & tell him.

As insulin was only discovered in 1921 Gordon was one of the earliest patients to be given the treatment; he needed daily injections of insulin and careful monitoring of food intake for the rest of his quite short life. There is no indication in the letters of how much his diabetes affected his education and whether he returned to Eltham College but neither is there any hint that his condition impeded his studies because he too began his medical course in Edinburgh and was fully qualified in 1932.

Bessie stayed on in Edinburgh until 1926. Towards the end of that time Tom in China was restless about a number of issues. The first political situation was becoming fraught with the skirmishes between the warlords trying to gain power and the strongly Communist leanings of much of the country – particularly the south. The negotiations between the Wesleyans and the London Missionary Society in Hankow over uniting to build a much bigger hospital blew hot and cold; Tom, having been in China for more than forty years, was beginning to be concerned about the timing of his next furlough, his impending retirement and the need to find some someone to replace him and above all, he was missing his wife very badly.

With all four of her children settled in their chosen career and in the light of all these uncertainties Bessie took the decision, with their blessing to sell the Edinburgh house and rejoin Tom.

TEN

The end of the journey

P robably the biggest worry on Tom's mind following his return to China after his 1922–23 furlough was the resolution of the difficulties between the London Missionary Society and Wesleyans over the building of the new hospital in Hankow. This was the project close to his heart and he longed to see the building completed before his retirement. The political situation in China was precarious, there was a struggle to obtain sufficient funds, and he felt that the Wesleyans were wavering in their commitment.

Although they had not been given clearance to start building, Tom and others on the spot, had been preparing two possible plans – Alpha and Beta. It was not until the middle of 1926 that agreement was reached with the Wesleyans and before her return to Hankow in October Bessie wrote to Mary Black, 'I have good news to tell you about Hankow – something has happened which enabled Mr Hawkins to approach the Wesleyans again and this time with caution they agreed to sanction the 'Beta' scheme so <u>that</u> has been cabled out – it is the complete Union Scheme that all out there wanted so much – won't Tom be delighted'.

Keith, their eldest surviving son, qualified in medicine in 1925 and after some practical surgical experience under the consultant Henry Wade he applied to the London Missionary Society, was accepted and was posted to Central China – to the delight of his parents.

Following the revolution of 1911 there was a modicum of unity under Dr Sun Yat Sen but the war lords fighting for their own supremacy up in the north and the movement towards Communism in the south lead to civil war. There were riots; fighting took place in Hankow and Shanghai; there was resentment concerning

Foreign Concessions and unfair foreign trade arrangements; Christians were targeted and violent demonstrations took place in a number of cities. Tom had written to Bessie in June 1925:

> *The internecine war – Military misrule – planting of fields with opium – perhaps millions of acres under Military compulsion – unjust taxes to support the military – bandits & soldiers as bad as bandits – shortage of wheat rice because displaced by the poppy – drought & floods – have all worked together for evil, raising the price of food to a height scarcely ever known before – depreciation of the dollar because of debased copper coinage (3000 coppers to one dollar!) have all combined to create discontent & rightly so, among the working classes & the poor. Bolshevists have been at work in this prepared soil & have stirred up the students – & got them to strike – Schools – both Government and Christian have been compelled to close their doors & the students have gone on the streets orating – shouting against Imperialistic countries such as England & Japan – demanding the abolition of extraterritoriality – & unequal treaties – the return of all concessions & many other things which you will read in the papers – and then came this Shanghai incident of which lighted all into a great flame – and then followed the Hankow incident of which I send you a reprint – or rather, a 'print-off' – I want Mr Allen to see it – Please pass it on to him when you have read it & I should like him to see the papers also – The shooting was done about 100 yards from my door – and on the street at our corner here – we nearly had a repetition of the same half an hour later – but the crowd, altho howling, ugly and threatening- thought better of it and didn't come down the street*
>
> *The Lewis guns & men with loaded rifles were just outside Wilson's door and I heard the Commanding Officer – issue his orders – to fire when they heard him whistle. Fortunately this was not necessary – and the Chinese Military took possession of the back street – and although the guards with Maxims – Lewis guns & loaded rifles were at their posts nothing occurred*

– There is reported to be a large gathering tomorrow – and there is full preparation to protect the Concession against it tonight. The atmosphere is electric – Mounted soldiers – British – American etc, – ride past my window constantly – & close vigil is kept.

The Japanese who was killed by the Chinese mob belonged to the house next door to mine – He was buried today – The bodies of the poor fellows who were killed or wounded were taken to the R.C. hospital – We saw a number of them carried along. It was a sad sight.

If that crowd had not been warded off – the whole Concession might have been in flames & few foreigners left to tell the tale – The Military Governor's co-operation with the foreigners gives us a comfortable assurance – that all will be well. Our Missionaries have been brought in from Wuchang & from Griffith John – & Dr Byles & Miss Bell are being brought in this evg. at least for the week end.

It was against this background of civil war which had been going on for two years that Keith was beginning his missionary service. Keith had sailed on the S.S.Khyber in August 1926 and his mother was not far behind as she was on board the S.S.Della in October. The fighting was seriously affecting the work of the missions and there was great uncertainty about where Keith should be sent. Tom wrote to Bessie when she was en route for China:

12th September 1926

A fortnight ago the Southern forces were fighting the Northeners in Hunan and were said to have Wuchang as their goal – It seemed fairly remote at the time – & in many ways highly improbable that they would get further than the borders of Hunan and Hupeh – (e.g. Yochow). Today Hankow and Hangyang are in their hands – and Wuchang is besieged and about to capitulate – and Wu Pei Fu [21] has been driven out – Southern soldiers with their red, white & blue neckcloths or ribbons, are everywhere in evidence and have been welcomed by the populace who absolutely hate Wu Pei Fu. The taking of Hangyang Hill was done with comparatively little difficulty for, although it is fortified and contains the Arsenal, yet it was practically handed over through the defection of Wu Pei Fu's generals.

The Southerners have advanced up the Peking Hankow line – beyond Hwang Pei station – but we have not heard that Hsiao Kan has yet fallen into their hands. Today I have just had a letter from Mr Geller. I must show it to others or I would enclose it – (I may send it to you later). The city was more or less in a panic – & was still in the hands of the Northerners. Mr.G didn't know whether his letter would get through or not, but it came by post all right. Dr Wills had (I am glad to say) left Tsao Shih – having come to Hsiao Kan to operate on Dr Shaw's little girl for appendicitis – He will have to wait some days before he can operate – & besides – it is doubtful whether he could return to Tsao Shih in the present unsafe conditions of the roads – (bandits, disbanded troops etc)…....We have taken many wounded soldiers into the hospital – as in the Revolution year. Many horrible compound fractures. (Humerus 4 femur 1 Tibia & fibula 1. Ulna 1) – We have also a number of cases of cholera in.

I am wonderfully well in spite of having been here all through the summer – I hope you have had a nice voyage so far – but I shall not hear much till you arrive, to which event I ardently look forward – After nearly four years' separation – I shall be extra pleased to be a family man once more – I may send you a short note to Aden & a decenter letter to Colombo – & perhaps some papers. I have not heard from you for some time – due probably to the interruption of mails through this sad war – Send this letter on to Howard to show to Gordon & forward to Jean & so save me writing so fully to them.

On her return to China Bessie and Tom moved out to Hwang Pei, a train journey away from Hankow. Bessie sent this letter to Mary Black and her mother:

December 1ˢᵗ 1926

> *We have now been just one week at this place (about 3 hrs railway journey from Hankow) which is to be our home we hope, for about 18 months. It is what we call a country station of the Hankow district. Hwang Pei is a small rather quiet Chinese town surrounded by a city wall. Our London Mission has had work here for a long time – Missionaries named Wasson have been living here and there is a large boys' school and also a good girls' school close to the garden of the Mission house and a Women's Home and Work-room where industrial work is done (founded to help poor destitute women). All seems to be working well. Mʳ & Mʳˢ Wasson have just gone on furlough. It was essential for some one to come & look after things here & no-one seemed available, so, as there was a young doctor & his wife who had had a year at Language School glad to go to do Tom's work in Hankow, Tom offered to come here with me & our Committee was very grateful.*

However such was the turmoil politically that the quiet life they had expected to enjoy at Hwang Pei soon reached crisis point and Bessie wrote to Jean:

January 1ˢᵗ 1927…

> *… We have had exciting times, soldiers swarming into Hwang Pei – 5000 of them & over 100 coming to our Boys' School Building. Our boys were rejoicing in being in the foreign house with verandahs next to us & then patients were always coming in – soldiers & others. It has been hard to write letters. Then yesterday exams finished, both schools were closed, pupils mostly wanting to go away, some having to be arranged for, escort to homes found for girls etc. Lots of women & girls, a bit afraid of soldiers, wanting to leave – i.e. women & girls in workroom; then the last 4 days news of serious trouble at Hankow.*

The end of the journey

We have put off & put off going there. Don't see quite when we can go in & we really must wait now till we hear that all is quiet there. It was such a shock yesterday to see the headlines which I enclose in our paper (Paper pf Hankow 6th Jany/27).

'Gigantic Anti-British Demonstration Held in Hankow, Kuomintang Flag is hoisted on Top of B.M.C.Building. Reinforced troops & Pickets quell further disturbances in British Concession. Rain brings monster parade to abrupt end. British Women & Children Evacuate Port.' ...

... We do not know yet how many women & children did evacuate the Port. We much hope that with the Kuomintang Flag flying & Chinese soldiers in command it was possible for them soon to return. Yesterday some soldiers were shot (court-martialled) outside our compound very near the place we stood to be photographed. We heard the shots fired & after saw the bodies & saw coffins brought for them later, from the verandah. Today after breakfast the General of this whole Division of the Army called & he wanted to see the empty house close by that the boys cleared out of today & he says he would like to bring his wife & live in it himself. Isn't it dramatic? or as we are all saying 'God is in it, working out His purposes thro' us – in unexpected ways.' The Chinese are so pleased about this latest phase – especially our woman who lives here & does our laundry work. She thinks we shall be quite safe now.

I fear the papers these days will distress you all but so far we have not really suffered at all. The strain & anxiety in Hankow this week must have been bad. I am sure Miss Coxon & the Wilsons & all on the Concession have been alarmed. Last night's paper said that things were calming down.

A week later Bessie and her friend Edith Wills were on the steamer bound for Shanghai. Bessie wrote to Jean:

271

14th January

    ... *We got thro to Hankow without difficulty & our baggage & the Chinese Christian, a country preacher, were awaiting us at the Lutheran Mission House, Old German Concession, Hankow, where we went & ate our lunch. We travelled in an open truck with no seats the 2nd half of the way. On the little branch line to Hwang Pei, we had seats & there was a man of the student agitator class in the compartment who had lots of posters that he was going to stick up & who wanted to let us know how iniquitous England was, how wickedly we had stolen land from China, how our blue jackets killed poor coolies etc. I told him we had been in China more years than he had lived, & what kind of work father had done, saving hundreds of lives, how we and all missionaries loved China & the Chinese etc. He said that no doubt there were very good English people but it was the duty of patriots to oppose our Nationalistic Government etc. When we parted he said 'When you go to the British Concession you must say you are Germans or something.' I told him I could not tell a lie & I was proud of my country as he was, that England I knew had goodwill to China etc,etc. It was good to have a talk rather than an enemy threatening violence. Oh we have very, very much to be thankful for, so many have had worse experiences – lots on this boat.*

Bessie's stay in Shanghai was to last until October 1927 and all that time Tom remained in Hankow trying, with colleagues, to keep the medical work going in Hankow and the outlying districts. Not least of the problems was that of paying the salaries of all those that worked in Mission establishments, such as the hospitals and schools, owing to the precarious position of the banks and the high rate of inflation. He was also in a position to keep the wheels turning for the building of the new hospital thus facilitating its opening in 1928.

For the Gillison family however there was some good news. In April Keith announced that he and a fellow missionary Kathleen Sanders had become engaged. They had been travelling companions on that notorious slow boat to China and were also fellow students at the Peking language school. Having completed the six months course, Keith had come to Shanghai to take the place of Dr Davenport, whose sudden death had left the Lister hospital in Shanghai very short staffed. Kathleen went to her posting in Siaochang but, in common with all missionaries in the north after only three weeks there, she was temporarily evacuated to Japan. Bessie wrote to Mary Black:

April 10ᵗʰ 1927

I want to let you & Aunt Jessie know by a letter to your two selves that Keith is engaged to be married. He is here with me now and I am very happy to have him & happy about his engagement. The girl is Kathleen Sanders, her home is in Plymouth where her father is Inspector of Customs. She came out under the L.M.S. with Keith and has been at the language school with him. You may remember that there was considerable mention of her in some of his letters written on the voyage! I gathered then that they seemed to be quite helpful to each other as comrades in board-ship enterprises & I am not surprised to know they are engaged. She is two months younger than Keith – is a certificated teacher & she did all the work for a B.A. degree but was prevented by illness (purely temporary) from sitting the exam. She did a few years of teaching before offering to the L.M.S. I imagine she is very capable & just the one to be a real helpmeet to Keith – but oh what a time for these young people to arrive in China! I expect that she today is a refugee in Tientsin just as I am here – all North China folk are evacuating – Keith at present has his job in the hospital here but of the future we know nothing – Tom is still in Hankow, one of the very few Britishers there at present.

By May things had got even more chaotic and Tom wrote to Bessie:

May 18th

The Kung-Wo is going out tonight and I will get off this to you – along with one or two other local letters – I am sorry I have not managed to get off one to England by this mail – I expect you have got my letter & parcel by Mr Rowlands – I haven't very much more to send you now! I note what you say about Kathleen going to Japan – She will enjoy seeing that beautiful country – though she and Keith will be sorry to part. However I hope it is not for long, and that they will be able to marry in September. As to where to spend the honeymoon – you might find a more cheery spot than sulphury Unzen, but there is plenty of time for that yet – I have been pretty busy today – I did a T.B. glands of neck, and an amputation of the leg today in the women's hospital. The ovariotomy is doing splendidly.

Today there is a great panic on – among the Chinese. People are moving their effects by the hundreds – from East to West & West to East. Rumours abound about the enemy advancing – up the Canton Hankow Railway – also down the Han etc, etc. but our houseboy tried in several shops to buy rice today and failed – He went out later to make another trial – & I don't know whether he has succeeded or not – The Central Bank paper money is being more heavily discounted and in some places it is being refused – There may be truth in the rumours or they may be exaggerated. Pastor King and D^r Hu both came anxiously to inquire about the state of affairs – I tried to assure them. There was an attempt made to commandeer the Wesleyan Hospital – but it was frustrated through the intervention of the Board of Foreign affairs.

The Tang Pu demanded our Boys School in Hwang Pei – and also the two Foreign Houses. I went to the Foreign Office with Mr Lin Shou Shan – who came down to Hankow to see me about it and Mr Chang (a Christian Secretary there) said he would write & put a stop to them taking the foreign houses. I said I didn't mind loaning the Big Boys School Bdg for 6 mos. And so the play goes on. The Communists are much hated here – They seem riding for a fall – but O poor China – she suffers whichever side wins.

The political situation gradually eased over the hot summer months mainly due to a split in the Kuomintang between Chiang Kai Shek and the other Communist leaders[22]. The National Party with Chiang at its head asserted its power and the 'red' revolutionaries temporarily took to the hills; life in the mission stations gradually returned to normal.

In August Kathleen returned to the mainland and the wedding of Keith and Kathleen took place in Shanghai on September 10th attended by both Keith's parents.

Keith and Kathleen had hoped to go to Kuling for their honeymoon but because of the political turmoil they went instead to Japan. Tom and Bessie stayed on in the mission compound of the nearly completed Union Hospital and handed their old house to Keith and Kathleen on their return from Japan. My mother's diaries record many instances of continual unrest and fighting in the city as one political faction held sway over another until the Kuomintang finally managed to gain control. The new hospital was opened in February 1928 and the credit for this lay largely with Tom who had seen the project through from conception to reality in spite of seemingly insurmountable obstacles.

Wedding group at the wedding of Keith Gillison & Kathleen Sanders.
Front row: Bessie, Keith, Kathleen and Tom Gillison.
Back left: Rev Ernest Box (Senior) and Mrs Box of Shanghai, Ernest Box (best man), Dorothy Doidge (bridesmaid), others unknown.
September 10th 1927
(The veil worn by my mother was the same one used by my grandmother in 1893 and much later by me in 1953).

It was in 1929 that Jean, Keith's sister, now a fully fledged and experienced nurse joined her brother Keith on the staff of the Union Hospital.

In 1929 Tom and Bessie came home on furlough leaving the work of the mission and the hospital in capable hands and on their return they moved into their retirement at Griffith John College which was about six miles outside the city. By 1929 Tom had been working in China for forty seven years and Bessie for thirty two and at the ages of 70 and 61 they were entitled to consider their future plans. There was never any possibility that they would return home to retire. Tom had said in a letter to Bessie some years earlier, 'I cannot see that it is right in my present state of good health to settle down at home to a bucolic life'. To him the perfect retirement would be to live within a reasonable distance from his beloved hospital in Hankow and to spend his time in translating medical books and religious pamphlets into Chinese. Bessie's dream would be the freedom to run a small clinic in just such a spot. Those dreams were eventually realized when they retired to the Griffith John College compound at Han Chia Ten where Tom made a valuable contribution to Chinese medical education by translating standard texts in chemistry and paediatrics; Bessie ran her clinic seeing some fifty patients a day. A small hostel of five beds allowed Bessie to accommodate male patients who needed more than one out-patient visit but did not need to be sent to the hospital in Hankow. The clinic was financed by donations from some of the churches at home but often the patients would bring a chicken, eggs or fish to pay for their treatment. It was a remarkable achievement for a woman in her late sixties.

With Tom and Bessie no longer involved directly with the hospital, Keith and the staff of seven resident doctors and nearly forty nursing staff enjoyed working with the facilities of the new building. My parents' first child – my sister Meili

View of the hospital from the Sun Yat Sen Park next door.

276

Hospital entrance.

Some of Bessie's patients arrive for treatment on a buffalo.

Three sisters who lost parts of their lower limbs through frostbite

The girls much happier after being fitted with artificial limbs at the hospital

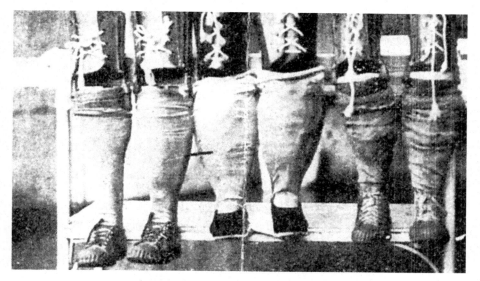

Artificial limbs made by the hospital carpenter

– was born in June 1929. The Union Hospital had only been open barely three years when disaster struck in the form of the savage flooding of the great Yangtze. On July 31st 1931 the river banks collapsed and water rushed in. Fortunately my mother and the baby were in Kuling for Meili to recover from a serious bout of dysentery. My father described the flood in his book "The Cross and the Dragon":

> *I was having breakfast with some of my colleagues when we noticed water seeping into the hospital compound. By the time we finished breakfast the gardens were an inch or two deep in water, so I took off my shoes and socks and paddled back to our house. It was obvious that the water was rising and by making pencil marks on the wall we found it was increasing in depth by about five inches an hour. We had never been flooded before and had no idea what to expect, so as to be on the safe side, with domestic help I moved things like upholstered chairs upstairs and tied knots in curtains to keep them clear of the water.*

The ground floor and downstairs verandah were about three and a half feet above ground level and when the water in the garden was about three feet deep, a Chinese stranger came by on a raft. He asked permission to unload things on to our verandah hoping no doubt that the water would rise no higher.

By bedtime on the first day of our flood the water was three to four feet deep in the ground floor rooms of our house and the hospital, the patients having been moved to higher floors. The next morning I found the water was about six feet deep in all the downstairs rooms, so I swam through the dining room, sitting room, study and other rooms, rescuing pictures curtains and anything else worth saving. It is surprising how little room there is for swimming in one's dining room when the table, chairs, sideboard, bookcase etc are all floating horizontally, instead of standing upright on the floor.

My next job was to find out how to travel to the hospital. My visitor had disappeared, fortunately leaving behind his raft. I think he had found a boat willing to convey him and his belongings to an un-flooded part of the city, so all I had to do was to improvise a pole and paddles in order to travel by raft to the hospital or other parts of the compound. Our carpenters made another raft or two and we hired a sampan for travelling the mile and a half or so to the un-flooded parts of Hankow for shopping and other purposes ...

Thousands of native Chinese became refugees and it is estimated that an area the size of England and Wales was flooded that year in China. Cholera, smallpox and typhoid were rife and millions must have died of drowning, starvation or disease. To quote Keith again:

The four storey main part of the hospital, with its framework of reinforced concrete, withstood the flood better than any of the other buildings and needed very little structural repair.

For more than sixty years, in conformity with most mission hospitals in China, the Hankow Hospital had had separate buildings for men and women patients. This meant two outpatients departments, two or more operating theatres, two kitchens, two laundries, two business accounts departments. To rebuild as before was going to be a big expense; was it all necessary? A bold decision was taken to break away from the customs of the past and build not two hospitals but one, to serve men, women and children.

It took two more years to complete and cost approximately 80,000 Mexican dollars. (For years Mexican silver dollars were the main currency in China). Eventually the Hospital, Nursing School, Institute of Hospital Technology and Church were better housed and equipped than ever before. The money came from the sacrificial giving of hundreds and thousands of believers in the value of the work being done.

It took the Israelites a week and thirteen marches round the city of Jericho to topple its walls, and it took Sophia Jex-Blake and her supporters

Chinese Customs House at the end of the flooded street.

Refugee shanty town.

Ferrying medical supplies.

The Flood of 1931.
Hospital staff going
to work by boat
and raft.

At the hospital
the waters rose
15 feet.

One of the wards at
the hastily erected
reed-matting
hospital.

Flood refugees'
huts on the railway-
line.

Two views of the Gillison house in the flood.

years of marching round the walls of Edinbugh University before women were allowed into their medical faculty. In Hankow the drastic but necessary action was taken by a flood.

After the hectic events of the flood and its aftermath work at the hospital got under way again. Tom and Bessie, officially now retired but hardly idle, were living and working at a house in the compound of Griffith John College. Keith and Kathleen were due for their first furlough and left for home in March together with their two little daughters. Travelling the other way were his bother Gordon, and his new wife, Gerty Sangster. Gordon and Gerty had married at the Morningside Congregational Church in Edinburgh before sailing to China and the voyage was to be their honeymoon. Owing to his diabetes Gordon was not eligible to be on the pay-roll of the London Missionary Society and furthermore he had certain reservations about his religious convictions which made him reluctant to call himself a 'missionary'. However he was anxious to apply his medical knowledge to benefit those who needed it and it seems that his mother arranged for Harris money to support him, as it had for herself and Mary in the early days, enabling the young couple to join the rest of the clan in China. There was a vacancy for a doctor at the small Kuling hospital which normally catered for its winter residents but which was very busy in the summer months as so many thousands of visitors came there to escape the damp heat of the plain and the health hazards that went with it.

That summer of 1932 spent in Kuling for Gordon and Gerty was a very happy time. Both Gordon and Gerty enjoyed working in such beautiful surroundings – Gordon in the hospital and Gerty helping in the school for foreign children. She was pregnant and together they were looking forward to the baby's arrival in January and, for some reason, they seemed convinced that the baby would be a boy. Work at the hospital began to ease off as the summer came to an end; as he was no longer needed in Kuling in the winter, plans were made for Gordon to come down to Hankow to join the staff of the Union Hospital as a locum for Keith who was still on furlough.

Gordon wrote to his sister Jean down in Hankow:

11ᵗʰ September

The first and most important question is re OUR IAN! We are of course hoping you will come and help him see the light of day, but after he, or his sister, has come there will still need to be someone in the house to help Gerty and him during the first ten days or so of his life. Mrs.W on her own tackled Miss Li on her plans for the future and found that she intended trying to get a little time off this winter to go and see her friend in Hankow, thereupon Wha Suumon hinted that she might find a job awaiting her chez nous. She seemed thrilled at the idea. Well, before we make any definite move in the matter ourselves we would like to consult you on the pros and cons and on the question of what alternative arrangements could be made, what nurses are available, what salary is usually paid to a nurse for such a job etc. Provided we don't have to pay Miss Li's travelling expenses we don't mind if we have to pay a little more than we would have to give some local nurse, in order to get someone we know and who knows us.

And to Jean from Gerty:

I do hope you will be on the spot when Ian sees the light of day and Miss Li is very keen to take her holiday in January so that she can attend to us both. We asked her about payment, but she utterly refuses to take anything, so we have had to think of a present for her. Ian is due to arrive about 15ᵗʰ January, or maybe a little earlier, so as there won't be much time for making his trousseau for some days after we come down. I have been feverishly knitting & have got two vests & a 'piece de resistance' in the knitting line in the shape of a cot blanket. The blanket has still to have woollen daisies embroidered on it, but it has been pressed & looks rather nice.

Gordon and Gerty's wedding at Morningside Congregational Church in Edinburgh, March 1932. His brother Howard was best man.

Gordon and Gerty settled in to their life in Hankow. In a circular letter to her family and friends at home she wrote:

December 1932

> *Even although we had had another two months in Kuling after we sent off the last part of our Journal and the month of August continued to be hectically busy and full of varied experiences – some sad, some just worrying and quite a lot of happy ones – I find it difficult to pick out the ones which would be interesting for other folks to read. As the sad and worrying experiences were all connected with the medical work, which for two months was simply tremendous, I think I shall just try and tell some of the picnic jaunts we managed to get in before we left.*

> *One item of medical news might interest you, however, it is of an operation performed by Dr Gillison Senior, who by the way is 73 and theoretically retired, on a Chinese girl who managed to get the side of her face blown off. She had seen something lying on the ground which looked 'good for food', but unfortunately for her it was a home made bullet wrapped in a potato or some such thing and put in a field by a farmer to put an end to some wild beast. There was a great hole in her face exposing such upper and lower teeth as were left. After one long and tedious operation in July Dr. Gillison had greatly improved her appearance, but was not too pleased with the corner of the new mouth he had made, so a little later on he did a second operation and improved the mouth, but alas some of the stitches gave way leaving a small hole in the cheek which was rather unsightly. This worried the old doctor so much that although he had to return to Hankow he made arrangements to come back to Kuling on his way to a medical conference in Shanghai. The detour added two days to his journey and cost him quite a bit, but he felt well rewarded by the final result which was really very good. The conference referred to was one of the Chinese Medical Association, (similar to the B.M.A.), at which he was asked to give a paper on 'Fifty Years in China'*

. *(Excuse me trumpeting my father-in-law but he is well worth talking about, and is a well known and much loved person in Central China!)* …

… *The first weekend after coming down from Kuling we went out to Han Chia Den – where the Griffith John School is – and came back to find the house more or less habitable. It is still suffering somewhat from the effects of the Flood two summers past, and is a distinct change from our conveniently built house at home. Like the majority of houses built for foreigners it has very high roofs and a superfluity of windows, but I expect we shall be glad of this in summer when the really hot weather comes. This is an experience we have yet to have. Gordon soon started work out at the Union Hospital which is two miles out of town. He is there in the forenoons, and after Tiffin goes to the Hwa Lo Dispensary, near our home, where the very poor are treated. The troubles and diseases he meets with here are very different from those we hear most about at home. In this ward he has quite a few soldiers with gunshot wounds received while fighting the bandits and communists which swarm over China, while very many of his patients have horrible skin troubles, particularly filthy ulcers of the legs.*

We are living in a very pretty Compound and it is a great relief to the eyes to see the wide lawn and pretty flower beds between the houses after being on the busy street. Hankow is perfectly flat and being a commercial town is very ugly and uninteresting with its many factories and offices and the busy streets with motors and rickshas flying up and down. The Chinese love noise, just noise for the sake of noise! The people in private rickshas keep ringing their bell incessantly, most of the bicycles have the bell fixed to the wheel in such a way that it rings all the time, and as for the motorist they seem to think the horn is there for the amusement of the driver. At least that is the opinion of most foreigners and is evidently solemnly believed by one of my small pupils at the Private School for foreign children where I teach in the forenoons. One of the questions in his exercise was 'Why do motor cars have a horn?' and he came and asked me if he could put, 'For the amusement of the driver', and when I said that that was wrong he said 'But they are in Hankow, Mrs Gillison'! He had evidently heard his father say that at some time This same little boy informed me that Oxford was famous because it was where the ox crossed the ford!

We are now expert in the use of chopsticks and thoroughly enjoy Chinese food, particularly the everyday kind. We have been to one or two feasts, but they are rather long drawn out affairs and although the different courses are very interesting one feels one has had quite enough when about half way through! It is rather thrilling to dine off Lotus seeds and Lily buds! We have also eaten boneless chicken and 'elephant's ears'. The latter are really a kind of fungus (horrid though that word sounds) which grows on trees while the boneless chicken is ordinary chicken which has been boned in some mysterious way which leaves the bird quite whole. This way of serving chicken is a distinct boon to young husbands who find carving a bit of a problem! To show how Chinese-y we are becoming I now wear a Chinese gown when I teach in the Chinese school. It is of blue silk lined with yellow fur and is very necessary in this cold weather. This is the season of 'ten coat' and all but the very poorest ricksha men wear at least one padded garment. The idea is to put on as many as one can afford and some of the kiddies look like the advertisement for Michelin motor tyres they are so much padded …

… I must just mention what has been jokingly called the 'Pasteurization' of Dr. Gillison, Senr. The Chinese Church wishing to honour him on the occasion of the 50th anniversary of his arrival in Hankow decided to make him an honorary Pastor in recognition of his devoted services to the Church. So far as we know he is the only foreigner who has been ordained by the Chinese Church.

Our adventures since we left England have been many and varied. First the voyage, then Community Doctor's life amongst foreigners at Kuling and now we have begun what we really came to China for, work among the Chinese, and if there is to be any more Journal it will be to tell of our experiences as missionaries. We are not actually members of the L.M.S. but are closely connected with it.

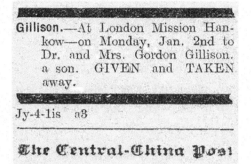

Gillison.—At London Mission Hankow—on Monday, Jan. 2nd to
Dr. and Mrs. Gordon Gillison.
a son. GIVEN and TAKEN
away.

Jy-4-1is a3

The Central-China Post

BABY
SON OF DR AND MRS G.GILLISON
GIVEN AND TAKEN AWAY
JAN. 2ND. 1933

Sadly on 2nd January Gerty's baby was born and died on the same day.

Gerty must have written to her mother when she was quite naturally deeply depressed and possibly feeling that the baby's death was in some way her fault. She was nine years older than Gordon and at thirty five perhaps her guilt could be attributed to her thinking that she was too old to bear children. I sometimes detected a wisp of jealousy of Gerty on the part of my aunt Jean. For the whole of her life she was always fiercely protective of her brothers Howard and Gordon and I think she felt that only she knew best how to look after them. There is a letter from Gordon to Jean written in 1931 at a time when Gordon and Gerty were not actually engaged to be married in which there are some indications of a slight problem with the family's view of the relationship.

31.1.31 My birthday eve

> *... I was commenting on page 2 on my failure to write, the thought uppermost in my mind at the moment is that something very strange has happened for I haven't had a letter from China for over three weeks now bar one from mother re Gerty & that came via Howard. However 'no news is good news' so I wont worry.*

> *Re Gerty, I am not wishing to open up old wounds, & I have said to Mater & Pater that I think the 'problem' should be dropped, – for a time anyway, – but I simply cant write a letter to you without saying how very*

much I appreciate your action in sending Gerty that comb. Gerty, who seldom shows much disturbance of her emotions, was verging on the ecstatic when she told me she'd got a present from China, – I confess I guessed 'Keith and Kath', when asked who I thought it was from, but I was wrong, it was from someone else, someone who clearly gave more pleasure in giving it than anyone else could have done. I don't know how better to express it than to say she was deeply touched by your action.

It's awfully strange this friendship of ours & yet it doesn't seem forced it 'comes very naturally'. We have both wondered (independently) whether it is a sort of trial or temptation & yet somehow we don't feel it is; however 'love is blind', there's no doubt about that, & so we are determined to follow God's lead as best we can & not hinder him any more than we can so in the end we hope that that which is best for us both will come about.

I know I hope, at present, that we may remain close friends always, perhaps that is 'begging the question' – however it would be false to pretend that I hoped otherwise & to stifle my desires by brute forces seems pretty poor psychology too!

My brother understood from family comments of those who were there at the time that in fact the delivery had been mis-managed by the doctor, and had a decision been made to perform a Caesarian section, the baby might have been saved. The following letter was written by Gerty's mother from Edinburgh:

February 17th 1933

My dear Gerty,

I was so relieved to get your letter yesterday the 16th written on Jan. 9th because you must have been pretty well by that time to be able to write a letter; but I know there would be still a good deal to come through.

I think I can just see the baby as you describe him, I have only got to remember my first sight of you. Like you, I think it does seem strange that he didn't live, you were evidently all right, & so was the baby & as for being punished for looking forward so happily, well, you were only doing what was right for both you & baby, so there could be no question of punishment. That would be a queer idea for a Loving Father, & my own opinion is that God himself did not intend the baby to die. Would an earthly father promise his child something, say for instance a lovely doll, & then just when the child was reaching for it, dash it to the ground and destroy it? No, I can't believe that. Would God make a thing so perfect & beautiful & in a moment deliberately crush the life out? I think not. I'm afraid there is an earthly reason. Doctors have before this lost babies through letting the mother carry on herself too long before giving help. I was disappointed at the very first, you remember, when you said how no woman Dr. could have managed to save both you & the baby as Dr. MacDonald saved me & you. However it's all in the past, & we will just try to forget the disappointment, but if ever you are expecting another I think you had better come home & we'll put you into the Simpson if we can't afford anything more select. I wish it had been possible for Gordon to have done the whole thing instead of being called in at the last.

Much love to you both,

Mama.

There was never any question that Gerty was not welcome and deeply loved by the family after the marriage for she coped magnificently with the difficulties of looking after a husband with severe and unrelenting medical demands. In addition to looking after Gordon she took on the guardianship of my sister Meili and me in 1939. The future must have looked bleak to her with an uncertain outcome for her husband, the responsibility for two little girls and the clouds of war menacingly overhead. Yet she proved herself to be someone who could provide the love, stability and a commonsense humorous approach to life which made her a wonderful guardian.

Gordon's work in Hankow included the setting up of a special clinic for treating pulmonary tuberculosis with artificial pneumothorax[23], a technique which was

Frances, Meili, Gerty, Bessie, Kathleen, Jean, Tom, Keith and Gordon

used extensively in Europe and America. The disease was a terrible scourge in China in those days. The treatment, by collapsing the affected lung and allowing air into the chest, would rest the lung and improve its blood supply. If later there were signs of recovery the lung would be re-expanded. Gordon wrote in his journal of one of the first patients to receive this treatment, a pretty little girl called Chuin Wha, 'Spring Flowers'. The improvement of her condition following nearly a year with other treatments greatly encouraged him.

The annual summer exodus of the missionaries to Kuling meant that, in the summer of 1934, for a brief period there were nine Gillisons – including two children – 'up on the hill' .

The family enjoyed a peaceful summer holiday in Kuling and returned to Hankow ready for work but sadly Gordon and Gerty received yet another set back. On Christmas Day Gordon coughed up some blood but said nothing at the time so as not to spoil the family celebrations. Later, not unsurprisingly, he was diagnosed with pulmonary tuberculosis. There was no alternative but to return home for treatment and rest and this brought an end to the work he was doing in China.

After an initial stay in the Brompton Sanatorium at Frimley Gordon was well enough to help his brother Howard in his General Practice in Ilkeston while Gerty took the opportunity to train in chiropody as a way to earn a living should Gordon remain unfit to work as a doctor. I remember speaking to some of Howard's patients who had been treated by Gordon all those years before and hearing from them how much he was admired and respected for his lovely bedside manner and his obvious concern and care for them as patients.

By 1937 Gordon's TB lesion had not healed and he needed further treatment. He was offered a post at the Buckinghamshire and Berkshire Sanatorium both as a patient and a member of staff – surely an ingenious and unusual arrangement – he worked as a doctor when he was well and was a patient when he was not. I have many happy memories of Uncle Gordon, although I was only seven at the time. On one occasion I remember Aunty Gerty was out shopping and Uncle Gordon and my sister and I had instructions from her that we were to ice my birthday cake. The icing that we made turned out to have the consistency something between concrete and glue and when it came to putting in eight candles Uncle Gordon decided that the only tool to use was a bradawl. How tooth-friendly it was when consumed I cannot recall.

Just two years later Gordon was admitted to Frimley Sanatorium but sadly his condition worsened and he died on Palm Sunday 1941 at the age of 32. This was the obituary published in *The Lancet* on 26th April 1941:

Gordon Colebrook Gillison M.B. Edin, who died at Frimley Sanatorium on April 6, put more into his thirty two years of life than he ever attempted to take out of it. Meeting the handicap of diabetes as a student, he accepted it dealt with it and carried on. Following his family to China where he had been born into a medical family, he met another foe, the tubercle bacillus. Once again he took it as a medical opportunity; he would 'cure' first himself then others. To that end he returned to England and found at Frimley the double opportunity for study and for 'cure'. Emerging with an Artificial Pneumothorax a year and a half later, he plunged into Sanatorium work at Peppard Common.

Not for him however the easy and careful path; every patient that came his way had not only a body to be tended but a mind to interest, a spirit to encourage, relations to help. Every member of the staff was his friend and neighbour, their problems his. His life was brief but enough for the sowing and reaping of a rich harvest of affection.

Tom and Bessie lived in the compound of Griffith John College at Han Chia Ten and, in spite of their years, never let up on their chosen work of translating and healing the sick. In 1935 the Yangtze river flooded again and the work of Bessie's daily clinic was seriously interrupted. The river is over a mile wide at Hankow and in summer is forty feet deeper than it is in the winter but in some years it rises considerably more than that. That year the water was ten feet deep in the garden and more than four feet deep in the downstairs rooms of their house and the clinic. It was not until the autumn that the water receded and the clinic was able to open again. Almost twelve thousand patients were treated by Bessie in 1935 in spite of the months of closure. There had been ninety operations under anaesthesia and of these forty had been for opening abscesses, removing dead bone, or extracting teeth. Bessie had undertaken a course in dentistry as well as medicine when she trained at The Royal Free Hospital and this was to prove very useful on many occasions.

Bessie made regular visits into the city once a week to visit Keith, Kathleen and the family in the Union Hospital compound and Tom continued his work of translation, as well as taking over the responsibilities of pastor to the villagers and chaplain to the college. This way of life continued calmly until one day in November 1936 an old man came in with a mouth full of broken and infected teeth. Bessie did her best for the patient removing the worst teeth but in doing so she scratched her own thumb on one of the broken teeth. Within a short time septicaemia developed and on November 30th she died. Tom wrote this letter to Howard, Gordon and Gerty in England:

Dec 1ˢᵗ 1936

   Today is Saturday. On Tuesday – just five days ago, Mother was seeing her patients, and was drawing a tooth for one of them and noticed a little blood on the handle of the forceps or on wiping her hands on the towel, and found it came from a scratch on the end of her own thumb. She put some mercurochrome on it and finished her morning's work – had tiffin – and then went into town – as Tuesday is her day for going in. She put through a good many jobs and came back between 6 and 7 and told me what she had been doing – and was well satisfied with what she had put through. She came back and said she was going to bed a bit earlier because she was tired and her thumb which she had dressed with her favourite – Izal lotion – was paining her a bit. I looked in on her about 10.p.m. and she said the pain was a bit worse and she was afraid it might keep her from sleeping. I suggested 5 grains each of Asprin and Dover's powder and she at once agreed. I then retired to my bedroom but got up again about 1.30. and found her in a dozing state from which she kept waking up with the pain and then dozed off again. I again looked in at 4.a.m. and found her in much the same state as before. She needed little persuasion to stay in bed to breakfast. I got her some porridge and coffee. I attended to her patients that forenoon, and later on as it was the day I was due in for the monthly meeting of the Tract Society's Board, I asked her 'Shall I go in or shall I stay with you?' She said 'Yes! go in.' However after tiffin I took her temperature and finding it had jumped from 99.2 at breakfast time to 103.2 at 1.p.m. I resolved not to go. Besides there was another curious feature viz. her mind was beginning to wander a bit – at intervals – and she was still dozing and speech very slow. I decided to ask Keith to come out and see her as I was anxious. ...

   Keith and Kath arrived in another car in two hours time. Keith examined and agreed the condition was a curious one – when he e.g. asked her questions in English she replied – but replied quite correctly – in Chinese. We agreed that she should go back with Keith and Kath in the car.

...I remained behind and well it was that I did so for one of the servants of the school fell and got sub-coracoid dislocation – under an anaesthetic we got it in all right – I saw Mother's patients next morning and had to give an anaesthetic to two of them – Strange to say one was an acute suppuration of the thumb in a young girl in great suffering. After tiffin I went in by ricsha to see how Mother fared, I had heard by telephone in the morning that she had stood the journey well and had had a fair night but mind was wandering a bit and the skin over the palmer aspect of the end of the thumb had risen like a blister. The pain was less – so in the evening I returned to Griffith John School so as to be there to do the patients next morning – I did not want her to worry about them. The phone next morning was not quite so good so after seeing the patients (the women helpers are splendid and see all the old cases and some of the simpler new ones) – had again to give an anaesthetic to a child for a large abscess, – sent one or two cases into the hospital.

I again went in after tiffin. There was less pain in the thumb. – Temp oscillating – General condition doubtful – Yesterday I again saw patients and again came in but prepared to stay as I was anxious both about the thumb and her resistive powers. Dr. Chapman is in charge of the case – along with Keith – while Jean and a number of the nurses are in charge of the nursing so she is having the best of care – The temperature has been coming down but it again took a sudden jump to 103.4 or thereabouts. My heart sank very low when I saw the arm and hand dressed. <u>Her life absolutely hangs in the balance,</u> and in my deepest soul I fear the worst – and can scarcely keep from breaking down – but that would hinder and not help – All are so good and kind. ... There is a long black slough (on the thumb) It is still adherent. Keith thinks it perhaps does not go very deep. It is however not the thumb that causes anxiety. The whole hand, the forearm and half way up the upper arm is intensely swollen (?streptoccocal cellulitis). Her mind has been wandering from the beginning – but has been a little clearer at intervals. I think it is a little less clear tonight. What causes anxiety however is the pulse It actually reached 200, then came down to 172, then 160, and the last taken two or three hours ago 156. She is being given glucose and saline intravenously ... by the drop method now for 9 hours, coramine added every four hours. Then to keep the swollen arm warm without having to change the fomentation too often Keith has devised a string of small electric light bulbs around a sort of cage. It answers very well. Poor Keith is pretty well tired out. Last night in addition to all his care for his mother, he had to do an acute appendix between midnight and 2a.m. It was a pretty bad case but he hopes to save it. I must now go on duty for a few hours to relieve the others. Will post this with the latest bulletin tomorrow.

December 1st.

All is over and the dear one is to be laid to rest today. These last few days have been days of special watching and waiting on her and I shall just finish first the story of the illness to the end. On the 29th.Nov. (Sunday) she continued having the glucose and saline and coramine & stropanthin and it seemed to help a bit – but the poor poisoned heart muscle got weaker. She wandered more and became less and less conscious of her surroundings and I was afraid the heart might flicker out suddenly – so I resolved to stay near her that night. I arranged for the head night nurse to be on the qui vive – to notice any change. Keith and Jean were taking a needed rest – they were simply worn out. I lay down on a hospital bed and said I was to be called at once if any change was seen. At 5.15.a.m. the nurse called me and dear Mother was breathing rapidly – air hunger – I sent for Keith and Jean but the end came too quickly for them. Keith and Kath arrived two minutes after she passed away and Jean a minute or two later. She would not have recognised them even if they had been some hours earlier. Jean and the nurses and Kath attended to the dear body. The face looked so peaceful – just as if she were taking a natural sleep.

I told Keith & Kath I would not stay for breakfast – I felt I could not face the children without breaking down – so I went to the C.I.M. about 7.45.

Bessie Gillison

Dear Mother passed away at quarter to six. The children did not see her after she passed away for the body was not taken to the house till after they had had their breakfast and had gone off in a ricsha to school in town. They are there with the L.M.S, for two days and will only come back when the funeral (to which they will not go) is over.

Mr Onley is to conduct the funeral service in the Union Hospital Ch. and Mr Rowlands and several Chinese and foreign will take part – the service being partly in Chinese and partly in English. Mr Withers Green will take the committal service at the grave and we will sing in English and in Chinese 'Guide me O Thou Great Jehovah' – You will hear more of the services later.

Today tens and tens of beautiful wreaths with loving messages of sympathy have kept pouring in. The grave is to be next to Mr. Wang Kwang's and diagonally across the path from Dr. Byles' – a very suitable site. Mr Felix Wei lent me his beautiful car all yesterday afternoon or I could not have got through.

I must close so that you will get this as soon as possible. You can imagine the blank in my poor old heart – but God is love and will draw me nearer to Him for the Strength and comfort you need.

Bessie's grave with the flowers laid on it from Tom's funeral.

In June 1937 Tom himself developed pneumonia and after a short illness he died. A circular letter was sent to their many colleagues and friends by Keith, Kathleen and Jean:

> *We are writing to tell you of Father's home call. It is not seven months since Mother's passing and now Father has left us too.*
>
> *While Mother was here with us, Father left a great deal to her and devoted most of his time to literary work. Mother, with occasional help from Father, carried on the medical work she loved among the sick poor, and did most of the letter-writing, but when Mother was taken, Father threw himself heart and soul into carrying on what Mother had done. He told us he would continue the medical work, at least until the summer, and do it he did, just as Mother had done, and when the time for Kuling came, he wound up the work, settled up the accounts and left everything just as Mother used to leave*

it. In addition he personally wrote about 300 letters to those who had written about Mother, allowing his own literary work to suffer.

In March Father had an attack of influenza with slight involvement of one lung. He recovered, but his health never seemed quite the same after this, though his energy was unabated.

On Wed. June 9th, the monthly missionary prayer-meeting was held at the Griffith John Compound and Father was asked to take the chair. He had not felt very well but accepted, and spoke at the meeting of Mother; how she had come out to do medical missionary work but family ties soon made that impossible, so she took up the training of Bible-women in her own home and did that for many years instead. Finally, in the evening of her life, the way opened again for medical work, and she did it as though she had never stopped it. 'Mother's life had shown repeatedly', Father said, 'that when God closes one door, He opens another'. It was a beautiful meeting and many spoke to Father afterwards thanking him. It was Father's last appearance in public a door was shutting and another opening for him, as it had done for Mother.

From that time onwards Father was confined to bed with fever, cough, breathlessness, and increasing weakness. For years he has had a chronic cough, and for some time an irregular heart, and now his symptoms became acute again and in spite of all that could be done he was taken from us on the 22nd. June less than a fortnight from the start of his illness. He did not suffer a great deal and right up to the last was full of his old cheery spirit. The first few days of his illness he insisted on spending in his house at Griffith John, because he was comfortable there, and because he had certain matters he felt he must finish off before leaving, and no amount of persuasion would move him, and finish he did – directing his cook and coolie from a long chair till everything was fixed to his satisfaction. Then after that he consented to come in and stay with us.

On Monday June 21st. there was to be a Hospital Staff Social, and we were asked if it could be held in our garden. Some of us thought it might

302

disturb Father, so we asked him, but he wouldn't hear of it being anywhere
else. They came and he was delighted to hear the laughter and merriment,
and asked for a big helping of ice-cream (it was an ice-cream social) not for
himself, but so that he could give some to our kiddies and the faithful coolie,
Han Sz Fu who was helping to look after him.

That night when Mei Li went to bed, she said in her prayer, 'Please
God, try to make Grandpa better', and next morning when Frances who was
sleeping on the verandah near Grandpa's room, heard him talking to his
servant, she said, 'Grandpa, you mustn't talk so much, you'll cough if you do'.
The kiddies did love their Grannie and Grandpa, and Grandpa was always so
interested in and concerned about them.

Father's cook Liu, and his coolie Han, were, at his special request,
allowed to help look after him, one doing day and the other night duty. Father
was most attached to them, and they were devoted to him.

The night after the social Father slept well, but during the day
of Tues. the 22nd. June, he became very breathless, and said three times
to Liu Shih Fu, 'Ts'en liao' – 'It is finished' and later dozed off to sleep.
He dozed quite peacefully that evening giving us no special cause for
alarm till quite suddenly about 10 p.m. the call came. In a wonderful
way those words were true. They were said, half dreamingly – thinking
perhaps of the Master Who said them first – and Whom Father
had loved and served so long and so faithfully, but they were certainly
strangely appropriate. Work for the Master begun here 55 years ago had
been finished, the hospital of which he had dreamed, and for which he
had worked and collected for a quarter of a century was standing there
complete, and making steady progress, the medical work at Han Chia Ten,
left to him by Mother had been concluded as in previous years, accounts
settled up, wages paid. The house had been tidied, things packed away and
all left in order. Less than a month previously Father had brought up to
date his will, written it all out in his splendid copper-plate handwriting,

*beautifully clear and business-like
– signed and witnessed. One of the
things over which Father spent most
pains and trouble during his last
months, was Mother's grave and stone.
He took infinite pains over the wording
and design – the English and the
Chinese and made frequent trips in
to Hankow to see that the work was
being properly carried out. Father's old
friend, Mr. Lewis Jones helped him
with the task and on Monday, June
21st (the day before the passing) Father
had the joy of hearing from 'Uncle
Lewis' that the stone was up and the*

The last photograh of Tom and Bessie.

*work complete. It was a tremendous satisfaction to him, and he said to
Jean with his love of fun – irrepressible to the last – 'Jean dear, if you are
ever in need of a stone, Lewis is the man to see to it for you'.*

*Father's call came about 10 p.m. on Tues. 22nd. of June, and all next
day, as with Mother, the Church leaders, former colleagues, students of the old
Hankow Medical school and friends of all sorts came and paid their respects
in silent reverence.*

*The funeral service, in our Ling Kwang Church, was a truly inspiring
one, the building being packed to the doors with representatives of all the
Missions, doctors, nurses, and friends, rich and poor, Chinese and foreign.
The apse and front of the Church were heaped high with flowers and the
walls were covered with scrolls sent by the various country and city churches
or by individuals. Several of Father's oldest friends took part, of course. Dr
Hu spoke most feelingly in Chinese of his 30 odd years of colleagueship
with Father, and Bishop Roots spoke in English. The latter had just returned*

Written on Bessie's grave stone is 'Well done good and faithful servant'
and on Tom's 'Enter thou into the joy of thy Lord'.

*to Hankow from a visit to Ichang and began by saying that it was less than
an hour since he heard of the death of his life-long friend Thomas Gillison.
Speaking though at such short notice he was positively inspired and one
could not but be stirred and challenged.*

*We laid the earthly remains to rest, side by side with Mother's, Mr.
Onley conducting the service at the graveside and all, Chinese and foreign,
joining in the hymn 'The King of love my shepherd is'. Surely Goodness and
Mercy have followed Father all the days of his life and he will dwell in the
house of the Lord forever.*

*The blank left in our hearts by the taking from us within so short
a time of first Mother and then Father is not easy to fill, but we do thank
and praise God for His great goodness and guidance given to our parents
throughout their long lives, and we pray that we may be enabled to follow
worthily in their footsteps.*

Sunset at Kiu Kiang (1929).

Tom had worked in China for fifty-five years and Bessie for forty-four – nearly a century between them. The hospital grew from being staffed by only one doctor for thirty-six years and without a single qualified nurse for forty-five years to twenty doctors, twenty qualified nurses and training schools for all hospital departments by 1950.

ELEVEN

A personal perspective

Wuhan (as we should call Hankow from now on) suffered badly from the bombing of the Japanese and although I was only five I remember having to shelter under our stairs with candles for light and listening to the falling bombs. So recent were these memories that when, in 1939 and 1940, the bombing of London began and we were in boarding school in Kent under the flight path of the enemy bombers, I could not understand anyone making a fuss about going under cover in an air-raid –

Walthamstow Hall School for the Daughters of Missionaries, in Sevenoaks, Kent. (Photograph taken in 1938 the year the author and her sister entered the school.)

to me it was a normal part of life. We, as a family, were due to go on furlough in 1938 but the bombing threat was so serious to Hankow that several missionary families sent their children down to Hong Kong to be out of harm's way. My sister and I were sent to stay with missionary friends in January 1938 with the intention that our parents would then collect us in August at the start of our journey to Britain. In a way those few months were a dummy run for the long separation that was lying ahead for my sister and me. My recollections of that time in Hong Kong are mainly that I had an attack of ringworm and both my sister and I had a tonsillectomy – neither memories to treasure.

We sailed in the 'Empress of Asia' from Hong Kong first to Nagasaki via Shanghai then across the Pacific Ocean to Canada in order to visit Grandmother Bessie's brother Joe Harris and his family in Vancouver and New Denver. The ship sailed early in the morning and in the late afternoon a raft was sighted with a fisherman on it. I remember very clearly everyone on deck rushing to the side rails to watch the lifeboat being lowered and I could see that the old fisherman was almost cardboard-stiff with cold and exposure as the crew brought him on board. It was gratifying to find that I had not imagined the incident for in my mother's diary for that day was this entry:

> *Empress of Asia sails at 7.a.m. About 5 p.m. sight a raft with one poor fisherman on it. Stop boat and pick him up. There 4 days. Blown out of fishing boat by gale. Called Liu, 62, native of place near Swatow. 1ˢᵗ Class collected $200 for him. Company sent him back home at their expense.*

I also remember hearing on the tannoy an announcement asking passengers who spoke any unusual dialects to go to the Purser's office to help with communicating with the old man. I think my father volunteered but I doubt that he could help for his Chinese, though good, was either Mandarin or a North China Peking dialect.

We called at Shanghai and Mother writes, 'Difficult not to have feelings of resentment as we sail up Shanghai river and see Jap flags flying from buildings.' Japan was already making substantial land gains in China.

The rest of the journey across the Pacific was free of dramatic incidents but my memories of Canada are unforgettable. Quite apart from enjoying 'Bosun Ranch' [24], the Harris family home in the most beautiful setting on Lake Slocan, we crossed Canada by the Canadian Pacific Railway and the views of the Rockies from the train made an indelible impression on a six-year-old. Our family visited more friends and relations en route in Winnipeg, Toronto and Montreal and we were taken to see the Niagara Falls. So special was that journey that it has remained a crystal clear episode in my memory for over seventy years.

From Canada we sailed on the 'Empress of Britain' which was described by mother in her diary as, 'Certainly a luxury liner with its Mayfair lounge, Cathay lounge, swimming bath, gymnasia etc. Spacious cabins. Service in Mayfair in morning and orchestral concert at night – excellent.' As it was a Sunday the 'service' referred to must have been a religious one – my mother would not know of any other kind of service.

The swimming pool made a great impression on mother for she described it as 'gorgeous'. However she apparently decided against using the ship's barber to have my sister Meili's hair cut because it would cost 2/- which was far too expensive. Reading her diary it seems that mother spent most of her time on board sewing name tapes on to our clothes ready for boarding school so I doubt that she sampled any of the facilities on offer.

The September term was already underway when we landed at Southampton, so the first thing to do was to get us into school. For the first few months my parents had the use of a house for missionaries on furlough in Sevenoaks and although we were officially boarders we were allowed to go home quite often. This must have been fitted in to the busy schedule of the meetings and services which they were addressing up and down the country but who looked after my young toddler brother during this time neither he nor I can remember; there is no mention of him in mother's diary.

The start of 1939 was also filled with deputation work but my parents must have been dreading September. Our summer holiday was spent camping in Scotland and although we must have been told that our parents and brother were returning to China without us I cannot recall being prepared for the coming parting; it was only when I read the family letters as we were transcribing them that I discovered that the plan to leave us at school in England had been made as far back as 1935. My mother wrote to Mary Black saying:

June 16ᵗʰ 1935

> *... Now dear Aunt Molly, we do hope you are flourishing too. I am so glad we had the opportunity of getting to know you a bit when we were on furlough. I hope you live as long as your Mother & then we are sure to. We expect to be home again in about 5 years' time. Then it will be to leave Meili & Frances at school. That time doesn't bear thinking about.*

The education of their children has always been a difficult problem for missionaries. A hundred years ago diseases such as dysentery and typhoid were common and young children were especially vulnerable. There were few schools which could provide adequate teaching on the Mission stations. All missionaries were faced with this dilemma and often they had little option but to send the children to suitable boarding schools back in Britain. This could mean a separation of many years with little contact between parents and children other than letters which could take a month or more to arrive. It was difficult for both parties – perhaps harder for the parent – and in some cases affected their relationship permanently. By the time my parents faced this dilemma the situation was further complicated by the shadow of war which added enormously to the uncertainty.

All my life I wondered how they were able to carry this plan through and it was not until shortly before my mother's death that I talked to her about it. My last conversation with her was a couple of days before she died in June 1991 at the nursing home in Nottingham where she had lived since she had had a slight stroke a few months earlier. She had only partial speech and it meant that conversations sometimes had to be prompted by asking leading questions to which she would respond with a head shake of yes or no but on the whole we were able to communicate reasonably well.

My sister, Meili, told me about a conversation she had had with mother the day before. She said mother had seemed rather agitated as if she had something on her mind, so Meili chatted to her touching on things that had happened in mother's life including her first years in China. They talked about her childhood, her family and her life as a missionary and Meili commented on the fact that it must have been daunting to marry into a family which had been established on the mission field for so many years. Meili got the impression that mother had indeed felt slightly overawed when she joined the family but she agreed that my grandparents were very gentle, good people and the feeling of being an outsider faded with time as they made her so welcome.

We knew mother was very near her end and I felt that I in my turn should try to talk things over with her, especially as my relationship with my parents had always been rather prickly. After their return to England from internment camp in 1945 adjusting to family life was not easy. My parents came under the influence of Moral Rearmament (M.R.A. for short but now called Initiatives for Change) during their first furlough in 1932 and had been deeply impressed by it. From 1933 onwards they were keen disciples of the movement and I have no doubt that during their internment by the Japanese it was a tremendous spiritual and practical support. The great disappointment for them was that, on their return to Britain and with the family together once more, I was so unreceptive for I am sure that, throughout their internment they had dreamt that we would eventually be a united family within the Group. I was a slightly rebellious teenager and was reluctant to join with the family in their daily 'Quiet Times'. I was not at all comfortable with being 'guided' by God using pen and paper to write down what He 'said' to me; neither was I willing to share that guidance with all and sundry including the many full time MRA adherents who were invited to stay at our house; nor did I like attending group meetings where public confessions were made which seemed to me, as an unwilling observer, like some kind of religious voyeurism. However I was prepared to accept that MRA was right for them but not for me and that was the tacit agreement between us which they seemed to accept. I was married soon after leaving teacher training college and for the rest of their lives the normal relationship of parent to daughter, grandparent to grandchild, were observed with friendliness but without any real closeness.

On that June day in 1991 we talked in Mother's room for an hour or so and it gave me the opportunity to ask her about the one thing that had always puzzled and amazed me: how it was that in 1939 she, my father and their four-year-old were able to go back to China leaving her two little girls, then aged ten and seven, not knowing with any certainty if she would ever see them again. I was as gentle, sympathetic and non-judgmental as I could be and said that I could not have carried it through had I been in that position. However I could imagine that it had been a really terrible experience for her. She nodded in great agitation and managed to say, 'I didn't want to – I <u>had</u> to, I <u>had</u> to'.

This remark of my mother's seems to me to sum up the extraordinary attitude that was expected of missionaries in those early years. Partly borne out of practical necessity because of lack of educational facilities on the mission field and partly because of the unsuitability of climate and prevalence of disease, parents knew that a time might come when they would have to say goodbye to their children for many years at a time. However separation was not always harmful. From my own experience the years apart from my parents were in no way unhappy. I was fortunate in having guardians I loved and was the type of child who adapts well to boarding school life. Nevertheless I cannot understand how any parents could bring themselves to allow a separation of that kind from their children. My grandparents, surprisingly and unusually, countenanced separation from their children during their secondary school years but for a few years they themselves separated during the children's tertiary education. This might strike the reader as an odd way round – but that was the way it was.

It was while writing this book that I was struck by the fact that I knew very little about the childhood experiences of my contemporaries who were also missionaries' daughters. At the time I was aware that in some cases my friends were not altogether happy with their guardians, particularly if they were not related, but as school girls we always took things for granted and never questioned the status quo. I knew one of my friends had had a very difficult childhood but when I got in touch with her recently to ask her about her experiences I was astonished to hear what she had had to endure.

My friend was born in Brazil and brought to England as a baby. She was left in the care of dedicated staff at a 'Home for the Children of Missionaries' in South London. On returning for furlough four years later her parents decided to put her in the care of two friends of her mother whom she had not previously met.

The death of one of these ladies in addition to the strain of the war years on the other 'Aunty' led to a very unhappy period in her childhood. After eight years absence (longer than usual because of the war) her parents returned with a five year old brother. This long awaited reunion did not come up to her eager expectations and in due course they returned to the mission field after a year's furlough taking her brother with them.

Then followed a miserable, but fortunately a short stay, with another couple in Sevenoaks. They were wealthy, childless and total strangers to her. She was attending Walthamstow Hall as a daygirl at this time, having been awarded a scholarship, and when the couple suddenly decided they no longer wanted her to live with them it was arranged that she would become a boarder; the best thing that could have happened to her. A member of staff of the children's home in South London, who over the intervening years had formed a close bond with her, became her legal guardian and a much needed 'mother' figure – a relationship that was to remain very close until the guardian's death in 1980.

In our time there were many missionary daughters at Walthamstow Hall and sons at Eltham College and the arrangements for the care of the children varied widely. In at least three families among my contemporaries the mother remained in England while the father was in the Mission station. Whether this was from choice or force of circumstances because of the war I cannot tell. There have been a few missionary parents honest enough to admit that it was they and not their children who made the choice to serve on the Mission field and frankly admitted and regretted the high price the children would be made to pay. My own view is that having made that choice, parents should appreciate that in following the demands of their calling they might also have to surrender the right to the close ties with their children enjoyed by normal families; they did not always do so. In retrospect I find it most surprising that while we were growing up, even among our closest friends, we never discussed or compared the arrangements made for our guardianship or our holiday arrangements; we just accepted that we were all more or less in the same boat, stood on our own feet and got on with life.

Looking back I am sure that much of my interest in reading and transcribing the letters lay in trying to understand this aspect of my family's missionary history. I feel I have grown to understand my relatives a little better through the letters and can only admire their selfless dedication to their faith. The jury is out as to whether those sacrifices were justified.

The first three years after my parents' return to China in 1939 had been spent in Hankow and the Mission had carried on the work as best it could although the Japanese had overrun the city. However after Pearl Harbor all foreign nationals were interned and for two and a half years their confinement made many demands on their physical strength, stamina and above all on their spirit. Not least was the almost total absence of news from either their families at home or the progress of the war itself. The camp was liberated in August 1945 and the 600 inmates repatriated a few weeks later. Once home they gradually built up their physical strength and tried to pick up their lives where they had left off. It was not an easy time for anyone. This was when the strain between my parents and me was at its greatest. I had been used to the strong moral and religious standards of a school staffed by thoroughly good Christian women who were completely dedicated to bringing out the best in the girls and acting in 'loco parentis' to the best of their ability with kindness and sensitivity. In return, for the most part, they had the full respect and affection of the pupils – in many cases forging a friendship which lasted a lifetime. I failed to see what MRA could offer which was not already expected or available in the conduct of the spiritual life to which I was accustomed; I became by default the black sheep of the family and a sad disappointment to my parents. (One black sheep became two in later years when my brother was older and allowed to think for himself.)

For my father especially, much though he needed the rest, his main aim was to return to China and try to help in re-establishing the Union Hospital. Like his father before him the pull of China was irresistible and was indeed one of the most important aspects of his life. In 1947 he returned to the Union Hospital on his own not knowing what state the hospital would be in. Expecting the worst Keith found that the Relief Agencies, the Red Cross and others had worked hard to re-equip the hospital in a most generous way. Former doctors and missionaries had quickly come out of retirement to help clean, re-condition and staff the hospital in readiness for the internees to return. Mother joined him in 1948 and was able to take on a good deal of the secretarial and financial side of the hospital work. By late 1948

This is the certificate recognizing Keith Gillison as Medical Superintendant which authorized the opening of the hospital. It states: Gillison, who is aged 48 years and born in England, is applying for opening of the privately owned Hankou Union Hospital. The application has been checked as conforming to the three management rules for hospitals and clinics. The application is approved. Signed: Mayor Xu Hui-Zhi Republic of China 37th year, April.

the Union Hospital boasted 298 members of staff including 20 Chinese doctors, 20 Chinese graduate nurses and 110 Chinese student nurses in addition to 10 foreign doctors and 6 foreign nurses. My father was appointed Medical Superintendant in spite of the fact that he had suggested to the Hospital Board (made up of Chinese as well as foreign members) that a Chinese doctor should be given the post. However his appointment coincided with the rise of the forces of Mao Tze-Tung and the Cultural Revolution; those influences were so strong that by 1949 continuing their work became incredibly difficult especially for foreign staff. Reluctantly my parents and the other missionaries felt that they should leave and after nearly 150 years, in 1950, the London Missionary Society's link with Wuhan and the Union Hospital was broken.

During the years following their return to the UK in 1950, much to their regret, Keith and Kath had virtually no contact with the Union Hospital except for a few occasional links by letter with one or two members of staff. In 1955 after a spell of five years working in his cousin Allan Gillison's General Practice in Bermondsey, my father accepted an invitation to work as a GP to the staff and students of the University of Ibadan, Nigeria where he stayed for seven years. He finally returned to the UK in 1962 setting up in General Practice in Letchworth which occupied him until his retirement at the age of 79.

The 1980s brought about a complete change of direction on the part of the Chinese authorities. Keith was invited to get in touch with the Union Hospital again and in the first instance he sent them some of the old annual hospital reports at their request as they seemed interested to know the history of the hospital. He was getting on in years, rather frail and felt unable to accept their warm invitation to make the journey out to Wuhan. However both my parents were very pleased to think that after so many years of isolation China was opening its doors to those who longed to be their friends once more.

From my vantage point in 2010, looking back over the hundred years of missionary work in Wuhan from the middle of the nineteenth century to 1950, it is hard to assess how much of a lasting contribution it made. The three main areas Missions aim to influence are education, medicine and of course, 'converting the heathen'. The political upheavals of one sort or another which lasted throughout the whole of the period that my family were in Wuhan affected much of their work and the Cultural Revolution virtually severed all ties with foreign missionary societies. I have no knowledge of any legacy left by the missionary societies in the field of education, nor any clear idea if the many Chinese Christians in Wuhan were able to continue observing their faith. One Christian family, who knew my parents, is still occasionally in touch with us but I have no idea of how easy it is for them to observe their faith or how large a group of Christians exists in Wuhan.

In the field of medicine the picture is quite different. During the last twenty years the Union Hospital has actively acknowledged its non-Chinese origins. In 2001 my brother Walford received an invitation to go to Wuhan to join in the Union Hospital's 135th celebration of the founding of the hospital. This very generous gesture was repeated in 2006 for the 140th anniversary and this time my brother, his wife and I, together with forty or fifty other guests of many nationalities, were given a magnificent reception and treated to three days of amazing hospitality. We were present at the opening of the magnificent new surgical block and attended an imposing rally, which was graced by many government, local and hospital officials. The work of Dr Griffith John in starting the hospital was recognized and my grandfather was celebrated and honoured as the first President of the Union Hospital. An imposing bust of Dr John has pride of place at the entrance to the building.

The bust of Dr Griffith John at the entrance to the Union Hospital.

The Chinese characters on the left certificate read as follows: Dr Thomas Gillison is the first President of the Xiehe Hospital. He made an extraordinary contribution to the development of the hospital. To commemorate Dr Gillison and to inspire a new generation, I am honoured to appoint Frances Clemmow, Dr Gillison's granddaughter, honorary member of staff of our hospital. President Wang Guobin, Union Hospital.

Although our grandfather was singled out for special honour he was merely the representative of the very many hundreds of doctors, nurses, and other staff who gave everything to further the work of the hospital over many years. The hope of all those men and women was that the hospital and the medical school they established would provide Wuhan with a worthy place of healing and the opportunity to educate the Chinese men and women in medicine. They could not possibly have envisaged the magnificent hospital and world-famous university that now stands on the site of the old hospital. The Union Hospital, part of Tongji Medical College, Huazhong University of Science and Technology, is right at the forefront of medical techniques, treatment and research.

The Union Hospital 2006.

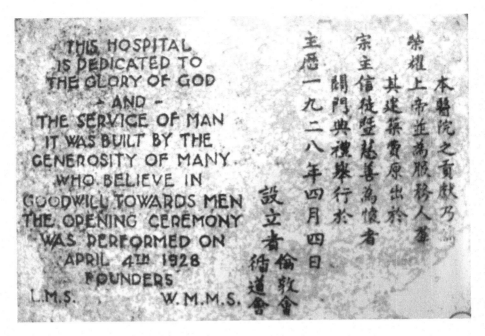

This plaque reads:

THIS HOSPITAL
IS DEDICATED TO
THE GLORY OF GOD
- AND -
THE SERVICE OF MAN
IT WAS BUILT BY THE
GENEROSITY OF MANY
WHO BELIEVE IN
GOODWILL TOWARDS MEN
THE OPENING CEREMONY
WAS PERFORMED ON
APRIL 4TH 1928
FOUNDERS
L.M.S.   W.M.M.S.

At the 2006 celebrations my brother and I were also very honoured to be presented with 'Honarary Credentials' acknowledging our grandfather's contribution to the establishment of the hospital.

It is touching that the old foundation stone of the 1928 hospital has been preserved and can be seen in the entrance hall of one of the buildings.

Since our visit to Wuhan in 2006 we have kept up our contact with Dr Hao Zhou, a young doctor who was one of our 'minders' in 2006. He gave me invaluable help in translating Chinese words and phrases when we were transcribing the family letters and although there is no longer any need to consult him on that front we enjoy a continuing friendship with him and his family. Were my grandparents able to see the magnificent hospital now, the amazing advances in medicine and surgery, the transformation of world communications and transport, they would think it a miracle. I would agree with them.

Afterword

The responses from different parts of the world following the original publication of *Days of Sorrow, Times of Joy* in 2012 astonished me. Several distant cousins from Australia, New Zealand, Canada and the USA got in touch and one particularly interesting letter came from California. It was from Thomas Rittenburg, who wrote saying that he had come across the book and had worked out that we shared the same Scottish great-great-grandparents – which was indeed the case. Furthermore, he was in contact with yet another cousin in Canada who, to my great delight, sent me a photograph of my widowed great-grandmother and her family. It was a picture I had never seen before and I was thrilled to add it to my collection. The studio portrait was almost certainly taken in 1882 on the eve of the departure of my grandfather and his older brother, John, to foreign parts – my grandfather, Thomas, to China and John, to Australia. It was to be the last time the family were together and, by their sombre looks, they seemed aware that this might be a defining moment in their lives (*see page 8*).

For seventy years I had taken my family history for granted and thought it unremarkable. It was only after reading the letters and understanding something of the lives of those early missionary families that I began to reflect on how my own childhood fitted in to this pattern. The course of my young life changed by a planned event in 1939. Our family – my father, mother and three children - had been on leave in the UK from China in 1938 but in November 1939, my parents and young brother returned to China leaving my sister, then a ten year old and me, aged seven, in England. We were in the care of a loving aunt and uncle as guardians for the holidays and in a sympathetic boarding school during term-time, where many of my peers were also daughters of missionaries, and in a similar situation.

We had almost no contact with our parents during those six years. Theoretically, twenty-five word messages could be sent through the Red Cross , but they would take months to arrive. I remember receiving two or three during the internment years, but my brother told me he can recall only one from us. (He also told me that the internees suspected that all the letters intended for them were set alight in a huge bonfire with other papers as soon as the camp guards realized they had been defeated.) Little that is worthwhile can be said in twenty-five words of the physical and emotional development of a seven and ten-year-old on the one hand or of the hardship and deprivation of an internment camp on the other. At school, time was set aside for writing letters home and as there was no way our weekly letters could be forwarded to China, (although I did not know it at the time) my guardians had the good sense and imagination to save our letters so that they could be handed over to my parents to read on their return.

For six years, my mother and father only figured in my life as 'Dear Mummy and Daddy' – the four words I wrote at the top of my weekly letter; neither were there photographs to remind me of what they looked like – an oversight which I am sure was not deliberate, but I suppose it had not occurred to anyone to take account of what a seven-year-old would or would not remember in subsequent years. I developed a certain amount of sturdy independence and self-reliance and even though I longed for us to be together again, the reality of fitting into a family unit which turned out to be deeply involved with the religious movement called Moral Rearmament, proved to be extremely difficult in practice.

In the last chapter I have already recounted the difficulties we had to readjust to family living because of their preferred daily religious observances. For my parents it was a way of life that had enabled them to face, positively, the privations of their Japanese-occupied mission hospital, and later the internment camp. I was always prepared to accept that it was right for them but I resented having MRA imposed on me. Its intentions were well-meaning but as a teenager I had neither the experience nor the confidence to challenge its principles or its methods and, as time went on, I found it harder to feel or display the affection my parents expected. In the end, we learned to co-exist, but our relationship remained strained and the uneasiness, sadly, carried over into my parents' relationship with my own children.

All this happened many years ago so it was a shock recently to discover that in her 2010 thesis *Protestant Missionary Experience during the War in China 1937-1945*, Jocelyn Chatterton, referred to my father Dr. Keith Gillison's letter (dated 1945) to Rev.T.C.Brown, Foreign Secretary for China of the London Missionary Society, about the consequences of the six-year-long family separation. My father wrote that after his youngest daughter (me) no longer believed in God which he attributed to the separation. In 1949, he resigned from the L.M.S. Dr Chatterton writes:

> ...Gillison, convinced that time in the internment camp had not been wasted, experienced grief over lost years with his children and this was the main reason given for his resignation to the Board in 1949. Gillison had experienced parent/child separation in missionary work having been the child of missionary parents. The Gillisons had left their children for over six years in their previous term in the field and felt they could not leave their children again for a similar period of time.

I had had no idea that my beliefs had ever been mentioned outside the family, but more importantly, I had never discussed my thoughts about God with my parents. At this stage they knew that I disliked the daily rituals of MRA, but we had never discussed my own views. I am sure they knew that I had joined the local Congregational Church as a member when I was fifteen but looking back, and if I am honest, that step might have been partly in a spirit of defiance as much as conviction. Perhaps my father's passionate belief in the principles and practices of MRA and his disappointment that I could not accept them, blinkered him; they had dreamed for so long of united family working together to 'change the world'. Today, however, my parent's misconceptions about my beliefs no longer concern me – it was all so long ago – but it is a matter of regret that the life they chose distanced us, and also made it more difficult for me to feel love for them without reservation.

In the years since my parents devoted their life to China, the missionary ethic has of course changed as society has learned to accommodate different concepts of religion, and politics. Global relationships have been transformed in the period of de-colonization which occurred in the second half of the last century. The world has shrunk in terms of travel, and technology has totally transformed communications. The story of the Gillison family is very much of its time and as such has a fascinating place in the long history of missionary work. Above all it is a monument to the human capacity for compassion, a belief in God and dedication to an idea of service in the face of overwhelming odds.

Frances Clemmow, June 2016

Notes

Chapter 2 Jane's engagement

1   p. 40 Taken to mean the constellation of Cassiopeia.

2   p. 43 Warrender Park Road (the Gillison address). Pounds, shillings and
pence

3   p. 57 Three islands in the Italian part of Lake Maggiore

4   p. 59 The Vaudois was a Christian sect which originated in 12th century France.
Its members believed in the Bible; did not recognize the trappings of the Roman
Catholic Church; refused to take the Sacraments or to accept the cult of the Saints.
In 1655 the Duke of Savoy ordered them to attend Mass or be turned out of their
homes in twenty days. The Duke's army was ordered to attack and what was to
be known as the Massacre of Piedmont took place. The brutality of the massacre
roused the indignation of Europe. Cromwell, then Ruler in England, began writing
petitions and letters raising money on behalf of the Waldensian victims and
threatening military action. He sent out emissaries but it seems unlikely that he
actually built a wall. However, because of his intervention he became known as the
Protector of the Vaudois or Protestants. It took another forty to fifty years before
the Vaudois were permitted to return to their homes in the Alpine valleys thus
ending two hundred years of persecution.

Chapter 4 Edinburgh – revisited

5   p. 82 The eighth Duke of Argyll had posts erected in treeless areas of his
estates for cattle to rub against for relief from midge and fly bites and other
irritant infestations. His verminous herdsmen also took advantage of the
posts and gave thanks for this relief by blessing the Duke.

6   p. 90 In Scotland wedding cakes were, and still are, decorated with 'favours'.

These could be rings, flowers, horse shoes or butterflies and at a particular moment of the ceremonies these could be given to chosen guests – or 'favourite' people. The meaning of a particular decoration (in this case the rings) can vary from one area of Scotland to another.

Chapter 5 Slow boat to China

7   p. 107 Yamen – HQ of Chinese official

8   p. 107 pengtze – shed or hut

9   p. 109 Ji Yi Sen – one of the Chinese versions of 'Gillison'.

10 p. 110 Another Chinese name for Dr Gillison.

Chapter 6 Valley of the shadows

11 p. 138 His reference to James Gilmour and the Mongolian Mission is interesting. James Gilmour (1843–1891) was a very unconventional missionary who tried to preach the gospel to a people who were steeped in the Lamaist Buddhism of which the Dalai Lama is the religious leader. He spent the summers with the nomadic Mongols and his winters in Peking where his wife lived as she was physically unsuited to the hard life he lived in Mongolia. His unconventionality extended to his marriage for he wrote and then proposed to a girl whom he had never met but whose portrait he had seen. Gilmour had earlier boarded with the Rev. and Mrs S. Meech in Peking where he had seen the portrait of Emily Prankard, Mrs Meech's sister, who was living in London at the time. That the lady herself was agreeable to the suggestion and entered into correspondence with James Gilmour before travelling out to meet and marry him, shows an equally free spirit.

Chapter 7 Unscheduled furlough

12 p. 180 Peking now known as Beijing

13 p. 180 The British Consul in Hankow

Chapter 8 The South African Connection

14 p. 194 Jan Hofmeyr (1845-1909, known as 'Onze Jan' (our Jan), was a journalist

and politician who was extremely influential with the Stellenbosch Dutch Cape Farmers. His 'Farmer's Protection Union' which combined with the Rev. Stephanus Du Toit 'Afrikander Bond' transformed the approach and programme of the Bond and made it the strongest party in the Cape Colony by the mid 1880s. In contrast to Du Toit, who favoured a narrow exclusive linguistic definition of 'Africander', Hofmeyr defined it as embracing 'everyone who, having settled in this country, wants to stay here to help to promote our common interests...' He was anxious to avoid war and wanted equal rights for the English and the Dutch Africander. John Gillison's assertion of Hofmeyr as an 'arch-plotter' would seem to have been both harsh and premature. (*Source*: W.K.Hancock *Smuts: The Sanguine Years 1870-1919*)

15 p. 201 The Battle of Jameson's Raid (January 2nd 1896). The Great Trek of 1835–1854 had established two Boer Republics – S.A.R (Zuid Afrika Republic), or Transvaal Republic (1852), and the Orange Free State (1854). Following the discovery of gold in the Transvaal in 1886, thousands of foreign speculators and adventurers – 'uitlanders' ('outlanders') – poured into the area. Ten years later the population of Johannesburg was more than 100,000. The idea behind Jameson's Raid, dreamt up by Rhodes, financed by Alfred Beit, and clandestinely supported by Joseph Chamberlain in London, was that the 'uitlanders' in the city would rise up against the oppression of the Boer government and, simultaneously, Jameson's force would cross the border and support them. Jameson was frustrated by delays and decided to act on his own with the result that serious mistakes were made and the attack ended in disaster.

The Jameson affair was a fiasco and it strained the relationship between the governments Britain and Kruger's Transvaal still further, particularly after Kaiser Wilhelm ll sent a telegram of congratulation to Kruger a few days after the raid. This created anti-German and anti-Boer feeling back in Britain and Jameson became a hero in British eyes. It was said that Jameson was the inspiration for Kipling's poem 'If' because Jameson had been discreet about the involvement of the British government in the raid, particularly of Chamberlain, and the lines, 'If you can keep your head when all about you/

Are losing theirs and blaming it on you' were intended to reflect Jameson's courageous silence on the matter. Although he was initially imprisoned for his actions he was released after a few months on the grounds of ill health and returned to South Africa. Eventually he became Prime Minister of the Cape Colony (1904–1908), was made a baronet in 1911 and died in 1917.

16 p. 206 Boer War (1899–1902). Following the fiasco of Jameson's Raid there were 4 years of unquiet peace. Rhodes, Beit and others, together with secret support in London from such government figures such as Chamberlain and Milner, were plotting to gain supremacy for Britain in South Africa and one method of achieving this was by demanding 'immediate voice' or a say in political affairs for foreigners in Johannesburg. Such was the pressure that President Kruger of Transvaal is quoted as saying, 'It is our country you want' and he issued an ultimatum on October 9th 1899. The British Government allowed this to expire by two days and then war was declared. Although the final outcome was a win for Britain, some aspects of the conduct of the war did not reflect well on the British. The British forces outnumbered the Boer fighters by 5:1. Some of methods the British commanders adopted were condemned by many, for instance: the burning of Boer farms, and the destruction of their crops and cattle; the creation of concentration camps in which women and children were kept in appalling conditions; and the indiscriminate shooting of prisoners on the battle field. Chief among the critics at home was the leader of the Liberal Party, Campbell-Bannerman, who was quoted as saying, 'When is a war not a war? When it is waged by methods of barbarism in South Africa.'

17 p. 207 The Battle of Elandslaagte (October 21st 1899). Elandslaagte was a village on the railway line between Ladysmith and Dundee in Natal. The British were defending both towns when General Kock, the Boer commander, sent a scout party to the railway and cut the telegraph lines. Their troop of about 1200 men camped in an area surrounded by a horseshoe of hills outside the village. Major-General John French and Colonel Ian Hamilton were sent with a force of 3500 men to attack the Boers and their tactic was to approach

the enemy in a two-pronged assault. The Devonshires attacked from the front and the Gordon Highlanders and others by a flanking movement targeting the Boers' left flank. Although some of the Boers surrendered with a white flag, General Kock made a counter attack which nearly succeeded. The General himself was killed and many of his fleeing men were cut down by the British cavalry which followed them. Because of this infamous chase the battle became known as, 'Ell and slaughter'. This battle, and that of Talana Hill a day earlier, preceded the famous Siege of Ladysmith which lasted from 2nd November 1899 until the 28th February 1900.

18 p. 216 Pneumonic plague. There are three types of 'plague' – bubonic, pneumonic and septicaemic. Bubonic is the most common and about 60% of patients die from this form which is caused by the deposit of bacilli through flea bites in the lymphatic system causing large, inflamed and painful swellings. Septicaemic plague occurs because the same bacillus is deposited directly into the bloodstream and the result is usually fatal. Pneumonic plague is the most deadly. The bacilli attack the lungs and severe pneumonia develops resulting in death within two to three days. The disease is spread by droplet infection and is extremely contagious. It is interesting to note that the famous Indian spiritual and political leader, Mohandas Gandhi (later known as Mahatma Gandhi), was in Johannesburg at the time when bubonic plague broke out in the Indian settlement and he himself helped with organising the nursing of patients with plague and even became involved with the nursing himself. It is possible that Frans's patients, from whom he contracted the disease, also came from this settlement.

There is one other interesting connection with Gandhi and the Marais family. Jessie (Marais) and her husband John Hoyland were missionaries in India and their daughter, Rachel, told me that her parents were great admirers and friends of Gandhi. In 1931 Gandhi came to England and stayed at the Quaker College in Birmingham where John Hoyland (who had been invalided out of his missionary work) was then a lecturer. John persuaded Gandhi to lay his hands on 5-year-old Rachel's head and bless her.

Chapter 9 The next generation

19 p. 231 Jessie Marais

20 p. 234 The concessions were parts of Hankow that had been begrudgingly ceded to foreign governments for their nationals to live in. There were British, Russian, French, German and Japanese concessions in prime positions along the Yangtze bank for a distance of several miles; their wide streets and foreign style buildings contrasting sharply with the narrow streets and closely packed housing of the native city. They were exempt from Chinese jurisdiction. The British returned the Hankow concession in 1927 as a result of serious anti-foreign rioting. The Japanese held the Hankow concessions from 1938–1945.

Chapter 10 The end of the journey

21 p. 268 Wu Pei Fu was a significant figure in the struggles that took place between the war lords who dominated Northern China between 1916 and 1927. He had joined the 'New Army' of Yuan ShiKai in 1902 and proved himself a brilliant strategist in many confrontations with other war lords and the emerging Kuomintang after the abdication of the Emperor in 1912 and as a result earned himself the name of 'the Jade Marshall' . His strongest base was in the provinces of Hunan and Hubei and it was there that he came up against the Kuomintang army of the South under Chiang Kai Shek in the so called 'Northern Expedition'.

22 p. 274 The civil war of 1925–1927 was basically a struggle between Chiang Kai Shek, leader of the Kuomintang Nationalist forces and the Chinese Communist Party. Many of the skirmishes took place in and around Wuhan but finally by 1928 Chiang had established supremacy and the Communist forces retreated to the south until they were able to re-group under the leadership of Mao tse tung.

23 p. 293 Artificial pneumothorax has not been used for the treatment of tuberculosis since the introduction of antibiotics.

Chapter 11 A personal perspective

24 p. 309 Bosun Ranch, New Denver, Canada. Joseph Harris, one of Bessie
Gillison's younger brothers, was something of a rebel, an idealist and
independent thinker, characteristics which had always fitted uneasily in the
well-to-do, God-fearing, Victorian Harris family. Joe was considered by his
father to be unsuited to a career in the family business of C & T Harris and it
was decided to send him to study agriculture in Guelph, Ontario. Following
his studies there, Joe farmed for a few years on Vancouver Island in British
Columbia. In 1896 he bought land above Slocan Lake at New Denver where
recent discoveries of silver deposits had brought miners to the area. Joe
was interested in farming to provide food for the local population rather
than exercising the silver mining rights on his land which he sold. Joe had
befriended a boatswain and offered him work. He was to help in building a
log cabin, clearing land and planting an orchard.

Although it was a struggle to make a living out of the farm largely owing
to the fluctuating fortunes of the mining industry, Joseph and his Scottish
wife Margaret, whom he met and married during a trip to England in 1897,
worked hard and brought up their family in the valley. During World War II
the farmstead was requisitioned to accommodate Japanese evacuated from
the Canadian coast, but has been continuously owned and cared for by the
Harrises. For over one hundred years now, each generation of the family
has been captivated by the magic of 'Bosun Ranch' and, because of their
generosity in inviting friends and distant relations, so have its many visitors.

The author's grandparents, Thomas and Bessie Gillison in the garden of
Bessie's parents in Calne, Wiltshire in 1914.

BIBLIOGRAPHY

Griffith John – The Story of Fifty Years in China
R.Wardlaw Thompson (*1908*)

Griffith John – Founder of the Hankow Mission, Central China
William Robson (*1888*)

Griffith John – Apostle to Central China
Noel Gibbard (*1998*)

The Birth of Communist China
C.P. Fitzgerald (*1968*)

China – A New History
John King Fairbank & Merle Goldman (*2006*)

Mary Hart – Memories & Letters
S.S.Harris & E.M.Gillison (*1896*)

The Cross and the Dragon
K.H.Gillison (*1988*)

Chatterton, J. M. (2010) *Protestant Medical Missionary Experience During the War in China 1937–1945:The Case of Hubei Province*, PhD Thesis, School of Oriental and African Studies, University of London

The author wishes to express her gratitude to Dr Simon Pooley, of St Antony's College Oxford, for his invaluable help and advice with particular regard to South African history.

Lightning Source UK Ltd.
Milton Keynes UK
UKOW05f1956040117
291404UK00024B/639/P